UNDERSTANDING AND TREATING CODEPENDENCE

James A. Kitchens, Ph.D

Prentice Hall
Englewood Cliffs, New Jersey 07632

Library of Congress Cataloging-in-Publication Data

Kitchens, James A.
  Understanding and treating codependence/James A. Kitchens.
    p. cm.
  Includes bibliographical references.
  ISBN 0-13-933482-3
  1. Co-dependence (Psychology)--Treatment. I. Title.
RC569.5.C63K58 1991
616.86--dc20

89-78398
CIP

Editorial/production supervision and
  interior design: KERRY REARDON
Page layout: AUDREY KOPCIAK
Cover design: MIRIAM RECIO
Manufacturing buyer: ROBERT ANDERSON

Printed in the United States of America

10 9 8 7 6 5 4 3 2 1

ISBN   0-13-933482-3

PRENTICE-HALL INTERNATIONAL, INC., *London*
PRENTICE-HALL OF AUSTRALIA PTY. LIMITED, *Sydney*
EDITORA PRENTICE-HALL DO BRASIL, LTDA., *Rio de Janeiro*
PRENTICE-HALL CANADA INC., *Toronto*
PRENTICE-HALL OF INDIA PRIVATE LIMITED, *New Delhi*
PRENTICE-HALL OF JAPAN, INC., *Tokyo*
SIMON & SCHUSTER ASIA PTE. LTD., *Singapore*

To Rachel, my love.

CONTENTS

PREFACE

Several summers ago, I attended a retreat at which we did a brief exercise that changed my counseling, my teaching, and the way I lived my life. The retreat leader turned the lights down low and led us through a brief meditation. Classical music played in the background. She spoke in a soft voice as she took us back into our childhoods. With her direction, I saw myself at the age of ten living in Biloxi, Mississippi. I went through the house in which I had lived at 1417 West Howard Street. The child I saw sitting in the dark bedroom where I slept was a lonely, fat, and unloved kid. He felt like he was all alone in the world and that life was a heavy burden.

I had always known that my father was an alcoholic and that my mother, a rigidly religious woman, had enlisted me in the battle against his drinking. What I had not realized until that evening was that the experience of growing up in that family had left a mark on me that was similar to the experience of others who had grown up in dysfunctional families. We feel alone and unworthy. I came to realize that I had spent the larger part of my adulthood trying to overcome the effects of that childhood pain.

The retreat leader concluded the exercise by reminding us that the wounded child that we had met in our guided imagery that evening was still very much present in us. I set off on a journey to find out how the fear and shame and doubt of that child of so many years ago had produced the man I had become. If, as she had suggested, that child had been hurt by those childhood experiences, and if he still lived in me with his pain and brokenness, how could I find him and help him to heal? Furthermore, how could I discover the ways in which I allowed the fear and insecurity of that child to influence my decisions and determine my life style as an adult? My search led me to a number of books that had been written by people like myself on the effects of growing up in a troubled family. They used the word *codependence* to describe the problem.

Many of these books were written about alcoholic families. But I discovered quickly that family problems other than chemical addictions could produce the wounded child. In my own experience, for example, I found that the rigidity of religion was a much more destructive force than my father's alcoholism. I discovered that what had hurt me was the family system, the whole web of troubled relationships that my family had been. I did not need to blame my father or my mother or isolate alcohol or religion as culprits. My parents were as much victims of the family mesh as I was. But neither did I need to protect my parents from my own honest recognition that they had hurt me by the choices that they had made. What I needed was to *understand* what had happened to me and how I had continued to practice the ways of thinking, feeling, and behaving that I had developed in reaction to that destructive system in which I lived as a child.

I began to incorporate what I was learning about myself and my recovery into my counseling. I had seen my first client professionally in the early 1960s, some twenty years prior to that evening at the church retreat. As I worked more and more of the concepts I was learning about dysfunctional childhood into my counseling, I found a new excitement about therapy. I found that the books written about the effects of a dysfunctional family were as helpful to others as they had been to me. I began doing group therapy for people who grew up in dysfunctional families. What I found was that as they dealt with the problems of the family in which they grew up (their family of origin), they were at the same time dealing with the problems of the family they had established (their family of orientation). Like me, my clients were more capable of living in the present when they healed the past.

This book is a result of my effort to incorporate my own personal healing as an adult child into the professional therapy setting. It is a practical handbook for people who presently are counselors or who are in training to be counselors. Other professionals, such as ministers, educators, social workers, and medical personnel, also will find it helpful in their work. Its major emphasis is on understanding the person who grew up in a dysfunctional family in order to help that person overcome the trauma of the past. There are ample books for the layperson. These books, written over the last six or eight years, are readily available to the men and women who suffer from the problems involved. This book is intended for those who want to learn how to work therapeutically with the adult child.

The book is divided into halves. The first half attempts to answer the questions, What is codependence? What causes it? How can it be assessed? Chapters One through Five look at these questions. The second half deals with the question, What can we do to help people with this problem? The last six chapters present methods of working with the adult child in individual, family, and group therapy.

I have included many case presentations because I believe that nothing communicates ideas more powerfully than real-life experiences. Every case presented is an actual and true case. I have changed names and have altered some biographical data to preserve anonymity. I have also quoted from written materials that my clients have given to me in the course of their therapy. I have not altered these materials in any way except to make them grammatically correct.

I would like to thank a number of people for their help in the writing of this book. First, I thank the individuals and families who have shared their lives with me over the last few years. I view your company on my journey as among the most rewarding experiences of my life. Truly, without these persons, I could never have written this book. I thank my friends Jack Shaw, John Shoop, and Nathan Church for their help in establishing the Relationship Enrichment Counseling Center in Dallas, Texas, where I was able to test out my ideas and do my therapy for a number of years. I am also grateful to the patients and staff at Twin Lakes Hospital in Denton, Texas, where I now do codependent group therapy. My thanks also to my students at the University of North Texas in Denton, Texas, who endured the long afternoons of discussion of these themes. My thanks to Bill Entzminger, Brenda Entzminger, Greg Stanley, Ann Love, Greg Gossett, Phil Christiansen, and Sharon Christiansen for reading various parts of the manuscript. Also, many thanks to the reviewers: Lawrence M. Brammer, University of Washington; Rick George, University of Missouri; and Paul W. Power, University of Maryland. And my special thanks to my wife, Rachel, whose love and care have helped to heal my wounded child.

At 11:30 A.M. on May 21, 1972, as the crowd left St. Peter's Basicila following the Pontifical Mass, a young Hungarian-born Austrian named Laszlo Toth leaped into the side chapel housing Michelangelo's *Pieta.* Pulling out a hammer he had concealed under his raincoat, he dealt the figure of the Virgin fifteen blows before being restrained by stunned onlookers. He crashed the hammer into her face repeatedly, smashing her left eye and her nose. He struck several blows that broke her left arm in three places and knocked off all the fingers of the left hand. The figure of Christ was unharmed.

The attack left the magnificent sculpture mutilated and, to the dismay of many experts, hopelessly mangled beyond repair. A team of seven sculptors, led by Ulderico Grispigni of the Vatican Museum, was assembled to do the impossible: Restore the Lady to the splendor and beauty to which her creator had originally designed her. Their first goal was to so enmesh themselves into the work of art that each stroke would be as much Michelangelo's as their own. They studied and caressed the statue, considering each little crevice and line. They looked and touched and examined until they felt that they were seeing the work with the eye of Michelangelo. Then they set about the task, working incessantly for seven months. Finally, four days before Christmas, 1972, they completed their assignment. The statue was restored.

Grispigni, on the anniversary of the tenth year of the restoration, was asked about the importance of the work. He replied, "If you ask any of us [his team of seven sculptors] twenty years from now what we did with our life, I think we would tell you that we gave this beautiful lady her face back."

I think the restoration of the *Pieta* to its original splender is not unlike the work we do with individuals who grew up in dysfunctional families. They have been struck repeated blows that have marred the uniqueness and luster for which they were originally intended. They are left mutilated and broken, sometimes hopelessly so, in their own opinion and in those of other people. But with care and persistence and always with great pain, they can reconstruct themselves and reproduce the beauty that lives in all of them. Given help, they can look back at their childhood traumas, finding there among the painful memories the broken child who emerged from the hammer blows as well as the beautiful child they were originally intended to be. They can learn to love and accept that beautiful child. In the love and respect that self-acceptance creates, they will find healing and joy and self-restoration.

James A. Kitchens
The University of North Texas
Denton, Texas

INTRODUCTION TO THE ADULT CHILD

Shannon was neat, attractive, and very shy. Now at age twenty-three she was thinking about killing herself. Her parents had divorced when she was five years old, and her father, an alcoholic, had committed suicide when Shannon was seven. No one talked to her about it. Suddenly her father was dead, and the family buried him. After her mother remarried, her stepfather made her lie in bed with him one morning after her mother left for work. He masturbated to show her "how men do it." Years later, in her midteens, she finally worked up the courage to tell her mother what her stepfather had done. Her mother responded, "That is not true. You must have dreamed it." Now in the midst of a great sense of hopelessness, Shannon wrote the following:

> My father's death has left a great void in me. Even though I did not know him, he is half of my heritage. I start to cry when I think I don't remember him ever holding me in his arms, ever kissing me or caressing my head. I can't remember him ever telling me it would be O.K. I never had that security.
>
> I was thinking last night about my past and how I never had any loving male guidance. This is probably what made me lose control. I never had anyone to just hold me. Someone I loved who showed me by doing this that he loved me, and that I was O.K. the way I was. Now I'm starting to cry again because I feel this loss again. How can you find something you never had?

It never really bothered me before, when I was younger, that my Dad was dead and I never knew him. But now that I'm older, there are things I need to ask him, advice I'd like to hear from him. I'd like to feel the arms of my very own father around me. I guess I have this great feeling that my world is not on stable ground.

Am I crazy?

Shannon is an adult child.

So is Libby. Although her story is different, her suffering was no less intense. The daughter of a successful Protestant minister, she was a very shy and self-effacing person. She worked as a secretary in a large company, had a stormy love relationship with a rather harsh young man who berated and made fun of her. She was about thirty years old and wanted to be married. She wrote the following:

> I must have been nine or ten when this event happened to me. We lived in a small southern town and the septic tank always backed up at our house. It was a cold, rainy, wintry Saturday night and I had to go to the bathroom. I was a skinny kid as it was—had those "cat eye" glasses and my mother always rolled our hair on Saturday nights in those pink cushion curlers. In order for us to use the bathroom when the sewer system backed up, my parents would put one of those blue plastic buckets with water in it on the enclosed back porch. That is what we were supposed to use to go to the bathroom. So I did that night. Picture this if you will. I am sitting on this bucket on a cold rainy night in my pink curlers, brown cat eye glasses and skinny body… got it? Well, I can still remember. One of my parents stepped out from behind the refrigerator which was right next to this area and took my picture!
>
> It was funny. However, it never stopped there. They have tortured me with that picture to this day. They made a slide of it. It is always a big joke and my parents and sisters and brother remind me of it and say that if I ever get married, they will be sure and show it to my fiancee and see if he will still want to marry me. I remember one time that it was shown to a boyfriend who was over when slides were being shown. It has always caused such a fright inside me every time I know they have been looking at old slides.
>
> As I have thought about it, I think it might relate to why I do not feel like I am any prettier than that little girl on that bucket. I don't really know what to think and maybe this is just silly. But that slide in my parents' hands has been a source of fear and irritation for me.

Both of these young women are caught in a syndrome that is now the subject of much careful thought as well as a growing amount of scientific research. They are known as *adult children of dysfunctional families*. The word most commonly used to describe their malady is *codependence*. In the introduction to her book on the subject, Schaef (1986, p. 1) says that the concept of codependence is "one of the most exciting ideas to evolve recently." I concur with this evaluation. I also see the concept as the foundation to innovative and imaginative approaches in counseling, approaches that have the potential to alter significant areas of the field.

PURPOSE OF THE BOOK

The purpose of this book is to help counselors and other therapists develop the knowledge and skills they need to deal with clients who are adult children of dysfunctional families, people who suffer from problems similar to those of Shannon and Libby. To carry out this objective, the book discusses in depth what codependence is, what its clinical characteristics are, what factors seem to be associated with it in a causal relationship, and how to treat it in group, family, and individual therapy.

As an area of clinical specialization, this discipline is only now beginning to develop. It emerged in the early 1970s in the field of chemical addiction, specifically among counselors of alcoholics. These persons began to look at how the addict affected the family. They wanted to help people who were married to and were the children of the alcoholic.

To do so, these counselors borrowed heavily from the theories and methods of marriage and family therapy, a field that had been rapidly expanding from its inception in the 1950s. Work in family therapy was adding new concepts, most notably in family systems theory. Therapy-oriented research in family interactions was expanding, and all of this material was available to chemical-dependency counselors who were interested in working with the effects of addiction on the family.

The early 1970s also witnessed the growth of interest in the area of addiction by social scientists, who began to research the effects of substance abuse on the family. Some of these scientists began asking about compulsions other than chemical addictions. They began to research physical abuse, sexual abuse, extreme religiosity, work addiction, adoption, divorce, and mental illness, among others, as abusive patterns that can lead to codependence in family members (Wright and Kitchens, 1976, pp. 55–84; Dutton, 1988, pp. 38–65). After a thorough review of this research, Feldman, Stiffman, and Jung (1987, pp. 3–30) conclude:

> Although biological influences, genetic predispositions, and stress-diathesis formulations can be invoked to account for childhood risk, it is obvious that socioenvironmental factors play a major, if not prepotent, role in the onset of childhood behavior disorders...the available data suggest that a substantial majority of high-risk children are likely to have *some* kind of major or minor sociobehavioral or psychiatric disorder as they progress toward adulthood.

The conclusion seemed inescapable that dysfunctional family patterns have a detrimental effect on the developing child and that these effects can spill over into adulthood. Abuse comes in many forms. Emotional violence is even more destructive than the physical pain and obvious destruction that addictions such as alcoholism cause. As Dorn (1983, p. 3) puts it, psychological abuse is just as violent as physical abuse, even though it "is often quiet, subtle, and pervasive. Discrimination and insensitivity [in the family] have a profoundly destructive and self-perpetuating effect on human development. The outwardly imperceptible hurts inflicted by ridicule, indifference, and disparagement can be devastating."

The combination of the efforts of researchers in all of these fields has given rise to the burgeoning and exhilarating growth of study, writing, and therapy dedicated to the adult who grew up in a dysfunctional family. Their efforts produced in the 1980s the innovative emphasis on the adult who grew up in a family that was, in whatever way and to whatever degree, abusive or dysfunctional. This research has led to the inescapable conclusion that persons who grow up in such families experience identifiable emotional and behavioral problems in dealing with life as adults. This adult retains the wounds, the pain, the emotions, and the destructive behaviors that he or she learned as a child. What that pain is all about and how to help individuals who experience it is the subject of this book.

CODEPENDENCE: A NEW TERM FOR AN OLD IDEA

The origins of the word *codependence* are obscure. The word probably emerged from the terms *coalcoholic* and *coaddict*. Cermak (1986, p.4.) notes that chemical dependency counselors began in the late 1970s to lump alcoholism and other drug dependencies together under the more generic name of *chemical dependence*. When they did, it was natural for them to speak of coalcoholics as *codependents*. Since that time, however, the concept has evolved to include a much broader set of ideas than that conveyed by the word *coalcoholic* or *coaddict*.

What is also apparent is that, although the term itself is new, the reality it describes is not. The family may be the oldest of all human institutions. It differs from one culture to another and from one historical period to another. But it has always served universally among human societies to carry out very specific human needs. Among those functions is the preparation of the young for satisfactory and fulfilling adult life in society. Some families, for a variety of reasons, simply fail to meet the needs of the child. These families are *dysfunctional* for that child, and he or she must bear the scars of that family experience in adulthood. Ours seems to be a culture in which many, if not the majority, of the families do not nurture and care for its young in a way that produces mature and emotionally healthy adults.

Winch (1963, p. 286), in his definitive study of the modern family, says that the family is "the setting for the expression of eagerness, interest, and the zest for living." His careful analysis results in the conclusion that the family as we know it in twentieth-century America simply does not carry out that function. Thus, we are a society largely characterized by emotionally disabling families and by people who are inadequately prepared for adulthood. The word *codependence* is merely the effort of contemporary thinkers to describe a phenomenon that has been prevalent in American society for decades.

Contrasting Models of Codependence

When one reviews the growing literature about codependence, it becomes obvious that there are two distinct models for the term. The earlier model seems to have arisen almost entirely from the chemical-dependency field. Later thinkers from the mental health fields have added a second and somewhat more complex model. Let us look at each of these models of codependence.

The addict-centered model of codependence.   In Model One (See Figure 1), the addict is the central character in the family, and *codependency* is the term used to describe the self-destructive things that family members do to cope with the addict's problem. In this model, the family goes awry because of the problem of the addict. According to this view, the addict acts and everyone else reacts. The logic of this model is that when one member of the family becomes deeply troubled, the patterns of the family are likely to become dysfunctional as a result.

As we have sharpened this model, family patterns other than those centered on chemical addictions have come to be regarded as capable of producing codependence. Families that are headed by parents who are rigidly religious, psychotic, workaholics, have various sexual disorders, or are overtly rageful persons are among the kinds of families that are capable of creating codependence in family members. Regardless of the problem around which the family is centered, the fundamental element of the model has remained intact: A troubled individual, usually a parent, stands at the center of the problem and the other family members react to that person in self-defeating ways.

Rex is an example of the addict-centered model. His whole life from childhood on was a reaction to his father's problems. Forty-five years of age, Rex was the epitome of American success. His law practice was growing and his salary was in the six-figure range. He lived in a new and very expensive suburban community in North Dallas with his beautiful wife and two preschool children. He attended a large

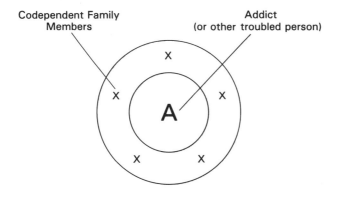

Figure 1: Addict-centered model of codependence.

Protestant church in Dallas. He was sincere in his beliefs and was a kind and sensitive man.

Rex got drunk at home nearly every evening and he and his wife fought about inane and inconsequential things. In their stylish and respectable lives, they were miserable. Rex was filled with an internal rage because he hated his father, who was a successful and wealthy businessman and also an alcoholic. Rex's father loved and approved of Rex's older sister who became a college professor. He was cold and distant toward his son. Rex made money to get his father's approval. He thought that making money would demonstrate his superiority over his sister. However, the more money he made, the prouder the father appeared of the academic and intellectual achievements of the sister. Rex tried even harder and hated himself all the more. He drank to cover the pain of his codependence. Rex followed a self-destructive pattern of thinking, feeling, and behaving that resulted as a reaction to the problems of his father.

The faulty family model. Model Two, on the other hand, regards the family system itself as the core problem (See Figure 2). The disorder belongs to the total system rather than to one person in the system. To survive, each member of the family develops ways of coping with a faulty family. Family systems theory has heavily influenced this model. The logic of this model is that when the family patterns are dysfunctional, members of the family develop problems as a result.

The MacAlaster family is an example of Model Two codependence. Martha, the wife and mother, had been the victim of sexual abuse in her childhood. Matthew, the husband and father, was the adult child of a domineering and alcoholic father. This was a second marriage for both partners, and they brought to their relationship all the baggage not only of their childhood but of their previously failed marriages. Martha was deeply insecure and attempted to overcome these feelings by controlling all the people in her life. Because she was so insecure, she needed from her family obedience that bordered on worship. That is the reason she picked for her second mate a man in great need of approval. His need of her approval served as the handle

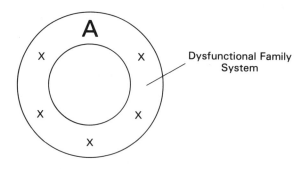

Figure 2: The faulty family model.

by which she controlled him. When he did what she wanted, she smiled approvingly and he felt great. When he did not, she frowned and he, sensing her rejection, raged inwardly. They then fought about some unimportant matter, Martha continued her disapproval, and Matthew got drunk. The next day, she disapproved of his drinking, they fought some more, and he got drunk again.

They had begun the process of bringing the children into this self-destructive dance. Martha coached the children to disapprove of their father's drinking and other behaviors she wanted to control. Matthew gave gifts and showered attention on the children to keep their love and to counter her influence. He tried especially hard to establish a coalition with his daughter to make her his ally in the family feud. Although only preschoolers, the children correctly sensed their own power in this situation. They learned to survive in this family and to get what they wanted by playing the game by the existing rules. Thus, the MacAlaster family had become an unhealthy system in which each member acted out his or her part and in so doing perpetuated the destruction to all.

APPROACHES TO CODEPENDENCE

Keeping these two models in mind, we will now look at some of the approaches that various thinkers have used in the development of their understanding of the adult child. A review of the available literature reveals that there are at least seven different approaches to codependence. While built around different aspects of the concept, these approaches emphasize many of the same characteristics and, therefore, overlap in significant ways.

Codependence As the Enactment of a Role

Many writers have viewed the codependent as the enactor of a learned role. For writers who take this perspective, codependence is primarily something that is *done* and only secondarily something that is *felt*. Larsen (1985) writes and speaks about codependence from this perspective. He is very behavior oriented. Larsen talks about six dysfunctional roles in the family that children of substance abusers usually take. The roles are *caretaker*, *people-pleaser*, *workaholic*, *martyr*, *perfectionist*, and *tap dancer*. He defines codependence as the living out of these roles, and he says that they are "self-defeating *behaviors*, greatly exaggerated and complicated by a pathological relationship to a chemically dependent person…that diminish our capacity to initiate or participate in loving relationships."

Black (1981, p. 4) also takes a role perspective. She refers to the syndrome in the spouse of the alcoholic as *coalcoholism*. According to Black, the coalcoholic becomes "increasingly preoccupied with the behavior of the alcoholic." Children in the family are "impacted not only by the alcoholic parent, but also by the nonalcoholic parent (if there is one), and by the abnormal family dynamics created as a consequence of alcoholism." The following are among the problems such children experience:

1. Increasing risk of becoming alcoholic themselves. Black notes that 50 to 60 percent of all alcoholics have at least one alcoholic parent. (Actually, that figure may be on the conservative side, as Black herself points out.)
2. They are prone to marry alcoholics.
3. They have a high risk of developing emotional or psychological disorders. Among these are difficulties identifying and expressing feelings. They become very rigid and controlling. They become overly dependent on others, feel no power of choice in the way they live, have a pervasive sense of guilt, are frequently depressed, and frequently have severe problems in intimate relationships.

Black (1981, pp. 16-27) describes four roles that the child of the alcoholic may take. She calls them the *responsible child*, the *adjustor*, the *placator*, and the *acting-out child*. We will look more carefully at these roles in Chapter Ten, when we consider how to help the adult child in individual therapy.

Wegscheider-Cruse (1984) has been perhaps most influential in describing *codependency* as a role the individual plays. She sees the term primarily associated with the alcoholic family. Such a family cannot produce a healthy individual. Rather, the person who grows up in such an atmosphere will adopt one, or possibly more, of four roles. She calls the roles the *hero*, the *scapegoat*, the *lost child*, and the *mascot*. The content of these roles is not unlike those of Black's four roles just mentioned. We will have occasion to return to these roles in greater detail in Chapter Ten.

Codependence as Internal Emotional Problems

Cermak (1986, pp. 1–7), a psychiatrist working in the area of alcohol dependence, makes an attempt to define codependence from the perspective of the American Psychiatric Association. Writing in 1986, he made use of the third edition of the *Diagnostic and Statistical Manual of Mental Disorders* (American Psychiatric Association, 1980). He notes that there is great diversity in defining the word and not much scientific precision. Thus, he makes an appeal for a more rigorous psychiatric definition. He suggests the following: "Codependence is a recognizable pattern of personality traits, predictably found within most members of chemically dependent families, which are capable of creating sufficient dysfunction to warrant the diagnosis of Mixed Personality Disorder as outlined in DSM III."

Cermak's discussion is helpful in distinguishing three different uses of the word. Codependence is, he says, a didactic tool, a psychological concept, and finally a disease entity. Codependence as a didactic tool "legitimizes many of the feelings family members have and gives them permission to begin focusing on their own dysfunctional behaviors." Codependence as a psychological concept is a useful abstraction that allows therapists and clinical theoreticians to organize data and to communicate about human behavior. As such, it is like any other highly sophisticated psychological concept. It helps us to study, understand, and communicate about human behavior. Finally, Cermak insists that codependence is a disease entity. Such an assessment implies "that a consistent pattern of traits and behaviors is recognizable across individuals, and that these traits and behaviors can create significant dysfunction. In other words, codependence is used to describe a 'disease entity,' just as phobia, narcissistic personality disorder, and Post-Traumatic Stress Disorder (PTSD) are diagnostic entities."

Whitfield (1987, pp. 5–27) also takes the approach that codependence is an inward emotional problem. He begins his helpful analysis with the concept of the *True self*. The term he uses to describe this self is *the child within*. When the basic nurturing needs of this child are not met in growing up, the inner child is "stifled." All authority figures, but especially parents, and all institutions such as education, organized religion, politics, the media, and even the helping professions can inhibit the proper growth of this child within. When this happens the person feels false and "uncomfortable, strained, or unauthentic." Whitfield refers to this false self as codependent. It is inhibited, contracting, and fearful. It hides and denies its true feelings. It is outer and other directed, and often inappropriately aggressive or passive. "Most of the time, in the role of our false or codependent self we feel uncomfortable, numb, empty or in a contrived state. *We do not feel real, complete, whole or sane.* At one level or another, we sense that something is wrong, something is missing."

Whitfield points out that, in the pathology of codependence, people believe that this false state is the normal way to be, the way they are supposed to be. To consider changing to relieve the pain is itself a frightening thought. He concludes, "The false or codependent self appears to be universal among humans. It has been described or referred to countless times in print and in our daily lives. It has been called such diverse names as a survival tool, psychopathology, the egocentric ego and the impaired or defensive self. It can be destructive to self, others and intimate relationships."

Codependence as Shame

For Fossum and Mason (1986, pp. 5–7) the essence of codependence is found in one word: *shame*. They explicitly point out that shame begins in a faulty family system. In their view, it is not the presence or absence of an addict of any kind that is the important factor in the development of shame. Rather, it is the quality of the family itself that is significant. Thus they refer to "shame-bound" families. Such families are based on "compulsive, abusive, or phobic behaviors." The individual growing up in such a family experiences shame that is "an inner sense of being completely diminished or insufficient as a person. It is the self judging the self. A moment of shame may be humiliation so painful or an indignity so profound that one feels one has been robbed of her or his dignity or exposed as basically inadequate, bad, or worthy of rejection. A pervasive sense of shame is the ongoing premise that one is fundamentally bad, inadequate, defective, unworthy, or not fully valid as a human being."

According to Fossum and Mason, guilt must be distinguished from shame. Guilt, on one hand, is a feeling of regret one has about behavior that has violated a personal value. Guilt is a feeling about what we have done. Shame, on the other hand, is about what we are. It is about the identity process and has to do with "who I am." Shame is the feeling or the cognition that "I am defective, inadequate, or incompetent."

"The roots of shame are in abuse, personal violations, seductions and assaults where one's sense of self has been trampled, one's boundaries defiled." According to Fossum and Mason, the source of this kind of psychological impact is the family of origin, or what they call the "shame-bound system."

Codependence as Conformity to Unhealthy Rules

Subby and Friel (1984, pp. 31–32) define codependence as "a dysfunctional pattern of living and problem-solving which is nurtured by a set of rules within the family system." For these writers, codependence is a family pattern that affects every member of the family. Behavioral and emotional characteristics of this codependent family configuration show up in individuals who exhibit the following:

1. Difficulty in identifying feelings.
2. Difficulty expressing feelings.
3. Difficulty in forming or maintaining close relationships.
4. Perfectionism in the form of too many expectations of self and others.
5. Rigid or stuck attitudes or behavior.
6. Difficulty in adjusting to change.
7. Feeling overly responsible for other people's behavior or feelings.
8. Constant need for others' approval in order to feel good about self.
9. Difficulty in making decisions.
10. General feelings of powerlessness over one's life; the feeling that nothing one does makes any difference.
11. A basic sense of shame and low self-esteem over *perceived* failures in one's life.

Subby (1984, p. 26), in another article, defines codependence in a similar fashion. He says that codependence is "an emotional, psychological, and behavioral condition that develops as a result of an individual's prolonged exposure to, and practice of, a set of oppressive rules—rules which prevent the open expression of feelings as well as the direct discussion of personal and interpersonal problems." Thus, it is the presence of the dysfunctional rules within the family system that provides the environment for codependence as well as other addictions.

Codependence as Rejection and Chaos

While he does not use the word codependent, the research of Ackerman (1983, pp. 25–45) is of great use to us in understanding the concept. Ackerman's focus is children of alcoholics who have not yet grown to adulthood. He notes that it is the dysfunctionality of the family that is so devastating to the children. He says, "Children of alcoholics are more affected by the disharmony and rejection in the home life than by the drinking. They see that the drinking stops once in a while, though the fighting and tension continue. This constant state of agitation affects personality development." Ackerman describes some of the behaviors the spouse of an alcoholic may exhibit:

- Hides and denies the problem of the alcoholic
- Takes on the responsibilities of the alcoholic (enabling behavior)
- Experiences difficulty in being open and honest with feelings
- Avoids sexual contact
- Gradually withdraws and isolates socially
- Has few feelings of self-respect and self-worth
- May use alcohol or prescription drugs in an effort to cope

Children who grow up in such a home show some of the problems the spouse experiences, as well as the following:

- May have birth defects
- Are torn between parents, because to be loyal to one may arouse the anger of the other
- Experiences little emotional, and sometimes, physical, support
- Avoids peer activities, especially in the home because of fear and shame
- Learns negative and destructive ways of problem solving and getting attention
- Has a lack of trust in others
- Develops poor values, standards, and goals because of the absence of consistent, strong parenting
- Suffers a diminishing sense of self-worth

Codependence as Addiction

Schaef (1986, pp. 4–43) offers the broadest definition of codependence. She calls it simply "the addictive process." She maintains that it is a disease that has an onset, a definable course, and a predictable outcome. It has many forms and expressions. An addiction is anything we feel we have to lie about. The addictive process, of which codependence is but one manifestation, "is an unhealthy and abnormal disease process, whose assumptions, beliefs, behaviors, and lack of spirituality lead to a process of nonliving that is progressively death-oriented." She sees the following as the characteristics of codependents:

- Dishonesty in the form of denial, projection, and delusion
- Not dealing with feelings in a healthy way
- Control, confusion, and thinking disorders such as obsessive thinking or overreliance on linear, analytic thinking
- External referenting
- Perfectionism
- Dependency issues
- Fear, rigidity, judgmentalism, self-centeredness, and negativism
- Depression
- Inferiority/grandiosity
- Loss of personal morality

Codependence as Family Culture

Another approach to the word codependency offers a breadth that, while it may be implied in these definitions, is not made explicit. St. John's Hospital in Salina, Kansas, has contributed to our understanding of the concept with the following definition and explanation:

> Codependency is a set of maladaptive, compulsive behaviors learned by family members in order to survive in a family which is experiencing great emotional pain and stress. These behaviors can be passed on from generation to generation whether alcoholism/chemical dependency is present or not. In other words, the original alcoholic or drug dependent person may have been a great-grandfather. No one else for three or four generations may actually become alcoholic, but most of the family members within these three or four generations will have learned to use a set of behaviors which helped them cope with the emotional pain and stress inherited from the original alcoholic/chemically dependent family member and which continues to create emotional pain and stress even to the present time.

In this view, codependency is so much a function of the family system that a chemically addicted person is not even necessary to keep it going. The destructive pattern becomes a part of the family ritual and is passed from one generation to the next in what appear to be normal and functional families.

This brief survey of the various uses of the term *codependence* reveals that the word has at least four different kinds of uses:

1. *Codependence* describes people's practices and feelings. In some literature, it is specifically reserved for the relationship between the addict and his or her

spouse. In this case, the codependent is an enabler. It may also be used in this sense to refer to parent-child relationships. When it refers to enabling, it is a term descriptive of the kind of relationship that protects the addict or other troubled individual from the negative consequences of his or her behavior. The codependent "enables" the user to continue to use by protecting him or her from the painful outcome of addictive behavior.

More frequently, the term describes the individual's effort to survive in the abusive family. When used in this way, the term is more inclusive than simple enabling of the addict. Any seriously dysfunctional behavior in the family, not just chemical addiction, may be the focus. In dealing with the "crazy" behaviors of the troubled family, the child develops ways of thinking, behaving, and feeling that help him or her survive in such an irrational atmosphere. These patterns help the child survive, but at an enormous cost. They are self-defeating in the long term because, while they dull the pain temporarily, they leave self-destructive scars on the personality and self-perception of the child. Furthermore, the individual continues to practice these patterns even after leaving home and becoming an adult. Thus, codependents are referred to as *adult children*. From this view, then, the word refers to personality disorders and self-destructive patterns of behavior that help the individual cope with the abusive family.

2. *Codependence* is a characteristic of a family. It may describe the present family of the individual or it may be a *multigenerational* phenomenon. In either case, the dysfunctional patterns of thinking, behaving, and feeling associated with codependence become a part of the family culture. As such, they are passed on from one generation to another *whether or not* there is an addict present in the family at any given time. This view of codependence is the broadest possible and includes aspects of the enabling and surviving tactics just discussed. Once initiated in the family, it feeds on itself, each new generation learning from the preceding one the self-destructive patterns of life. Incorporated into the family in this way, codependence becomes the primary problem. People develop addictive patterns to cope with the codependence rather than becoming codependent to deal with the addiction.

3. *Codependence* is a set of emotional and personality characteristics. As such, the term is a sociopsychological category. It describes a set of emotional, attitudinal, and behavioral attributes that are useful to clinicians and researchers in communicating with each other about the problems human beings can experience.

4. The term is a concept used by clinicians and laypersons alike to describe symptoms and to find therapeutic techniques. It gives a name to a very real syndrome that people experience at the deepest and most painful level. It helps adult children understand what is going on in their lives and why they do the kinds of irrational things that they do to themselves and others. It opens up a

way for individuals to find relief, to change their lives and to grow as human beings.

Now, we shall turn to some basic guidelines that will be of help to the counselor in working with the codependent.

REFERENCES

American Psychiatric Association. (1980). *Diagnostic and Statistical Manual of Mental Disorders* (3rd ed.), Washington: American Psychiatric Association.

Ackerman R. (1983). *Children of Alcoholics: A Guide for Parents, Educators and Therapists*, New York: Simon & Schuster.

Black, C. (1981). *It Will Never Happen To Me*, Denver: M.A.C.

Cermak, T. (1986). *Diagnosing and Treating Co-dependence*, Minneapolis: Johnson Institute Books.

Dorn, L., with Eldridge-Martin, P. (1983). *Peace in the Family: A Workbook of Ideas and Actions*, New York: Pantheon Books.

Dutton, D. (1988). *The Domestic Assault of Women: Psychological and Criminal Justice Perspectives*, Boston: Allyn & Bacon.

Feldman, R., Stiffman, A., and Jung, K. (1987). *Children at Risk: In the Web of Parental Mental Illness*, New Brunswick, N.J.: Rutgers University Press.

Fossum M., and M. Mason (1986) *Facing Shame: Families in Recovery*, New York: W. W. Norton.

Larsen, E. (1985). *Stage II Recovery: Life Beyond Addiction*, Minneapolis: Winston Press.

St. John's Hospital, "What Is Co-dependency?" Unpublished paper, Salina, Kans.: St. John's Hospital.

Schaef, A. (1986). *Co-dependence: Misunderstood-Mistreated*, San Francisco: Harper & Row.

Subby, R. (1984). "Inside the Chemically Dependent Marriage: Denial and Manipulation." in *Co-dependency: An Emerging Issue*, Pompano Beach, Fla.: Health Communications.

Subby, R., and J. Friel, (1984). "Co-dependency — A Paradoxical Dependency," in *Co-dependency: An Emerging Issue*, Pompano Beach, Fla.: Health Communications.

Wegscheider-Cruse, S. (1984). *Another Chance: Hope and Health for the Alcoholic Family*, Palo Alto, Calif.: Science and Behavior Books.

Winch, R. (1963). *The Modern Family*, (Rev. ed.) New York: Holt, Rinehart & Winston.

Whitfield, C. (1987). *Healing the Child Within*, Pompano Beach, Fla.: Health Communications.

Wright, J., and Kitchens, J. (1976). *Social Problems in America*, Columbus, Ohio: Charles E. Merrill.

2

BASIC GUIDELINES FOR COUNSELING THE ADULT CHILD

Gross (1974, p. 178) tells about a young man whom he once treated. The man's "earliest memory was that of walking under a doorsill astride his father's shoulders. He grabbed for the sill and became terrified. He could trust neither his hands nor his father's shoulders, and he began screaming." According to Gross, this child grew up to be a young man who saw himself as inadequate and his environment as overwhelming. He was depressed, hesitant, and insecure. He lived a life of disillusionment and despair.

Today, we would use the word *codependence* to describe the problem of this young man. Several approaches are available to today's counselor to work with this kind of codependent person. Wide-ranging problems come to the therapist's attention. Therefore, we should expect that counselors vary in their theoretical and methodological orientations. They do not disappoint us in this regard, and debates continue on the relative merits of the competing systems of therapy. This book makes no attempt to resolve those differences. In many ways, the debates are healthy for the discipline. However, what is needed in the area of codependence is some basic framework within which we may apply these various methods and theories. Such basic guidelines or broad principles will not only help different counselors do their work, but will assist them in communicating with one another despite widely disparate approaches to their clients. This chapter will present a set of suggested guidelines for consideration.

BASIC GUIDELINES

Following is a set of fundamental guidelines for all counselors who work with adult children. The guidelines are not a substitute for the therapist's theoretical or methodological perspective. Rather, they are a framework from which the therapist may work with codependence while retaining his or her own personal counseling orientation.

- There must be a conviction that codependence exists as an identifiable category of mental and behavioral disorders and that it has a recognizable set of symptoms.
- The family of origin—that is, the family in which the individual grew up—is central in the development of codependence.
- The problems that individuals acquire as they grow up in these dysfunctional families are of a wide variety and occur in various degrees.
- Effective therapy must help the individual to deal with the past in such a way as to get to the problems of the present.
- What is important in the individual's past is not the events themselves, but the individual's perception of the events and what choices the individual is making about that perception today.
- Therapy with a codependent client moves slowly and at the client's pace. Recovery is long term and takes place outside the therapist's office.
- This field is in the emerging stage, and much discovery is yet to be made. Some professional humility is called for, and a therapist must be open to new developments and research findings.

This book is written from the perspective of these basic guidelines. Therefore, we will have occasion in the chapters that follow to return to the guidelines on many occasions and to consider them in detail. Let us take a brief look at each one now.

There Must Be a Conviction That Codependence Exists As an Identifiable Category of Mental and Behavioral Disorders

As described in the previous chapter, the word *codependence* is a somewhat clumsy attempt to label a real phenomenon in today's society. It is perhaps unfortunate that such an unwieldy term has been selected to describe this very real experience. However, the awkwardness of the word must not deter us from seeing its utility.

Beth made me keenly aware of this truth. She was a freshman student in one of my university classes. Near the beginning of the semester, I asked that each class member write a brief autobiographical piece illustrating some concept from the text. The students were given free rein to select any concept they desired. Beth chose the concept of self-esteem. I had not mentioned codependence and had not lectured on the effects of a dysfunctional family. Beth had never heard of any of these ideas.

Her spontaneous and uncoached writing helped me to realize the inherent validity of the qualities that the term *codependence* is designed to describe. As part of her assignment, Beth wrote the following:

> I feel unworthy. I am not good enough to be loved by anyone. I expect rejection from men and that is usually what I get. My first rejection from a man occurred when my father left me. Daddy died when I was four years old. I never got to tell him how much I love him. Maybe that is why he went away. Maybe he left because I was a bad girl or because I was not pretty. Of course, I tell myself now that these thoughts are ridiculous, illogical, and irrational. I tell myself that Daddy died because he had a bad heart. Still, in the back of my mind, the thoughts I had as a little girl remain.

The nature of personality disorders.   Codependence is a distorted view of the world and an unhealthy self-concept that is the end product of faulty parent-child relationships. By the time the codependent is an adult, this way of seeing reality has been reinforced by many years of life experiences. Thus, it is built into the personality of the individual.

In his attempt to present codependence in psychiatric terms, Cermak (1986) tried to fit the concept into the categories of DSM III. We noted in Chapter One that he was the first to suggest that what we are calling codependency falls within the DSM III category of personality disorder.

We will look in depth at codependence as a characteristic of a disordered personality in Chapter Four. A brief overview of the connection is helpful at this point. The *Diagnostic and Statistical Manual of Mental Disorders, Third Edition—Revised* (American Psychiatric Association, 1987, p. 335) defines *personality traits* as "...enduring patterns of perceiving, relating to, and thinking about the environment and oneself...exhibited in a wide range of important social and personal contexts. It is only when *personality traits* are inflexible and maladaptive and cause either significant impairment in social or occupational functioning or subjective distress that they constitute *Personality Disorders*."

A personality disorder, then, may be said to exist in a condition that takes a normal human *trait* and by virtue of inflexibility and maladaptiveness converts it into a *disorder*. This is exactly what Beth had done with the normal human trait of grief at a time of great loss. Grief, experienced in a normal manner, functions to help an individual deal with loss. But for some reason, Beth turned it into a lifelong way of thinking about herself and her world.

DSM IIIR (American Psychiatric Association, 1987, p. 337) groups personality disorders into three clusters with some overlapping characteristics. The first cluster includes *paranoid, schizoid,* and *schizotypal personality disorders.* Individuals falling into this cluster exhibit mild forms of psychotic behaviors and appear odd or eccentric. More specifically, people who fit into this category suffer from unwarranted suspiciousness, have trouble forming social relationships, and are characterized by oddities in thought, perception, speech, and behavior.

The second cluster includes *histrionic, narcissistic, antisocial,* and *borderline personality disorders.* These persons often appear overly dramatic, emotional, or erratic. They may be overly reactive and need an abnormal amount of attention. Or, they may be grandiose and have an exaggerated sense of their own importance. Some may appear to have a conscience deficit and be overly antisocial. Or, finally, some persons who fall into this cluster may suffer from instability in interpersonal behavior, mood, or self-image.

The last category includes *avoidant, dependent, compulsive,* and *passive-aggressive personality disorder.* People in this last category are fearful and anxious. They are hypersensitive to the threat of rejection and abandonment. They are characterized by an almost pathological lack of self-confidence and at the same time are excessively devoted to perfection in all areas of their life. Some are indirect in dealing with their emotions, especially their negative ones.

Characteristics of personality disorders. Coleman, Butcher, and Carson (1984, pp. 233–258) attest that personality disorders stem from "immature and distorted personality development, resulting in individuals with persistent maladaptive ways of perceiving, thinking, and relating to the world around them." They refer to personality disorders as *character disorders,* perhaps to emphasize how perpetual are the nature of these problems. (The term *personality disorder* was introduced in DSM I in 1952 to describe this general category of mental problems. Prior to that, these mental problems were known as "disorders of character.") Furthermore, Coleman, Butcher, and Carson point out that personality disorders are generally recognizable by adolescence and continue throughout the individual's life. They list five characteristics of personality disorder:

- Personality disorder implies a pattern of disrupted relationships.
- Personality disorders are not "episodic." That is, the problems associated with this malady are longstanding and form a persistent pattern that occurs across a lifetime.
- Whatever the particular pattern individuals develop, it colors each new situation they meet and leads to the original paradigm of maladaptive behavior.
- These disorders are, in a sense, disorders of reputation: They are marked by the imprint the behavior has on others as well as the pain the individual feels. That is, the pain that the individual experiences may be extended to others with whom the individual has a relationship.
- Finally, the patterns of behavior reflected in personality disorders are highly resistant to change.

Codependency and personality disorders. St. John's Hospital has listed twenty-one characteristics as descriptive of codependence. The list is not exhaustive, but it is perhaps the longest such list. It is helpful to compare this description of codependence with the various clusters of personality disorders. In parenthesis after each description, I have given the specific personality disorder to which that characteristic pertains. Of course, in real life, these categories are not discrete and individuals do not fit neatly into them. There is considerable overlap as they blend and combine the characteristics in various patterns. The following list presents the St. John's descriptions of codependence rearranged under each cluster of personality disorder:

Cluster I: Paranoid, Schizoid, and Schizotypal

- Difficulty in developing or sustaining meaningful relationships (paranoid and schizoid).
- Overreacts to change (paranoid, schizoid, and schizotypal).
- Feelings of being different (paranoid).

Cluster II: Histrionic, Narcissistic, Antisocial, and Borderline

- Difficulty in following a project through to completion (borderline).
- Feelings of fear, insecurity, inadequacy, guilt, hurt, and shame that are denied (histrionic).
- Being either superresponsible or superirresponsible (antisocial).
- Being addicted to excitement (histrionic).
- Tendency to look for "victims" to help (narcissistic).
- Tendency to lie, when it would be just as easy to tell the truth (antisocial).

Cluster III: Avoidant, Dependent, Compulsive, and Passive-aggressive

- Inability to know what is "normal" behavior (compulsive).
- Difficulty in knowing how and allowing oneself to have fun (compulsive).
- Judging oneself without mercy and having low self-esteem (avoidant).
- Constantly seeking approval and affirmation, yet having no sense of self-identity (dependent).
- Confusion and an enduring sense of inadequacy (avoidant and dependent).
- Lack of self-confidence in making decisions; lacking a sense of power in making choices in life (dependent and passive-aggressive).
- A tendency frequently to split life problems into "either-or" categories. Inability to see alternatives to situations and thereby responding impulsively when making decisions (compulsive).
- Isolation and fear of people, especially authority figures (avoidant and dependent).
- Fear of anger and criticism (passive-aggressive).
- Dependency upon others and fear of abandonment (avoidant and dependent).
- Confusion between love and pity (dependent).

- Rigidity and the need to control (compulsive).

Consideration of this list leads to the conclusion that there is great similarity in what DSM IIIR calls personality disorders and what we are calling codependence. The conclusion is evident that while these are not identical entities, they are at least greatly overlapping categories. We may, therefore, think of codependence as an identifiable category of mental and behavioral disorders with a recognizable set of symptoms.

The Family of Origin Is Central in the Development of Codependence.

Virtually all thinkers who write in this area begin their analysis of cause with the family of origin. Schaef (1987) suggests that our society is based on addictive patterns. The family becomes the funnel through which these destructive patterns are conveyed to the child. Families become unhealthy when the needs of its members are inadequately met. In childhood the adult child first learns the self-defeating patterns that characterize codependence. They began as methods of dealing with perceived or real problems in the family. The individual continues to practice these ways of thinking, feeling, and acting after leaving the family of origin. These traits are deeply ingrained, with the individual either being unaware of them or rationalizing them as "the way I am."

The place of the family.   Writing about the place of the family in producing the character of the individual, Lidz (1968, pp. 46–47) says, "The family forms the earliest and most persistent influence that encompasses the still unformed infant and small child for whom the parent's ways and the family ways are *the* way of life, the only way he knows." Lidz notes that family ways and the child's patterns of reacting to them "become so integrally incorporated in the child that they can be considered determinants of his constitutional make up." Lidz concludes, "Subsequent influences will modify those of the family, but they can never undo or fully reshape those early core experiences."

Poets and sages have written eloquently across the centuries about the impact of these early experiences upon us. Freud's comment to the effect that "the child is father to the man" is a variant of this theme. The scars of the family of childhood are deep, and their pain is real and searing. A recent poignant description of the negative effect of the family can be found in the autobiographical writings of John Lee (1987). He describes himself as one who flies away from commitments, responsibilities, intimacy, male friendships, and his own body. He is, he says, "the flying boy," and that phrase is the title of his book. He says, "I saw maleness as exhibited by my drunken, angry father and wanted no part of such meanness." The trail toward healing and out of the depths of depression that those self-feelings produces is itself a painful and difficult experience, as Lee's book attests.

Research in the area of the family has shown that very subtle differences in parental response can produce specific behavioral differences in children *at very early ages*. For example, Michener and co-workers, (1986, p. 73) cite the work of Main (1973). Main observed the behavior of mothers and infants when they were reunited. Separation activates the infant's need for attachment, and the quality and intensity of the need can be assessed by simple observation of the child's behavior at the reunion. Using this technique with children in their first year of life, he identified three types of mother-infant bonds.

The first he called *secure attachment.* Children who are securely attached actively seek proximity and renewed contact with the mother. They express pleasure at the reunion. When observed at home in their natural, everyday activities, the children's mothers were sensitive to infant signals and responded quickly and sympathetically to their distress.

The other two types were forms of *anxious attachment.* Children in both of these types show distress at separation but are not happy when their mothers return. They show little pleasure when being held but cry when put down. These children are less responsive to strange adults and to other children. Main distinguishes between the two variants of anxious attachment. The first variety he calls the *ambivalent child.* This child mixes approach behavior with resistance to contact. At times, this child seems to express anger at contact with the mother. At home, the mother of the ambivalent child is slow to respond to the distress of the child.

The other variety of anxious attachment Main calls the *avoidant child.* These children avoid contact with the mother when reunited. Home observation indicates that their mothers consistently reject the child because of their own feelings of irritation and resentment. These mothers seem to view the responsibility for child care as interfering with their own interests and activities. These mothers also seem to have a strong aversion to bodily contact and tend to be emotionally unexpressive.

Three facts emerge from this research that are relevant to our work with codependents: (1) Children develop very specific patterns as responses to differing primary and family relationships. (2) Children begin the process of developing these patterns of behavior virtually at birth. (There are some thinkers who say that the process begins at conception and includes prenatal experiences of the fetus.) (3) These patterns of behavior are observable before the infant is one year old.

The significance of the family (or its substitute) on personality development is based on the fact that, at birth, the human infant is completely dependent on others for survival. Human infants are the most dependent of all newborns. This dependency makes the infant especially amenable to the social and physical environment. Face-to-face interaction and close bodily contact are essential not only for the child's physical survival but also for his or her emotional and spiritual well-being.

As the child grows older, other needs begin to emerge. Rosenberg, in 1965, discovered four such areas of need: (1) The child needs acceptance, affection, interest, and involvement of the parent in the child's affairs; (2) The child needs firm and consistent enforcement of clear limits on the child's behavior; (3) The child needs parents who allow latitude within these limits and respect the child's initiative; (4) the child needs noncoercive forms of discipline. That is, when the child's behavior calls for discipline, the parents deny privileges and discuss reasons rather than punish the child physically.

The healthy family. The healthy family meets the developmental needs of the individual; the unhealthy or dysfunctional family does not. Indeed, it is unhealthy *because* it does not provide the environment where these basic human needs are met. Several writers have attempted to distinguish between the healthy and unhealthy family system (Lewis et al., 1976; Curran, 1983). The following is a list of some of the traits that a healthy family would manifest:

- A healthy family feels safe to all the members. That is, they know that they may be open and do not need to hide what they are or what they think from one another.
- The healthy family encourages family members to reach out to one another. There is the expectation that family interaction will be caring and that family members will experience mutual support within the family.
- Confrontation in healthy families is open and honest. All persons, including children, are expected to speak for themselves. Disagreements are handled directly and immediately.
- In the healthy family, each person has both rights and responsibilities and these are fairly distributed between parents and children. Rules do not favor the more powerful persons in the family.
- Healthy families are flexible and do not have one "right" way of doing things. When considering problems within the family, they explore numerous options. If one solution does not work, they try another.
- All members of the healthy family demonstrate a high level of personal initiative and assume personal responsibility for their individual choices and interests. This includes both children and parents.
- In the healthy family, each person is taught to ask for what he or she needs openly and directly. When those needs cannot be immediately or completely met, the individual has avenues within the family to negotiate and compromise.
- Healthy families expect and encourage emotional maturity and autonomy that are appropriate for each member's age and experience. Meaningful allowances are made for exceptions based on level of stress and stage of life. Room is made for growth and learning from one's mistakes.
- Healthy families see themselves realistically. They share common perceptions of reality that are congruent with the social framework of their community.
- Healthy families are open and honest in their expression of emotions. Each member is encouraged to share feelings and talk about problems. Family members see themselves, not so much as responsible for solving each

other's problems, as the environment in which each can find his or her solutions.

- The prevailing mood in the healthy family is one of warmth, affection, and caring. Family members respect each other and recognize each other's talents and contributions.
- Healthy families have fun. Spontaneity abounds in the healthy family. Humor and wit are frequent in the healthy family, and family members like to be together.

Claudia Black (1985) has written eloquently about the effect of the unhealthy family on the child. She titled a workbook for the adult child *Repeat After Me,* a phrase that implies the repetition of things learned in childhood from the family. She introduces the book with these words:

> Once upon a time you were a child. That fact has an important bearing on your life today. As adults, we often try to ignore our lives as children and discount the impact it may have in our adult lives. *Repeat After Me* was written to be of help to you, the reader whose parents were not able to consistently attend to your needs, who were not able to help you believe that you were special and were not able to offer you a sense of emotional "safety" as you grew from childhood and adolescence into adulthood. These can be homes in which there is no identifiable problem...homes where a family avoids showing feelings, homes where there is little nurturing, homes where rules are rigid rather than fair and flexible, and homes where time is not given to the children. When these dynamics occur in a family, it is likely you reach adulthood not feeling good about yourself, having difficulty trusting people, having difficulty identifying needs and then allowing those needs to be met. These things can cause great difficulty in your ability to be close to others and create problems in your personal or professional life (p. 5).

The Problems Individuals Acquire as They Grow Up in These Dysfunctional Families Are of a Wide Variety and Occur in Various Degrees.

Kathy and Mary, both sexually abused in childhood, illustrate the very different consequences that codependence may have. Kathy's father sexually abused her from the time she was three until she was fourteen. An alcoholic military man, he saw Kathy as his special gift and used her as a substitute for the "love" he could never have with his cold and distant wife. Kathy tried to kill herself when she was fourteen. At that point, her father stopped his sexual advances. Today, after four years of therapy, Kathy at age thirty is sexually promiscuous, is still unable to have a loving relationship with a man, and is a recovering alcoholic.

Mary, on the other hand, was sexually abused repeatedly over a number of years by a cousin and grew up in a family with an alcoholic father. She got pregnant at age fifteen and later married the father of her child. Divorced twice, she finally married a man with whom she has established a wholesome relationship. Her therapy has produced a great transformation in her life. She has a full and active monogamous sex life and is a happy and well-adjusted wife and mother.

Codependence as a multivariate phenomenon.   Codependence, like alcoholism and other addictions, is not a unitary phenomenon. Rather, it is a multivariant. That is, it comes in different combinations of variables. There is danger in the simplistic view that sees codependence as a single set of symptoms. According to this view, codependence is either present or absent. Once it is diagnosed as present, a specific course of treatment is prescribed. The difficulty with this oversimplification is the assumption that once we know that the person grew up with an addicted parent, we know all that is wrong with him or her and all we need to know for treatment. Use of this either-or diagnosis forces individuals into a preconceived mold and interferes with both proper assessment and effective treatment.

Levels of severity.   A much more helpful approach is to view codependence as a continuum from the mild and nonproblematic to the severe and highly problematic. We will give attention in a later chapter to the methods of assessment. At this point, it is enough to indicate the differences in degree that the disorder can take. We can divide such a continuum into four categories:

1. Mild, non-problematic. Here the individual who grew up in a dysfunctional family has almost no emotional or behavioral scars from his or her experience. A number of factors can be identified that might be responsible for this fact. The dysfunctionality itself may have been mild. Or the individual may have had healthy emotional support systems outside the family (Ackerman 1983, p.24). At any rate, the individual comes through the early years of life relatively unscarred.

2. Moderate, slightly problematic. In this condition, the individual exhibits some behavioral and emotional problems as a result of his or her early experiences. The connection between the family of origin and these problems may be obscured under other complaints. For example, the person may complain about having trouble maintaining intimate relationships or having trouble at work or feeling depressed. Life goes on in an otherwise normal manner for this person and he or she needs help only in a minor way.

3. Serious, very problematic. This person experiences a number of life problems associated with his or her family of orientation. Not only the number but the degree of seriousness of the problems is of significance here. This person finds functioning in life to be of difficulty because of the patterns of behavior, feelings, and thoughts associated with the codependence. As in the other categories, the client may be unaware of the interrelationship of the problems of life and his or her family background.

4. Severe, problematic to the point of dysfunctionality. Codependency for this person is an almost totally inhibiting experience. Not only is a normal life impossible, side effects may affect physical health. Even at this most serious point, the individual may be completely unaware of the relationship of the problems and his or her childhood.

Such a continuum does not imply a progressiveness of codependence. That is, the individual does not begin at the minor end of the continuum and progressively develop deeper and deeper stages and symptoms as time goes by. Rather, the various points of the continuum represent different individuals who largely stay at one point indefinitely. That is not always the case, however. Some people may get progressively worse over their lifetime, and others may move up and down the scale depending on the level of stress in their life at any given time.

One of the most difficult problems of the therapist is to determine where the client falls on this continuum. Furthermore, as with most other areas of mental illness, theories and methods of treatment are designed for those at the most serious end of the continuum. The effect of this fact means that we withhold services from those with moderate and minor problems. People at all levels of the continuum deserve to get help in those areas where they need it. They do not need to be ignored because their pain is not as great as that of others. Nor do they need to be lumped into a category that is inappropriate for them.

Effective Therapy Must Help the Client to Deal With the Past in Such a Way as to Get to the Problems of the Present.

Any therapy that is designed to look explicitly at the client's history runs the danger of getting lost in the past and never finding a way out. The goal of therapy is to enable the client to live more fully in the present. Codependency tends to be associated with several social, psychological, behavioral, attitudinal, and emotional problems that originate in the past. Indeed, the nature of codependence is such that early patterns of thought and behavior learned in a dysfunctional family are carried over from the past to the present. Therein lies the pathology of codependence. In uncovering how the past is related to these present problems, the client may get caught up in blaming and in the release of anger about that past. He or she may not come back to deal with present problems. The therapist must be careful that this does not occur.

The problem of becoming embroiled in the past is especially troublesome in the area of codependence. Codependent clients are very adept at both denial and avoidance. Rehashing the past and attempting to understand the family of origin, so necessary to effective therapy for codependence, can actually become another tool of denial and avoidance. So long as the client can remain in the past, he or she does not have to face the problems of today.

Effective therapy for the codependent involves understanding how he or she got this way. It is necessary to remind many clients that what we seek is understanding, not blame. Some feel guilty and fear that they are betraying their families by giving away family secrets when they talk about problems of the past. We can help these persons most effectively by encouraging to continue delving into their personal history. Others are much more willing to look at how their family has hurt them. Allowing the long-pent-up pain and anger to come out is in itself therapeutic. There is both insight and relief involved in looking at where we came from. But that is not enough. Once having confronted the emotions and having gained the insights, the therapist must help the client to come back to today and deal with the here and now. The cycle is not complete until both parts have been done.

What Is Important in the Individual's Past Is Not the Events Themselves, but the Individual's Perception of the Events and What Choices the Individual Is Making About That Perception Today.

Perception refers to the rather intricate process by which the individual constructs an understanding of the social world out of the data he or she obtains from the environment. The data come from the events, people, and other stimuli available to a person in his or her everyday experience. But perception involves more than passively registering the stimuli that impinge upon the senses. Current expectations and past experiences influence the process of perception. It is a purely subjective process dependent more on what is in the individual than what is in the environment.

As an example of perception, consider two men who spend the night on the side of a mountain. The evening is cool and the stars are bright. Normal sounds of the night are all around them. For one man, an experienced outdoorsman, the night is beautiful and the sounds cheerful and heartening. For the other man, unfamiliar with the out-of-doors, the same sounds and sights are fearsome and overwhelming. The difference is in how each *perceives* the environment.

What is important, then, is not nearly so much what has happened to us in life as how we have interpreted what has happened. Take failure as an example. It is a rare person who has not failed in some important way in his or her life. What is most consequential is how the individual has interpreted that failure. If, for example, the person interprets failure as merely the lack of effort, he or she may feel some guilt and respond with renewed effort. On the other hand, if the person interprets the failure as a lack of ability, he or she may feel shamed and may despair and quit trying. The former interpretation is an external explanation and is subject to change. The individual feels a sense of control. That is, there is something one can do about the situation. The latter interpretation is more devastating. It is internal. That is, it belongs to the character of the person and to the individual. This fact may mean that it is not subject to change.

David and James are two boys who illustrate the origin of the sense of personal defectiveness and deformity called shame. Both are hypothetical ten-year-olds described by Fossum and Mason (1986, pp. 20-21). Each boy at some point in his life is attacked and beat up by a bully on the way home from school. "James' system has taught him to judge himself and his experience on a good-bad scale. He feels robbed of his dignity and feels that he is bad. When he arrives home he tells no one about what has happened to him. His response is dysfunctional for his growth, not because he feels the pain of having been treated abusively, but because he keeps the incident and his feelings secret." David however, "bursts into his house yelling, 'A terrible thing just happened to me!' He reacts with indignation to the assault, and as he does, he simultaneously feels the benefit of the supportive relationships and extends and deepens them. In effect, he expels the shame he feels and matures in his relationships."

For the therapist who is working years later with James, the significant thing is not the event of being beaten up. Rather it is the meaning this event had in the larger context of James's experience of his world at that time. In short, what did James do with the experience? How did he perceive it, and how has he responded to it? It is very important that clients be freed to get in touch with traumatic events of the past. And there is therapy in the simple catharsis of emotional release. It is a significant victory when a client comes to the point that she is able to say, "I have never told anyone this before in my life. When I was ten, my stepfather made me fondle him." But as relieving as it is to get these secrets out, the therapeutic work has just begun when it occurs. The client has discovered the blocks to a full life; now they must be removed. Too many clients and therapists are ready to quit when the client has achieved emotional release. It feels good to cry or get angry and let the feelings out. It is a relief to know where one's problems originated. But the major work begins at that point in restructuring one's perception of reality.

Therapy with a Codependent Client Moves Slowly and at the Client's Pace. Recovery Is Long Term.

As noted earlier, codependence is a way of thinking and behaving that the individual developed as a survival tool in a dysfunctional family. As such, codependence is a long-term and deeply ingrained set of characteristics. It also is a method that the individual uses to interpret and make sense of the world. Though painful, it nonetheless seems necessary to the person. He or she is reticent to give it up as a way of life. These facts in themselves make it a difficult problem to treat. Add to them that the client is frequently unaware of the connection of his behavior and the pain he or she is experiencing, and the problem becomes more difficult to treat.

As noted previously, it is the conviction of many thinkers and researchers that codependence falls within the DSM IIIR category of personality disorders. Diagnosing and treating personality disorders is very difficult, because they are based upon normal personality traits that for whatever reason, are made rigid and inflexible. It is at this point that they become maladaptive and begin to cause personal distress and impairment in social functioning. Nonetheless, to be asked to give up the dysfunctional patterns of thought or feeling or behavior can seem to the codependent like giving up his or her entire personality. It is not as simple as saying, "When you put your hand in the fire it hurts. So, stop putting your hand in fire." Codependents are much like the man who has been told that he has never needed the crutches on which he has depended all his life. Despite knowing this new truth, he holds the more fervently to the crutches, afraid that his legs are not strong enough to support him. If he throws away the crutches, he fears he will never be able to walk.

Cermak (1986, pp. 77–97) made an extensive description of the stages of recovery. He outlines four such stages:

> *Stage One: The Survival Stage.* During this stage, clients must dismantle their denial system, learn to focus on themselves, and learn to take responsibility for their own problems.

> *Stage Two: The Reidentification Stage.* At this point, the focus of therapy is to help clients accept and understand codependence, work through the grieving process as they accept the reality of their past, and become aware of their compulsivity. Clients must also set realistic limits for themselves and their own willpower.

> *Stage Three: The Core Issues Stage.* In this stage, clients work on the specific ways in which codependence has pervaded their lives. The issues are different for each individual in this phase. People tend to go at their own pace in this stage.

> *Stage Four: The Reintegration Stage.* This stage prepares the individual for termination of therapy.

These stages of recovery may have differing time frames from one individual to another. Also, recovery may not always flow smoothly from one stage to another. For some persons it may move back and forth repeatedly through various stages.

Entirely absent from this list is any reference to post-therapy recovery. For some, perhaps even the majority, recovery strategies are necessary after therapy is over. One may have to deal with relapses and, in some cases, the codependent may have to continue to deal with issues at increasingly deeper levels after he or she has left the care of the therapist.

This Field Is in the Emerging Stage and Much Discovery Is Yet to Be Made. A Therapist Must Be Open to New Developments and Research Findings.

No one who works in the field of mental health and chemical addiction would say that every person who grew up in an emotionally dysfunctional family suffers more emotional problems than those who did not. Some would even argue that while the term codependence is gaining popularity in magazines and workshops, we are making too much of the concept.

For example, Vince Hyman (1987, p. 3), editor of *Professional Update*, a newsletter of the influential Hazelden Institute in Minnesota, writes that the Hazelden

Family Center has chosen not to use the term *codependence* when dealing with family members of addicts. For them the word *codependent* is used to describe a phenomenon the manifestations of which have not emerged into a clearcut syndrome. Hyman notes that use of the term is a labeling process that may lead clients to focus on problems rather than on solutions. Hyman does admit that "...*any* chronic illness creates stress within the family system" and that, in that condition, "certain patterns of similar responses emerge."

Any therapist working in the area of codependence must remain aware that there is a great deal that is not known about the problem. One must avoid using the term as "treatment jargon." Simply knowing that a person grew up in a chemically dependent or otherwise dysfunctional family does not automatically provide sufficient evidence that the person suffers from codependence or for that matter from any other clinical disorder. Even when the behaviors, attitudes, and emotions of the individual lead toward the diagnosis of codependence, the therapist must remember that there are individual differences in degree. Therapists must move slowly and not lump individuals into preconceived categories. Scientists are just beginning to develop research to test these and related concepts. Time is needed to collect and analyze the empirical data necessary to answer the many questions that remain about codependence.

GOALS IN COUNSELING THE ADULT CHILD

All counselors can enhance therapy by remembering that the people they serve are complex, multifaceted persons who need a treatment plan that is unique and individualized. The counselor must recognize that no one goal or treatment outcome is apt to be appropriate for every client. A number of goals are available. Which one or which combination of them is appropriate depends on the specific needs of the client.

The following are some of the possible goals or treatment outcomes that a therapist working with the adult child may want to consider:

Understanding

The counselor is interested in helping the client to know *what* is actually going on in his or her life as well as *why* it is occurring. Sometimes this task involves overcoming the client's denial. It always involves a didactic element that is designed to give the client information and insight. Helping the client to see connections between present dysfunctional behavior and patterns learned in childhood is a major consideration in the development of understanding.

Helping the client to understand what is occurring and how it came about is a foundation to all other goals. All people are interested in the question, Why? They want to know, How did I get this way? Effective therapy helps them answer that question about themselves. Understanding, in the sense of having some sort of explanation for what is going on, gives us a sense of mastery and control. Taylor (1983, p. 1164) describes this need for explanation in persons with cancer. He concludes that answering the question, "How did I get this way?" helps create a sense of control that is useful in adjustment and coping. Bulman and Wortman (1977, p. 362) found the same thing in the rehabilitation of paraplegics. Codependent therapy must contain a teaching element that attempts to create understanding.

Change

This goal is a significant objective in most therapies. However, one must be careful not to assume that change is automatically an important goal for every client. Clients give lip service to their need for change. After all, one might reason, was it not for this purpose that the client came into the therapist's office? He or she is stuck and they want help in removing the pain and changing the behavior or thinking that causes the problem.

Experienced therapists realize that, more frequently than not, clients only want the pain to go away. Or they want someone else to change so as to solve their problem. That appears most true of codependents. To counter this tendency, the therapist must focus on keeping the client "within" himself or herself. Clients must be taught the difference between their wants and their needs. They need to be taught about the power of their own "self-talk." They need to learn about their own rituals and, most importantly, the ways they avoid becoming aware of and expressing their own true feelings. In these and similar areas, the therapist must focus on the *client's* need for change.

Self-Efficacy

Self-efficacy has to do with the internal locus of control. In effect, it is the belief that one has the competence and strength to cope effectively with one's environment. It is the sense that one is not merely the victim of outside forces over which one has no effective control. The presence of such a belief has an impact in all areas of one's life. It affects the way one thinks about oneself and the evaluation one makes of oneself. It has an impact on self-esteem and affects performance. Bandura (1982, pp. 127–128) explains:

> If self-efficacy is lacking, people tend to behave ineffectually even though they know what to do.... The higher the level of perceived self-efficacy, the greater the performance accomplishments. Strength of efficacy also predicts behavior change. The stronger the perceived efficacy, the more likely are people to persist in their efforts until they succeed.

Adult children do not have a strong sense of self-efficacy. They are characterized more by a sense of powerlessness. Some may overcompensate for this feeling by brave shows of grandiosity. The therapist must keep in mind the client's need for a more intrinsic sense of self-control.

One word of caution is necessary at this point: Codependents must learn to *give up* some types of control. They are frequently "rescuers" and "fixers" and believe that they are supposed to make a perfect world for others. Adult children learned early in childhood that they must control the environment for the benefit of others or control others within the environment. This type of control causes great stress in the codependent and is one of the beliefs that he or she must give up. Obviously, it is not to this kind of unreasonable control that the term *self-efficacy* refers. Codependent control is almost always control of others. Self-efficacy is control of self, in the sense of having viable choices, even in a changing and unpredictable environment.

Development of More Rational Stress Response

Adult children need to learn options other than their compulsions for relieving their stress. Because of poor coping skills and a sense of personal incompetence in solving their problems, codependents frequently develop patterns of stress relief that are themselves dysfunctional. They can find relief in the area of stress response by learning to face and understand their own personal reality. We can encourage them to know and express their feelings and to deal realistically with their own needs. Possibly most helpful of all, they can discover a sense of optimism and hope based on the belief that life does not have to be the way it has always been. Change is possible.

Spiritual Growth

The adult child must be led to deal with the most core belief about his or her basic value and meaning. Codependency is based on the belief that one is unworthy and thus deserves to be rejected and abandoned. Codependents come to be satisfied with second best and to accept the idea that they deserve what they get in life. The process of therapy invites the adult child to consider greater self-meaning and purpose in life. Essentially this is a spiritual step and it serves as an antidote for the feelings of unworthiness.

Calhoun (1976, p. 248) describes the spiritual nature of humankind:

> Our self-sense centers in our immediate awareness of our bodies engaged in social, cultural, and economic relationships. In the whole picture we must make room for what we may call the spiritual dimension of the self. *Spiritual* does not necessarily refer to an immaterial "soul" (although it may), but to a part of ourselves that transcends both our animal imperatives and our social role playing.

Thus, the spiritual describes the part of ourselves that is beyond the senses. It is the part of us that strives to push beyond ourselves, beyond the necessities of life, beyond the strictly natural world of the senses to the unattainable. William James (1900, p. 192) calls this self the "true, the intimate, the ultimate, the permanent me which I seek."

Spirituality, as it is understood here, is essentially the first three steps of the Twelve Steps of Alcoholics Anonymous.

1. We admitted we were powerless over alcohol—that our lives had become unmanageable.
2. We came to believe that a Power greater than ourselves could restore us to sanity.
3. We made a decision to turn our will and our lives over to the care of God, as we understood Him.

Spiritual growth fundamentally alters the understanding that codependents have of themselves. They discover that they are neither alone nor abandoned. They are not bad or unworthy. To the contrary, they are loved and valued both by a Higher Power and by the community that surrounds them.

Restructuring of Healthier Relationships

As the adult child changes through the various stages of recovery, a natural result is the restructuring of relationships. We must help the individual to anticipate that some unwanted results may occur in this area. Relationships amount to an ongoing stage play in which all participants have a role and follow a script. Recovery means that one begins to change the role and alter the script. That process is uncomfortable to the adult child and even more so to the other parties in the relationship. Frequently, the codependent feels that he or she is letting others down by the new behavior or attitudes and experiences internal pressure to return to the old ways. At other times, the pressure may come from others as they try to force the situation back into its old grooves.

The restructuring of relationships is a very important goal in recovery. And it is as difficult as it is important, even when the therapist is working with an entire family. Codependency begins in childhood in the context of a faulty relationship. Its patterns are developed to cope with this problematic and troubled relationship. Some of its most destructive and humiliating feelings and thoughts are involved with intimacy in present-day relationships. Among the most challenging aspects of working with adult children is the attempt to help them undo the prior hurt of early relationships and develop the skills to restructure present relationships in a healthier fashion.

Now, let us turn to how codependence looks in real life. What are its characteristics and what are its causes?

REFERENCES

Ackerman, R. (1983). *Children of Alcoholics: A Guide for Parents, Educators, and Therapists*, (2nd. ed.) New York: Simon & Schuster.

American Psychiatric Association (1987). *Diagnostic and Statistical Manual of Mental Disorders (3rd. ed.,-Rev.)*, Washington: American Psychiatric Association.

Bandura, A. (1982). "Self-efficacy Mechanism in Human Agency," *American Psychologist*, 37, 122–147.

Black, C. (1985). *Repeat After Me*, Denver: M.A.C.

Bulman, R., and Wortman, C. (1977). "Attributions of Blame and Coping in the 'Real World': Severe Accident Victims React to Their Lot," in *Journal of Personality and Social Psychology*, 35, 351–363.

Calhoun, D. (1976). *Persons-in-Groups: A Humanistic Social Psychology*, New York: Harper & Row.

Cermak, T. (1986). *Diagnosing and Treating Co-dependence*, Minneapolis: Johnson Institute Books.

Coleman, J., Butcher, J., and Carson R. (1984). *Abnormal Psychology and Modern Life* (7th ed.), Glenview, Ill.: Scott, Foresman.

Curran, D. (1983). *Traits of a Healthy Family*, Minneapolis: Winston Press.

Fossum, M., and Mason, M. (1986). *Facing Shame: Families in Recovery*, New York: W. W. Norton.

Gross, H. (1974). "Depressive and Sadomasochistic Personalities" in J. Lions Ed., *Personality Disorders: Diagnosis and Management*, Baltimore: Williams & Wilkins.

Hyman, V. (1987). "Some Thoughts on Co-dependency," *Professional Update*, February, 1987, 5: 3.

James, W. (1900). *Psychology*, New York: Holt, Rinehart & Winston.

Lidz, T. (1968). *The Person: His Development Through the Life Cycle*, New York: Basic Books.

Lee, J. (1987) *The Flying Boy: Healing the Wounded Man*, Austin, Tex.: New Men's Press.

Lewis J., Beavers, W., Gossett, J., and Phillips, V. (1976). *No Single Thread: Psychological Health in Family Systems*, New York: Brunner/Mazel.

Main, M. (1973). *Exploration, Play and Level of Cognitive Functioning as Related to Child-Mother Attachment*, Unpublished doctoral dissertation, Baltimore, Md.: Johns Hopkins University.

Michener, H. et al. (1986). *Social Psychology*, San Diego: Harcourt Brace Jovanovich.

Rosenberg M. (1965). *Society and the Adolescent*, Princeton, N.J.: Princeton University Press.

St. John's Hospital, "What Is Co-dependency?" Unpublished paper, Salina, Kans.

Schaef, A. (1987) *When Society Becomes an Addict*, San Francisco: Harper & Row.

Taylor, S. (1983). "Adjustment to Threatening Events: A Theory of Cognitive Adaptation," in *American Psychologist*, 38, 1161–1173.

3

CODEPENDENCE IN EVERYDAY LIFE

Mental health professionals are still in the process of defining codependence, and therefore some ambiguity surrounds the term. This vagueness can detract from effective therapy. The counselor interested in helping adult children needs a clear understanding of what the concept means as well as how people and families become codependent. The purpose of this chapter is to offer a concise definition of codependence and discuss its causes. Two questions are central in the chapter: (1) What is codependence? That is, what does it look like in the individual and in the family? How is codependence formally defined? (2) What are the causes of codependence? That is, what are the specific factors that cause codependence?

CODEPENDENCE IN EVERYDAY LIFE

An Example

Ben and Marty had been lovers for five years before they divorced their respective spouses and married each other. Marty had a seven-year-old son and a three-year-old daughter when the two married. The couple was fairly certain that Ben was the father of the three-year-old daughter. Ben also had two teenage sons by his first wife. They worked together in a large insurance firm. Ben was a million-dollar seller and Marty was an administrative assistant to one of the vice-presidents. They were both attractive and physically healthy persons.

Their combined salaries provided them a more ample living, and they led what appeared to be a very exciting life. They traveled throughout the United States and Europe. They bought fancy cars and boats and lived in expensive homes. They gambled in Las Vegas and Atlantic City, ate in the best restaurants, and exercised in the best health clubs. To the outsider, they gave the appearance of fulfilling the American Dream. On the inside, it was a great deal different.

They went for marriage counseling after being married only two years. Their presenting complaint was that they fought bitterly and incessantly. Marty disapproved of Ben because he was sharp-tongued and critical. She doubted his love because he made demands of her because she could not get along with his children. Ben complained that Marty was fearful and jealous toward his former wife and children. He felt controlled because he thought he had to have her permission to see his children. He was also afraid that she was not faithful to him, a fact Marty consistently denied while accusing him of infidelity to her. Ben laughed at that fear and denied his infidelity in such a way as to confirm Marty's fear.

Marty described Ben as a "stuffed rooster." He was too tough on her, she complained, while he gave in to the demands of his mother and children. For his part, Ben tried to be macho. He was quick witted and kept everyone at a distance with sharp verbal stabs. He pointed to his success in making money as proof that he was well adjusted and needed no counseling. In Ben's view, the problem was all Marty's.

Ben's parents were both alcoholics. His father was a "hard-drinking" man who had made a lot of money in real estate. Ben described him as a big man who drove Cadillacs. They had never been close, and even now Ben felt more awe of his father than love for him. Ben had always been much closer to his mother. She was a shrewd businessperson, and he still consulted her for advice. Ben said that he "admired her but did not know if he loved her." He never felt that she really approved of him. He said, "She loved me but never really liked me. I always felt that I could not please her, no matter how hard I tried." Despite a six-figure salary, Ben still borrowed money from his mother and frequently did not pay it back.

Marty came from a different background. Her parents divorced when she was two years old and she never saw her real father again after that. When she was about fourteen, she learned that he had committed suicide shortly after the divorce. Her mother married a "mousey little man who provided the family with an income but little else." Her mother "bossed him around" and he did everything her mother told him to do. Her mother was also a rigidly religious woman who made everyone in the family go to church "twice on Sunday and once on Wednesday night." Marty had no memory of her mother ever hugging her and telling her that she loved her. She continued to see her mother, making weekly trips back to her home town. But, she confessed, "I still feel like a little girl with her and that I have to do what she wants. I am still uncomfortable around her."

As a child, Marty had felt loved by her maternal grandmother, who lived in the same small town as she. For that reason, she spent a lot of time at her grandmother's house. She felt sad most of the time and believed that she had to get away from her mother if she was to be happy. She explained, "I despised my stepfather because he was weak and let my mother push him around." She fantasized about how much her real father loved and wanted her. She wished that he would come back and get her.

Ben and Marty were both classic adult children, and they had a codependent relationship. They were unhappy with themselves, with their lives, and with each other. They wanted to be loved and to love another person. Yet, everything they did resulted in less love and more unhappiness. They had all the trappings of a successful middle-class life. But they were filled with inner demons that they could neither understand nor control.

Let's look at some of the factors that Ben and Marty illustrate about codependence.

Characteristics of Codependence

Codependence starts in childhood. Ben and Marty did not get what they needed in their families of origin. Important gaps were left in the childhood experiences of each. They missed the love and acceptance that are essential for a healthy foundation upon which to build a life.

Beane and Lipka (1984, p. 18), educational psychologists and experts on the development of children, point out that there are relatively few homes today in which the child experiences acceptance and love. They explain, "Many parents are unhappy with their own lives or do not know how to construct a healthy environment for their young. A few even feel that an oppressed childhood will 'build character,' thereby leading to a healthier adulthood. In such homes, children may face constant physical punishment or abuse, tentative and conditional love, rejection and denial of self-worth. The message to children in these circumstances is that they are neither loved nor trusted and that they do not really belong."

To describe the family atmosphere that produces the healthy and well-adjusted child, they quote Hymes (1963, p. 25):

> Lucky is the child to whom body and hands speak an overriding message of pride and joy. Lucky is the child whose experiences with mothering speak to him of unconditional love! His parents are delighted with him, just as he is. There is nothing he could do to earn more love; there is nothing he could do which would take love away. He is loved with no strings attached.

Ben and Marty missed those experiences and they were paying an enormous cost in their adult lives.

Codependence creates inner turmoil and distress. Ben and Marty's presenting problem was their marriage, and their complaints were all about each other. Their *real* problem, however, had to do with the way they regarded *themselves.*

Codependence produces negative self-feelings. These feelings are the deepest and most painful problems in self-esteem. They are more destructive than merely not liking oneself. The nucleus around which the codependent builds his or her self-image is, "I am *worthless*; I have no value at all."

As noted in the previous chapter, this feeling is *shame*. Shame is the belief that there is something wrong with the way we are. This feeling arises out of the lack of love and acceptance that the child experiences in the family of origin. The child reasons, if there were not something wrong with me, they would love me and I would be okay with them.

Ben and Marty carry around in their inner being these negative self-feelings. These feelings produce a sadness and an anger that they must somehow assuage. Furthermore, they must keep anyone from seeing their real selves, because that self (as they perceive it through their shame) is deformed and inadequate. Much of their adult behavior is designed to help them get what they want from others in a manipulative and deceptive way. They are reduced to these methods because they believe no one will love and accept them as they are.

Codependence interferes with one's ability to establish intimate relationships. This inability to establish intimacy may be one of the most severe consequences of a dysfunctional family. Having grown up without intimacy, the adult child is condemned to establish dysfunctional relationships that continue to block that intimacy.

Dysfunctional families deny children access to love and acceptance. These children do not perceive themselves as worthy of love. Deep below the surface of their conscious mind, they believe that no one will ever love them as they are. They must continually conceal what they are if they are to have love and acceptance. Being loved is a major goal of their lives, but they cannot ever be trusting and vulnerable in such a way as to receive and give genuine intimacy.

Among Ben and Marty's deepest needs was the need to be loved. They were no different from any other person in this regard. Their lives had demonstrated their search for intimacy. Ben's affairs were his attempts to find acceptance and hide the inner pain that he was not lovable. Marty's efforts to keep him away from his children and former wife were her struggles to have his love exclusively. She could not share his love because of her fears that he would choose someone else over her because she is unworthy. The only way she could feel loved was to have his unrestricted attention. Their fights were motivated by their great need to be loved by the other person and their belief that they would not get their needs met. Thus, they tried to control the other person in the only way they knew how.

Codependent individuals communicate indirectly. As noted above, adult children believe that they are worthless and therefore will never get what they want and need. They become distrustful. They scheme and control and manipulate. They attempt to get what they want in devious ways. They seldom share their feelings directly and just ask for what they need. Rather, they are oblique and evasive and rarely get straight to the point.

Marty was afraid that she would lose Ben's love. But instead of talking directly about that fear, she attacked his former wife and children. She made fun of Ben's dependence on his mother. She tried to keep other people out of his life. She was manipulative and devious.

Ben, on the other hand, was afraid of powerful women. Rather than talk openly with his wife about her control in his life and ask her to give him more room, he belittled and mocked her. Then, to prove that he was not under her control, he did exactly the opposite of what she wanted.

Neither Ben nor Marty was getting their needs met. The harder Marty tried to control Ben, the more he resisted her control. And the more he resisted, the harder she tried. Neither one of them could stop the cycle by really dealing with what was going on in themselves or how they saw the relationship. What was true in their marriage was also true in the associations they had with their parents and children. They were just as dishonest and controlling in those relationships.

Codependence comes in different patterns.   Ben and Marty share a similar way of thinking and feeling about themselves and the surrounding social environment. But they have different ways of behaving to deal with those thoughts and feelings.

Ben was aggressive and competitive, sometimes bordering on antisocial. He was caustic, rude, harsh, and overbearing. To get what he wanted, he could be bullying and intimidating. Yet, he could be charming and winsome, as his acheivements in selling demonstrated. His competitiveness in the business world came from his insecurity. He felt he must succeed in the financial sphere to live up to his father's model and to get his mother's approval. Yet, as with many bullies, his aggressive behaviors were rooted in his fearfulness and insecurity.

Marty was very acquiescent. She never yelled and never bullied Ben. She was calm and submissive. Her anger was exhibited in her passive-aggressive style. For example, she tried to control Ben's contact with his former wife by telling him he had "his tail between his legs." She could be clinging, demanding to know Ben's every move and his whereabouts at all times. She was very dependent and tried to make him feel responsible for her fear and sense of inadequacy.

Codependent behaviors are persistent and repetitive.   The destructive patterns of self-thinking and feeling begin in childhood as methods of surviving in a family that fails to meet the child's genuine needs. They are learned coping mechanisms that perform *instrumental* functions for the child in his or her family. They are ingrained into the personality of the child and provide the bedrock for the way he or she sees the world. The child uses this mental map of reality as the foundation for strategies that allow the child to achieve positive reinforcements and avoid negative ones. These patterns of self-thinking and self-feeling are not, therefore, episodic like some other forms of mental disorders. Rather, they are an internalized and persistent part of how the adult sees the world and himself or herself in it.

Thus, these patterns of seeing the world and behaving in it become automatic, unconscious responses to specific situations. The adult child engages in these self-limiting ways of acting without any consideration of alternatives. In fact, the codependent may not even be aware of alternatives. "This is just the way I am," he or she may say, "and there is nothing I can do about it." Or, what is even worse, the adult child sees the behaviors as normal and perhaps even morally desirable.

Marty's need to control Ben because of her insecurity that he might not otherwise come back to her is an example of her belief that her behavior was desirable. Until she came to understand differently, Marty saw these behaviors as expressions of her "love" for Ben. "I am deeply in love with him," she explained to me. "I need him desperately and would be destroyed without him." Marty further justified her controlling behavior as love for Ben. "He is too dependent on his ex-wife and children and I want him to grow up. Besides, they hurt him by taking advantage of him."

In truth, Marty had learned in childhood that she had to define everything carefully and make specific boundaries for other people's actions, or her needs would go lacking. As a child, her controlling rigidity allowed her to stake out her space in her family of origin and make sure that her interests would not be ignored like her stepfather's were. Also, she saw this kind of thinking and acting modeled by her mother. For Marty, her mother's way was the normal design of femininity. She was only doing what she considered to be natural, and she was largely unaware of the destructiveness of her controlling behavior.

Codependency is a subtle and elusive form of addiction. Neither Ben nor Marty thought of themselves as addicts. They both were individuals whose friends thought they were well adjusted and happy. They possessed all the status symbols that are associated with success in American society. What they lacked was the peace and serenity that comes from feeling good about themselves.

They were addicted to the patterns of behavior and thinking they had developed in childhood to cover the pain and insecurity they experienced. These patterns had gotten them through childhood and they were still hooked on them. The problem was that those patterns had left them with no inner sense of their own value, so they looked for their worth outside themselves. They were incapable of approving of themselves and had to get approval from others. They tried to get a feeling of self-worth from the things they owned, the places they traveled, their promotions and job titles, and their "love" relationships. They had no sense of their own competency as human beings, so they had to substitute power over each other and attain victory in arguments.

Chemically addicted persons believe that the solution to their problems is found in the chemical. They are dependent on the fix. The drug relieves their pain and misery by producing an altered state of consciousness and the illusion of energy and strength. With most drugs, it takes more and more of it to achieve less and less relief. Ben and Marty were no less addicted. Their own lack of self-love and self-acceptance led them to a dependency on a fix that came from outside themselves. These external things produced in them an altered state of consciousness. And just as for the chemically addicted person, their addiction gave temporary relief and led to even more pain. More pain, in turn, created greater dependence on the compulsive and irrational behaviors and thoughts.

Definition of Codependence

This is the definition of codependence that I have found most serviceable in therapy:

> Codependence is a maladaptive bonding within a family system. To survive psychologically and socially in this dysfunctional family, the child adopts patterns of thinking, acting, and feeling that at first dull the pain but finally are self-negating in themselves. These patterns become internalized and form an essential part of the personality and world view of the individual. The child continues to practice these self-destructive patterns of thinking, behaving, and feeling in adulthood and in so doing recreates over and over again the bonding in which the destructive patterns originated.

How do these destructive patterns of behaving, feeling, and thinking make their way into the individual's personality? What may we say about the *causes* of codependence? These are the questions to which we now turn.

CODEPENDENCE AND THE DEVELOPMENT OF THE SELF

If Ben and Marty are to experience personal healing and develop a healthy relationship with each other, they must develop a new and different view of themselves. Whereas their self-perception had previously been negative and not clearly focused, they must come to see themselves in more positive terms. They must gain a healthier and more realistic view of their place in their psychological world. Where they have previously felt that they were limited in their life choices, they must come to see the legitimate power they have over *themselves*. Where they have feared that they were incompetent as persons, they must become experientially acquainted with their true value. In short, healing for these adult children must begin with the *self*. It is in the development of the self that codependence originally entered their lives.

The Person and the Self

James (1890) suggested that the self is both the "knower" and the "known." In other words, the self is both the capacity to see ourselves as an object and the object that is seen. The self can be simultaneously thinker and perceiver and the object that is thought about. James called the knowing part of the self the "I." The part that is the object, he called the "me." Thus, the "I" is the knower, the self as subject. It is the "I" that is aware of how we look to others. With the "I," we are able to be self-transcendent and stand outside ourselves, seeing ourselves as we imagine others to see us.

The "me," on the other hand, is the self that is seen. It is the self as object, ("I" see "me"). For example, let us say that I gave a speech at an intellectual club last evening. As I went through my speech, I was aware of how I was looking to the people in the audience. I saw myself talking smoothly and making a positive impression. For no apparent reason, I stumble over a word and can't pronounce it correctly. I am aware now of a different "me." Before the slip, the object I saw was a fluent and engaging speaker. After bungling the word, I see a stumbling and inadequate speaker.

In codependence therapy, the "me" is the part of the self with which we are concerned. The adult child has a self-perception that is negative and inadequate. The child's interaction with his or her social and psychological environment, beginning with infancy, has warped the "me" that the adult carries around in his or her head.

Self-Perception and Self-Esteem

It is necessary to differentiate at this point between the *self-perception* and the *self-esteem* of the individual. Most people use these two terms synonymously. They are not and must be clearly distinguished by the therapist. The former is the image which the person has of himself or herself. When I stop and think of me, what comes to my mind is my "self-perception or self-concept." According to Michener, DeLamater, and Schwartz (1986, p. 38), the self as object is based on *self-descriptors*. The normal person draws this image on the basis of two types of descriptors: (1) The first they call *roles*. Individuals see themselves in terms of roles they play in life. Some important roles are occupation, age, sex, group membership, and religion. (2) The second type of descriptor they call *personal qualities* or *attributes*. Individuals are aware of self-qualities like their interpersonal style (introverted, cool, friendly), emotional style (moody, optimistic), body image (good looking, fat), and material possessions (owns a Porsche).

Self-esteem, on the other hand, refers to the evaluation one makes of the self-perception. Individuals draw conclusions about themselves and have feelings about the self they perceive. These conclusions are usually based on the extent to which they succeed in living up to self-defined or other-defined expectations. These expectations may be realistic or unrealistic, conscious or unconscious. The point is that people feel proud of the self as they perceive it, or they feel shame and embarrassment about that self. Depending on whether or not they experience a sense of satisfaction, they either want others to see what they see, or they want to hide and keep their self a secret. Positive evaluations include a sense of competence (creative, clumsy), sense of self-determination (ambitious, self-starter), sense of moral worth (trustworthy, evil), and sense of unity (mixed up, a whole person).

Development of the Self

Beginning with Cooley (1902), social scientists have understood that the self develops in interaction with other people. He pointed out that self-perceptions and their attendant self-evaluations are a reflection (or mirror image) of the way we believe others view us. He referred to this concept as the "looking-glass self." Mead (1934) further developed the idea by suggesting that the self actually emerges in interaction with "significant others," especially in the family, and that all forms of games and play in which children participate are important in the development of the self. For Mead, the self is simply the collective culture of the society mediated through the family and internalized by the child.

Codependence and the self. The self, then, is the image the individual has of himself or herself (self-perception) along with the evaluation (self-esteem) the person makes of that picture. It is central to the emotional health of the person. How does the self develop? What are the processes that can keep the self from properly developing? How do these processes contribute to the development of codependence in the dysfunctional family?

The answer to those questions lies in the almost limitless malleability and amazing developmental potential that human infants have. Totally helpless at birth, human babies have the animal kingdom's longest period of immaturity. They are the most helpless and vulnerable of all newborns. Human infants are absolutely dependent on the environment for social, psychological, and physical survival. They take years to acquire the knowledge and understanding that are necessary for the living of life as a human being.

One of the first things that the baby begins to do is distinguish between *self* and *nonself.* Within the first few weeks of birth, the infant learns to draw a boundary between that which is "me" and that which is "not me." Naturally, the line of demarcation is at first fuzzy. Lidz (1968, p. 123) shows how important the family is in these early stages of self-development: "...during infancy...there is no clear boundary between the self and the remainder of the world, and the infant cannot differentiate between how he feels and what the mother does that influences his feeling."

Interacting with the environment, the growing child continues to get a picture of what the self "looks" like. At the same time, the child is developing a concept of the world. The perception of the self and the image of the environment is like a *cognitive and emotional map*, a map that will steer first the child and then the adult through the complexity of living. This map includes the sense of who the child is, what the child might or might not become, what is and is not important, as well as the nature of the environment in which the child lives. Some children come out of that early period with the sense that they are good and valuable and wanted and that their environment is warm and accepting and encouraging. Others get the opposite impression. They sense their environment to be harsh and uncharitable and themselves to be inadequate to cope with it.

Lidz (1968, pp. 117–118) commented on the importance of the first fifteen months of life in the development of the self: "These are a very long fifteen months. During no other period of life is the person so transformed both physically and developmentally. Yet what happens lies beyond the individual's recall, buried in the oblivion of wordlessness. At most a vague feeling, some amorphous recollection that eludes memory may upon occasion flit in and out of an adult's awareness....The inability to recollect our infancies sets limitations on our capacities properly to understand or depict the period."

Codependence and the life cycle. These beginning months start a process that continues throughout childhood. Indeed, as Erikson (1968) has shown, the individual spends the entire life cycle working through specific challenges to the development of self-understanding and self-acceptance. Childhood years set the tone for the rest of life. The child adopts a stance that acts as a filter that organizes raw behavior and helps the individual to interpret what is going on in his or her world. These perceptions are powerful because the child is largely unaware of them. According to Vallacher, Wegner, and Hoine (1980), we look *through* the rules but rarely *at* them. They are powerful because they do not easily change. Coleman, Butcher, and Carson (1984, p. 110) comment on the imperviousness of these filters:

> New experience tends to be *assimilated* into our existing cognitive framework, even if the new information has to be reinterpreted or distorted to make it fit. We tend to cling to existing assumptions and reject or distort new information that is contradictory to them. *Accommodation*—changing our existing framework to make it possible to incorporate discrepant information—is more difficult and threatening, especially where very important assumptions are challenged.

These authors further point out that, out of this understanding of our *self* and our place in our environment, we develop a consistent pattern of perceiving, thinking, feeling, and acting. They call this consistent pattern a "characteristic *life-style*." It brings with it a set of "inner controls" that give us direction and help us find meaning in our existence.

Thus, the neonate and the young child are extremely vulnerable in family relationships. Both the individual's self-perception and self-esteem unfold in those early, formative years. During this time, the child acquires the cognitive and emotional map that will filter future events as well as give them a general stance toward life or a life style. In the dysfunctional family, the basic psychological and social needs of the child go unmet. The dysfunctional family leaves a child with the perception of an inadequate self and a complex set of behaviors and feelings that the child developed to cope with that pain. Both the perception of the self and the attendant behaviors and feelings are codependence.

Charlie Brown, of the *Peanuts* cartoon strip, shows the pain of a broken self. According to Schulz (1975, p. 81), the creator of the cartoon strip, Charlie Brown is a "loser." He is "a put upon character." Charlie is depicted as a child, but he symbolizes the frustration and failure of the adult. Schulz (1963, p. 9) interprets the entire cast of characters as a commentary on the problems that adults maintain from childhood. He wrote, "Linus' affection for his blanket...is a symbol of the things we cling to....What I am getting at, of course, is the adult's inadequacy here—the inability to give up habits which really should be given up." It is not without significance that Schulz first called his comic, "Li'l Folks." This title correctly conveys the impression that, while these characters are drawn as children, they are adults. They represent the wounded and devalued child that still exists within the adult and the pain and delimitation the adult experiences through this child. For the adult child, it is painful to think, as Lucy frequently reminds Charlie, that "Your problem is that you are *you*."

Figure 3 shows in schematic detail the psychodynamic stages of codependence throughout childhood and early adolescence, and into late adolescence and adulthood. Each rectangle represents a cycle that begins in a specific stage and is carried into the next developmental phase. It begins with a set of dysfunctional childhood experiences (Stage 1) that result in an excessively dependent child. This negative cycle moves into and is repeated in Stage 2. The adolescent child responds to his or her unmet emotional needs by denial or by the development of negative self-feelings. By late adolescence or early adulthood (Stage 3), a set of rigid and compulsive behaviors and attitudes are added to the cycle developed in Stage 2. These further contribute to the negative self-feelings that give rise to one of several pain-reducing compulsions, such as various addictions, including those to chemicals, food, sex, rage, work, perfectionism, or religion. By late adolescence and early adulthood, the negative self-feelings are reinforced by the compulsive and addictively rigid behaviors in a vicious cycle of psychological, physical, emotional, and spiritual dependence.

Let's look at some conditions in the family that have been associated with codependence.

Family Relationships, the Self, and Codependence

Perhaps the most popular generalization about the development of codependence is the assumption that some form of early disturbance occurred in a family relationship. Before looking at some of the family conditions that result in children who grow up to have codependent problems in adulthood, we must look at the *circularity* of causality.

In our western heritage, we have become accustomed to thinking about causality as being *linear*. That is, everything moves in a straight line from one point to another. In the western concept of time, the present replaces the past and the future replaces the present. It all flows in a straight line from beginning to end, from cause to effect.

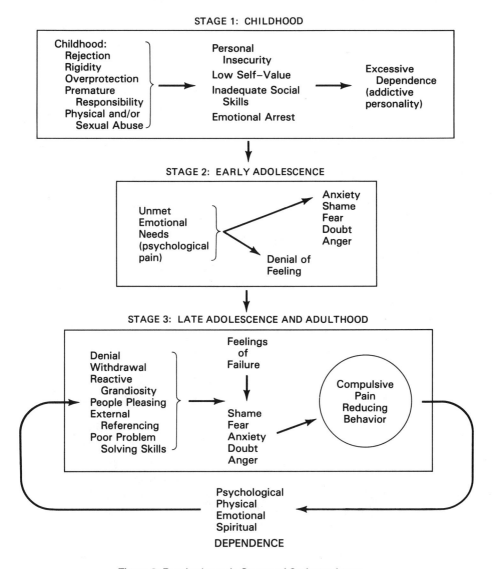

Figure 3: Psychodynamic Stages of Codependency.

In linear causation, A causes B, which causes C. The batter swings the bat (A), the bat strikes the ball (B), and the ball flies over the fence (C). Much of our thinking about family problems and mental and personality problems falls into this kind of limited thinking. Linear causality fixes blame. The parents are inadequate (A), Suzy is damaged in growing up (B), and Suzy becomes a codependent adult (C). Therefore, the parents are at fault.

By contrast, the concept of circular causality sees events as occurring in a cyclical fashion. Life flows more in an endless round, like a circle. Spring leads to summer, which gives way to fall, which leads to winter. Then it all starts over again. In circular causality, A causes B, and B causes A. Both have an effect on C which, in turn, has an effect on both A and B.

Let's take the Smith family as an example of circular causality. Mrs. Smith was busy with her job when Mary Beth was in elementary school. Mary Beth felt left out and became surly and irritable. Because of Mary Beth's behavior problems, Mrs. Smith felt inadequate as a parent and turned more to her job to get a sense of her worth. As a result, Mary Beth felt more left out and tried harder, through negative behaviors, to get Mrs. Smith's attention. Mr. Smith, in turn, was involved in providing for the family and in building his own career. He expected Mrs. Smith to do most of the nurturing. He was critical of both Mrs. Smith for her ineffective parenting (as evidenced by Mary Beth's behavior problems) and of Mary Beth's attitude and behavior toward her mother. Both of them felt worse about themselves because of his expectations. Mrs. Smith worked harder and Mary Beth got more aggressive in response to Mr. Smith's criticism. Mr. Smith responded with more criticism. In this manner, each person affected all others and was, in turn, affected by all others.

Seeing circular causality in most dysfunctional families means, according to Molineux (1985, p. 58) that we must be careful when placing blame. In most cases, there are no heroes and no villains, no good guys and no bad guys. What we, as counselors, look for in searching for the family's role in causing codependence is not *blame*, but *understanding*. Our purpose is to enlighten so as to find solutions, not to fix responsibility so as to assign guilt.

The concept of circular causality is also beneficial to the codependent because he or she has frequently assumed *self-blame* for the problems in the family. They come into therapy expecting the therapist to blame them for the problem. Helping them see that they, along with other members of their family, were victims of a system that had negative effects on everybody is, in itself, extremely therapeutic.

With this concept of circular causality in mind, let us investigate the conditions of family life that can produce the negative patterns of codependency in the individual.

Parental loss.   Many codependents report having lost a parent during childhood. Usually the separation comes through divorce or death, but for some, the trauma may occur through adoption. This fact is very important since sociologists predict that half of all marriages performed in the 1980s will end in divorce, and *half of the children born in the 1980s will spend a part of their childhood with a single parent* (Robertson, 1987, p. 366).

Hare (1970) suggested that a key factor was not the parental loss per se, but the emotional disturbances in the family relationships created by the departure of the parent. Children do not accept the separation automatically. They see their survival threatened and they feel abandoned. Persell (1987, p. 317) argues that the child cannot accept the term *one-parent family.* Emotionally the child considers this term inappropriate. She cites the work of Wallerstein and Kelly (1980, p. 307) as evidence. After a five year study of sixty divorcing families, one conclusion the researchers reached was that the self-images of the children "were firmly tied to their relationship with both parents and they thought of themselves as children with two parents who had elected to go their separate ways."

In other words, many children do not see the parent as *gone,* but themselves as *left.* Kristen felt that way. She wrote:

> He left for good at Christmas of 1978. He took with him my admiration and love along with a large share of my mother's heart and sanity. So began my long journey into rejection and hopelessness.

> I was a healthy and happy ten year old—thin, pretty, bright, doing well in school. When he left, I began to eat. Inhale may be the better word. I gained forty pounds in the spring and summer of 1979. I was lost in sadness.

> He called daily at first. We lived only a few miles from him in Houston and I saw him every week-end for about six months. Then the contact began to decrease slowly. My weight went up and my grades went down. First "B's" then "C's" and "D's." His tactics changed. He was "disappointed" in me and I had "let him down." I tried. I mean I *really* tried. I wanted to please him because I believed that if I were thin and smart, he would come back.

> My mom and I moved to Dallas in 1980. The phone calls became less and the visits non-existent. I stayed fat and continued to do poorly in school. I despised myself.

> Today, at nineteen I see him once a year, if that much, and talk to him once every few months. I still desire his attention and want his approval. (What I want is his *love.*) On legal forms next to "Father's Name," I write, "Not Applicable!" I resent that he has so little interest in me.

> So. Now all I have is *me.* I had that all along. And, oh God, please let that be enough.

Parental rejection. Some parents are cold and distant with their children. They do not encourage open and warm relationships in the family, and the children feel cut off and abandoned. The child always concludes that the parent does not provide warm, loving support because the *child* is inadequate. I have never seen a child who says, "My parents do not seem to want to love me. Since I am obviously a good and lovable person, something must be wrong with *them.*" Rather, the child makes negative assumptions about himself or herself. These disapproving self-feelings have destructive results on personality development. Coleman, Butcher, and Carson (1984, p. 130) point out that parental rejection produces feelings of anxiety, insecurity, low self-esteem, negativism, hostility, attention seeking, loneliness, jealousy, and slowness of consciousness development. They cite the work of Buss (1966), who found that children who grow up in cold, distant families become adults who are cold and distant in their relationships. They conclude that, "Although the child learns the formal attributes and amenities of social situations, he or she does not develop empathy for others or become emotionally involved with them" (p. 255).

Often the codependent individual grows up in a family in which one parent (usually, but not always, the father) is rejecting and the other parent is overly protective. These mixed signals further confuse the child. What appears to be a loving relationship develops between the emotionally protective parent and the child. Actually, the relationship is little more than a parent–child coalition in which the child becomes responsible for the well-being of that parent, a condition referred to by Boszormenyi-Nagy and Spark (1973) as *parentification.* Another name used to describe this circumstance is *emotional incest.* The child ameliorates the rejection of one parent by becoming responsible for the other parent. The child's need to be a child, to be nurtured and cared for by accepting and responsible adults, goes lacking. Bernard and Corrales (1979, p. 80) conclude, "The child becomes an adult prematurely."

Corley's father was a lawyer and land developer. She was the second child of a family that included four children. She was sixteen when I first met her. Her sister, two years older than she, had just had an abortion. The family was very religious, and the oldest child's sexual misconduct was more than the father could take. He brought her in for counseling and in the course of working with her, I asked that the entire family come in for a couple of sessions. They did. Figure 4 shows the seating arrangements when they settled in the room for the first session, an arrangement that symbolized the inner workings of the family.

Mother and children sat huddled together while father sat at a distance from them all.

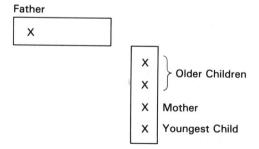

Figure 4: Family seating arrangement.

Corley was the "parent child." When Mother spoke, she looked at Corley for confirmation. Corley smiled, nodded, and gestured approvingly. She reinterpreted each person's comments when they were unclear. Mother was the family's designated "feeler." She cried, got hysterical, wrung her hands in bewilderment, and laughed for the whole family. Father was stiff, self-assured, confident, and controlled. For him everything was black and white. He was the family rule maker and conscience. Throughout the discussion, he stayed logical and analytical. At one point, late in the session, Bettiann, the daughter who had had the abortion, said that she had never felt close to her father. I asked her to talk about that feeling. She responded with a description of her father as emotionally absent from the family. In effect, she said that she had never felt that he loved her. After she completed her tearful and honest response to my query, I asked the father how he felt about what she had said. His response was to recite the historical events of her childhood and to justify his behaviors. Each time I tried to bring him into the present with questions about his current feelings about his daughter, he resisted with analysis or explanation.

Finally, I said, "Your daughter doesn't feel loved by you. That hurts her and she wants to talk with you about it. She's having a hard time feeling loved by anyone. What do you say?" He spoke with no expression on his face or in his voice as he said, "She is wrong. If she does not know by now that I love her, there is nothing I can do about it." I turned to Bettiann for her response, and she said, "I want him out of my life."

Unrealistic parental expectations.   In many families, the parents convey or the child comes to feel that he or she must live up to a set of impossible expectations. The demand for perfection and other unrealistic demands helps create in children a lack of spontaneity and a rigid conscience. These children are set up for severe conflicts. They struggle with guilt and a sense of personal failure. Children who come from such an environment very often lack a sense of playfulness. They are extremely serious and work hard.

This condition may occur in any family, regardless of its socioeconomic status. One or both parents may be either very successful or complete failures. In the family in which the parent is successful, the child may feel that he or she has to live up to the parent's example. In families in which the parents are not successful, the child may feel that the family honor and good name rest on his or her accomplishments.

This problem is most prevalent in families in which one or both parents, irrespective of their own personal accomplishments, suffer from low self-esteem. Coopersmith (1981) has shown that high self-esteem in parents is positively correlated with high self-esteem in children. There are a number of reasons for this:

1. Parents with high self-esteem model this behavior for their children. They show them what healthy self-esteem looks like. Parents with low self-esteem do just the opposite. They demonstrate to their children the feelings and behaviors of a person who thinks little of himself or herself.

2. Parents with high self-esteem are able to tolerate their children's differing ideas and emotions. They are more flexible and are therefore less likely to attempt to force their children into a preexisting mold. In such a family, the children experience themselves as persons who have worthy ideas and are valuable enough to express them freely.

3. Parents with high self-esteem are more effective disciplinarians for their children. They are firm but flexible and thus avoid the twin problems of being either too harsh or too permissive. With either of those extremes, the children experience themselves as not being valuable. When parents are rigidly strict, the children sense themselves as being secondary to the rules and therefore as having no value. When the parents are so permissive as to place no limits on the children's behavior, the children perceive themselves as lost and are unsure of what they can do to be worthy persons.

4. Finally, parents with high self-esteem are less likely to need to live vicariously through their children. Parents with low self-esteem, on the other hand, more characteristically live through the accomplishments of their children. They have a greater probability, therefore, of conveying impossible expectations to their children. In this situation, the children perceive themselves to have importance and to be loved and accepted only if they can perform up to the parents' expectations.

Billy was a workaholic. He was a fifty-seven-year-old college professor driven to produce more than anyone else on his faculty. He came from a blue-collar family in which the father was an alcoholic. His father was, to use Billy's term, a "falling-down drunk." Billy's mother had served as surrogate mother for her seven sisters and brothers. Although Billy was the oldest child in his own family, he grew up almost as a sibling to his uncles and aunts. While his father had been a wage earner as a carpenter, Billy's uncles had gone to college and entered the business world to become financial successes. One had become the manager of a local department store, and another annually paid more in income tax than Billy's father earned in a year. His aunts had married well and their husbands provided financially for their families. Only Billy's mother had married "beneath the family." They lived in a small ragged house on the edge of town. Billy was ashamed of his house and would not bring any of his friends home with him.

To complicate things even more for Billy, his mother was rigidly religious. She practiced a fundamentalist religion that condemned anything less than teetotalism. Thus, Billy's mother was able to cloak her resentment about her husband's financial failure under religious contempt for his alcoholism. She put the father down with infallible arguments that neither Billy nor the father could refute. She could vent her anger at her husband without taking personal responsibility for it.

Billy felt that, to gain his mother's love, he had to be the person in his family who performed up to the level of his uncles and aunts. He had to save his mother's honor. He learned early that his mother and others in her church noticed and praised him for working hard and for being "good." This latter term meant being religious and following the rules of morality in their religion. They made statements like, "You are not like most young people." Billy felt special. The result was that Billy became a person who felt comfortable and loved only when he was working. He could not relax. Even worse, Billy could feel accepted as a part of any group only if he did more than any other person in the group. To be accepted, he had to be unique. He could be unique only if he sacrificed himself in the service of the group. Thus, Billy worked hard to be accepted by the group, but he could not accept the rewards of his work. Billy lived with a carrot dangling perpetually just out of his reach. He could never work hard enough or be unique enough to get him the approval he sought. The cycle was unending, because Billy could never overcome his mother's loss that she and her husband did not live up to the other members of her family.

Chaos and crisis.   Some families are characterized by constant discord. In these families, one or both parents, or sometimes a child, acts in a gross or eccentric manner that keeps the home in constant emotional turmoil. In the chaotic family, the marital relationship can become disturbed in one of two basic directions.   (1) Sometimes both parents are embroiled in constant fighting.   Lidz, Fleck, and Cornelison (1965) refer to this condition as *marital schism*. The home is a place of continuous tension and chronic unresolved conflict. Both parents are too busy fighting to maintain their own equilibrium to give the child the love and guidance he or she needs for healthy growth.   (2) At other times, one partner is strong and dominant, and the other is weak and underfunctioning. In the interest of minimizing open disharmony, this second parent simply acquiesces to the bizarre behavior and beliefs of the overbearing partner.   This condition is called *marital skew*. In this situation, the chaotic parent acts out his or her erratic behavior, while the spouse and children wait for the storm to pass so life can return to normal.

    In either case, home life in the chaotic and discordant family is unpredictable, and the child never knows what to expect. The child is trapped in an unwholesome and insane environment and cannot make sense of his or her world. In this atmosphere, communication patterns are irrational. The child observes faulty parental models. Almost without exception, the child gets enmeshed with one parent or the other. The child blames and shames himself or herself, feeling responsible for correcting the situation. Some children follow the example of their parents and begin to act out their frustrations with antisocial behaviors. The chaotic family does not give the child the nurture and care that are essential for healthy growth. This family produces adults who themselves have a difficult time establishing and maintaining intimate relationships.

    Bernard and Corrales (1979, p. 45) reported on the effect of growing up in such a disturbed family. They note that experienced family therapists have demonstrated the "murderous hate" which children of these families experience for their parents. At the same time, there is paradoxically present in the child a "devoted love" that demonstrates itself in the child's willingness to sacrifice his or her emotional well-being for the parent. These families in the extreme result in the schizophrenic child. At any level, this family produces a codependent adult.

Carol Sue was a forty-seven-year-old social worker. She was anxious all the time. She bit her fingernails until they bled. She had a hard time sitting still. Compulsive about her home, she cleaned, and when it was clean she cleaned it again. Never comfortable at work, she wondered if she pleased her boss and whether her fellow workers liked her. She was a heavy smoker and had troublesome eating habits. Divorced, Carol Sue lived with her twenty-seven year old son. Her aged mother lived only a few doors away from her. Carol Sue's father had died when she was nineteen.

Carol Sue wanted to commit suicide. Her comment was that life had never been worth anything and she didn't think there was much chance for any real change. Carol Sue lived waiting for tragedy to occur.

Her father had been a severe alcoholic. Evidently a quiet, hard-working man when sober, he became a raging and cruel monster when drunk. Carol Sue's mother was dependent and weak and very afraid of him. Carol Sue felt isolated on the one hand, and responsible for her mother on the other. Her father drank nearly every weekend from the time Carol Sue was born until she was eleven. At that time, he gave up drinking in a sudden religious conversion. Even after that dramatic change, however, he remained uncomfortable with his daughter and she with him. Carol Sue reported being "nervous and fidgety" all the time and was "tired of life. It started bad and went down from there," she said.

Rigidity and nonadaptability. Parents in some families are inflexible. They have rigid belief and behavioral systems, and they expect the children to conform to their standards. The rules are not adaptable, and the parents cannot tolerate any deviance on the part of the child. This domination of the child produces submissiveness, lack of self-reliance, dependence in relationships, low self-evaluation, and fearfulness in attempting new things. Children who grow up in this kind of family have a hard time being creative and spontaneous. They have little self-confidence and cannot trust their own insights or feelings. They have a tendency toward guilt and self-condemnation.

Libby, who was described at the beginning of Chapter One, was a codependent who grew up in an inflexible home. Libby saw her father as a very successful Protestant minister. Religion was the pole around which he wound his rigidity. His understanding of the Bible was all the family needed in order to have the proper rules of life. Libby felt required to believe and behave as he did if she were going to get his love and approval.

Despite her obvious intelligence and attractiveness, Libby had no self-confidence. She looked to others to tell her what to think, what to feel, and how to behave. She wanted to be married but picked men who dominated and mistreated her. At twenty-nine, and after six months of codependent therapy, she gave up her job in Texas and moved home to North Carolina to care for her father when her mother became ill.

Sexual and physical abuse.   According to Dutton (1988, p. 103), widespread research evidence shows that children who grow up being physically or sexually abused or who witness such behavior in their homes have a much greater probability of becoming involved in a violent relationship as an adult. Straus (1977) found that the more frequently a woman was hit by a parent, the more likely she was to be in a relationship in which she was battered as an adult.

Battered children may, in fact, develop a pathological bonding with the parent who administers the abuse. There is strong evidence from studies both in the wild and in laboratories that such traumatic bonding occurs among animals. Harlow and Harlow (1971, p. 206) did a series of research projects with monkeys in which "evil surrogate mothers" were used as potential attachment objects. These mothers hurled the infant to the floor, struck them with brass spikes, exuded loud, noxious air blasts, and shook the infants until their teeth chattered. None of this abusive behavior deterred the infants from engaging in bonding behavior with the surrogates. What seemed to occur was that, as the punishment increased, the infants tried even more persistently to attach to the mother.

Dutton (1988, p. 109) reported on experiments with dogs in which the same surprising results were found. The data seem to show that inconsistent treatment (both maltreatment and affection intermittently from the same source) cause an animal to accentuate attempts to gain proximity to the attachment object.

With human children, the results are not radically different. Children who have a history of physical or sexual trauma grow up with deep psychological problems. The longer and the more traumatic the abuse, the deeper and more pathological the results typically are. Individuals who have been abused as children repeatedly put themselves into abusive relationships. They, like the infant monkeys, simply try harder to get affection from the very persons who abuse them. They may have a hard time leaving abusive relationships. They may suffer guilt that they are not what the abuser needs and therefore see themselves as responsible for the abuse. They may attempt to be more loving, more tender, and more caring so as to make up to the abuser for whatever they perceive themselves to lack.

Caroline's mother physically abused her throughout her childhood years. She whipped her, locked her in her room, spoke sarcastically to her in front of her peers, and ridiculed her in general. The mother alternated between sudden, unexpected rage and unexpected sweetness. When Caroline reached age fifteen or so, the whippings stopped, but the verbal abuse did not.

Caroline grew up to be a physically beautiful woman with a dependent personality. She gave love so as not to be abandoned. She married a very wealthy man with whom she quickly established a codependent relationship. Gradually he tired of her lack of self-worth and dependence on him. He became insensitive and then verbally abusive. He joined Caroline's mother in criticizing her. After seventeen years of marriage, Caroline was stuck in a marriage that replicated the life she had when she was a child. She could not end the relationship with her husband, and neither could she work at changing it. She could not stop her mother from verbally abusing her, and neither could she walk away. At forty-two, she had no place to go. "What's wrong with me?" she asked between sobs. "When will my mother love me?"

Keeping these causal features in mind, let us now turn to the clinical description of codependence. We will also look at the various types of adult children and how they differ from each other.

REFERENCES

Beane, J., and Lipka, R. (1984). *Self-Concept, Self-Esteem, and the Curriculum*, Boston: Allyn & Bacon.

Bernard, C., and Corrales, R. (1979). *The Theory and Technique of Family Practice*, Springfield, Ill.: Charles C Thomas.

Boszormenyi-Nagy, I., and Spark, G. (1973). *Invisible Loyalties*, New York: Harper & Row.

Buss, A. (1966). *Psychopathology*, New York: Wiley.

Coleman, J., Butcher, J., and Carson, R. (1984). *Abnormal Psychology and Modern Life* (7th ed.), Glenview, Ill.: Scott, Foresman.

Cooley, C. (1902). *Human Nature and the Social Order*, New York: Charles Scribner's.

Coopersmith, S. (1981). *The Antecedents of Self-Esteem* (2nd ed.), Palo Alto, Calif.: Consulting Psychologist.

Dutton, D. (1988). *The Domestic Assault of Women: Psychological and Criminal Justice Perspectives*, Boston: Allyn & Bacon.

Erikson, E. (1968). *Identity: Youth and Crises*, New York: W. W. Norton.

Hare, R. (1970). *Psychotherapy: Theory and Research*, New York: Wiley.

Harlow, H., and Harlow, M. (1971). "Psychopathology in Monkeys," in H. Kinnel, Ed., *Experimental Psychopathology*, New York: Academic Press.

Hymes, J. (1963). *The Child Under Six*, Englewood Cliffs, N.J.: Prentice-Hall.

James, W. (1890). *Principles of Psychology*, Magnolia, Mass.: Peter Smith.

Lidz, T. (1968). *The Person: His Development Throughout the Life Cycle*, New York: Basic Books.

Lidz, T., Fleck, S., and Cornelison, A. (1965). *Schizophrenia and the Family*, New York: International Universities Press.

Mead, G. (1934). *Mind, Self and Society*, Chicago: University of Chicago Press.

Michener, H., DeLamater, J., and Schwartz, S. (1986). *Social Psychology*, New York: Harcourt Brace Jovanovich.

Molineux, J. (1985). *Family Therapy: A Practical Manual*, Springfield, Ill.: Charles C Thomas.

Persell, C. (1987). *Understanding Society: An Introduction to Sociology* (2nd ed.), New York: Harper & Row.

Robertson, I. (1987). *Sociology* (3rd ed.), New York: Worth.

Schulz, C. (1963). "Knowing You Are Not Alone," *Decision*, Vol. 4, September.

Schulz, C. (1975). *Peanuts Jubilee: My Life and Art with Charlie Brown and Others*, New York: Holt, Rinehart & Winston.

Straus, M. (1977). "Wife Beating: How Common and Why?" *Victimology*, 2(3–4), 443–459.

Vallacher, R., Wegner, D., and Hoine, H. (1980). "A Postscript on Application," in R. Vallacher, D. Wegner, and H. Hoine, Eds., *The Self in Social Psychology*, New York: Oxford University Press.

Wallerstein, J., and Kelly, J. (1980). *Surviving the Breakup: How Children and Parents Cope with Divorce*, New York: Basic Books.

4

CLINICAL FEATURES AND TYPES OF CODEPENDENCE

All adult children are similar because they have a number of traits in common. Yet they are also different, because codependence shows up in the individual's life in several varieties or types. Each type seems to revolve around a specific characteristic or trait. This trait, in turn, is predictive of the kind of internal distress, behavioral problems, or disordered relationships the individual experiences. The purpose of this chapter is to present in detail the nature and content of these several types of adult children.

Before we look at these various types of codependent personality disorders, let us first look at the clinical traits they all share. The following are some of the traits that are associated with codependence. Usually, codependent individuals exhibit several of these traits in different combinations.

CLINICAL FEATURES OF ADULT CHILDREN

Identity Disorder

Adult children almost always are uncertain about identity issues. They are ambiguous about who they are, because they have an unclear self-perception. They may also be unsure about gender issues. While almost all codependents suffer self-esteem problems, what most codependents lack is self-awareness.

Codependents have trouble separating their "ideal self" from their "real self." The "ideal" exceeds the "real," and they experience guilt and shame because they believe that they must make the real match the ideal. They feel that they should live up to the ideal in every detail, and they cannot.

Because they cannot distinguish between the real and the ideal, they frequently cannot distinguish between their needs and their wants. Thus, they are unable to commit themselves to the goal of satisfying their own needs. Instead of moving directly and with self-confidence in the path of appropriate need satisfaction, they become frozen with *self-doubt* at the same time that they realize the need.

This trait shows up in statements like, "I don't know what I want (or think or feel)." "Is this God directing me or is this just my fear (or doubt or stupidity)?" "I can't tell if this is really what I want or if this is just a way of dealing with my shame." Clients are struggling with this issue when they show mistrust of themselves or when they belittle their ability to get their needs met.

Affective Deficiency

Although they may seem overly concerned about the needs of others, codependents seem incapable of taking care of their own needs. They do not care for themselves. Rather, they have a chronic feeling of their own lack of value. Sometimes, this lack of self-love demonstrates itself in an aggressive and harsh style of relating. Some adult children are able to cover their fear of worthlessness with a veneer of impudence. Most frequently, the codependent develops patterns of avoidance and dependence to cope with this perceived lack of value as a person.

Codependents are emotionally impaired. According to Cermak (1986, p. 23), emotions for the adult child are either enemies to be avoided or weapons to be used. For the codependent, to be emotional is to be "unnatural" or "weak" or, in the case of negative emotions, even "immoral." The adult child cannot, therefore, spontaneously experience and openly demonstrate emotions. Rather, emotions are to be brought under the control of the will. They must be restricted, controlled, and used. Rather than enriching the life and adding to its fullness, emotions become yet another area that tests the individual's ability to be in complete control of life.

Cognitive Disorders

Codependents have difficulty tracking reality. In many areas of their lives, they do not know what "normal" is and they have problems knowing their own feelings. Thus, they are dependent on the expectations of others to tell them what they want and what they should do. To deal with their emotions, they project them, and as a result they frequently think that they have no feelings. Because of these factors, adult children are typically confused in their thinking.

Adult children frequently say things like, "What is a person supposed to believe (or do or want)?" They have trouble solving problems and frequently do not seem to be able to distinguish between their own wishes and those of significant others in their lives. They get stuck in little things and cannot figure out what to do to get themselves out. They seem at times genuinely perplexed about the simplest things.

Woititz (1983, p. 24) concludes, "They look at things that appear to be normal and try to copy them. Yet, what they are copying may or may not be normal, so they are behaving as if they were normal, without having a sound basis for making that decision." Whitfield (1987, p. 30) explains how this cognitive confusion comes about. He says that the child begins by *repressing* observations, feelings, and reactions. By practicing this over time, the child eventually *invalidates* the feelings. Finally, the child loses contact with these essential internal cues, and this results in the codependent's living with chronic distortions of reality.

Boundary Distortions

Boundaries, or the ability to distinguish oneself from others, is an area in which all codependents have trouble. In the first few months of life, the infant has no sense of self and is not able to distinguish between the self and the nonself. Gradually the child recognizes where he or she ends and Mother begins, and by age three the normal child is capable of separating between the "me" and the "not me." In the dysfunctional family, however, the child's natural drive to individuation is thwarted, and the child is confused in several important ways about the distinction in self and nonself. The result is fused boundaries between the individual and others in the environment.

Dysfunctional families invade the inner space of the child and thereby distort boundaries in at least three ways:

1. **Emotionally.** The child is not allowed to learn to identify and experience his or her own feelings. Parents tell the child how he or she should feel and thereby discount the child's feelings. The result is a child who looks to others rather than to the self to know what he or she is feeling. In some families, rather than dictate feelings, parents prevent *any* expression of emotion. The rule is, "No feelings allowed." In either case, the child ends up incapable of experiencing his or her own feelings as separate from those of significant others in the environment.

2. **Physically.** Sometimes the body of the child is invaded through sexual molestation or physical abuse. The psychic effect is the same as in emotional invasion. The child experiences his or her body as having no protective barriers. Boundaries become distorted and the child has no effective identity in which there is safety and security. Thus, physically or sexually abused children have great difficulty distinguishing between themselves and their environment.

3. **Intellectually.** Fossum and Mason (1986, p. 73) refer to criticizing, blaming, mind reading, prying, and mind raping as intellectual boundary blurring. The effect on the child is the perception that the thinking and belief system of the adult is right and that the child has no right to intellectual exercise.

The result of these invasions on the inner space of the child over a long period of time is the loss of a protective screen between the child and others. The individual responds in one of two ways to this condition. Most commonly, he or she has no interpsychic or ego boundaries. What significant others think, feel, want, or need becomes what the individual experiences. Thus, these adult children typically make themselves extensions of other people or make others extensions of themselves. They have no effective barrier to protect the inner space of their ego. When they become involved with another person, they tend to expect themselves to take on the values, preferences, and attitudes of the other. They do not experience themselves as a separate person with feelings and needs distinguishable from those of the other persons in their life.

Codependents sometimes consider this boundary distortion to be a superior trait in themselves. They call it "sensitivity to the needs of others" and they are frequently hurt that it is not reciprocated. What they are actually doing is imitating the other person in the hope that the other will give them approval and acceptance. In so doing, they lose themselves. They also live on the border of anxiety, because any change in the other person or in the situation is a threat to their well-being.

The second boundary problem that may result from the invasion of a child's ego space is that he or she grows up to be an adult who builds walls that are impregnable and beyond which no one is ever allowed. This person may desire intimacy and may even seek it, but he or she never experiences it. Rather than having no boundaries, this person builds boundaries that are inpenetrable walls. This person risks no real contact with anyone else.

Poor Relationship and Friendship Skills

Disrupted personal relationships is a term that is most appropriate to describe the codependent's inability to establish intimacy. Whatever else is true of the adult child, he or she almost always leaves behind a trail of failed and usually hurtful relationships. And most frequently, the nature of the disorder is repeated from one relationship to another. For example, the "clinging vine" wears out one partner by his or her incessant and extraordinary demands. When that partner leaves, the codependent enters another relationship and repeats the same behavior. Adult children do not appear to learn from their mistakes. Rather, they seem to stay with dysfunctional behavior because they are unaware of other alternatives.

Compulsive and Obsessive Behaviors

Codependents are compulsively attached to certain self-damaging and self-defeating patterns of behavior. Sometimes these behaviors are in the area of familiar addictions like chemicals, gambling, shopping sprees, and sex. At other times, the obsession may be with love itself (being in love with love), a particular person ("If I lose Joanne, my life is over"), or even one's job.

These compulsions are primarily a defense system. For the codependent, engaging in the compulsive behavior or having the obsessed object is a method of preventing the pain associated with the codependency. In other words, engaging in the compulsive behavior allows the adult child to avoid certain unwanted emotions.

Inappropriate Anger

A real issue for almost all codependents is anger. They have denied throughout their lives most of the things they have needed. The result of that denial is deep, smoldering rage. Furthermore, the adult child has lived with great feelings of shame during most of his or her life. The primitive response to shame is rage. Their anger, therefore, is inappropriate, not because it is not deserved, but because it is expressed in an unhealthy manner. The adult child "stuffs" his or her anger and does not express it openly. It comes out as depression or, in some cases, psychosomatic illness. Or, it surfaces in sudden explosions of rage that the individual cannot control. The severity of the anger does not suit the situation and is frequently directed at the wrong person.

Most adult children also fear anger a great deal. Codependents typically experience *anger anxiety*. That is, when they get close to their own anger, they get anxious. What surfaces is the anxiety, not the anger. In the thinking of the codependent, anxiety is an appropriate emotion, and anger is not. Some codependents organize their whole life around the effort to keep covered the deep rage that boils beneath their conscious mind.

Sexual Maladjustment

Adult children typically have difficulty with their own sexuality. Many of them were victims of sexual abuse, and all suffer various types of identity conflicts. Most do not feel comfortable with their own self-perceptions. It is no surprise that they struggle in the area of sexuality.

Their problems generally fall into one of two categories: either they (1) act out sexually or (2) they avoid sex altogether.

1. Many of them are or have at one time been sexually promiscuous. A great number have been through more than one marriage and in some cases a number of affairs. Sexual behavior is used for purposes other than sexual ones. Sex is used in an effort to get intimacy. Or it is a way to get approval or acceptance. For some, sex is a way of achieving personal power.

   For such persons, their sexual history as they see it is another aspect of their shame. They may have memories of incest, rape, or both. They may feel guilty about early sexual behavior. Some may have abortions or sexually transmitted diseases in their past. For these persons, their sexuality is an occasion of both shame and grief.

2. The second category of codependent problems with sexuality is at the opposite end of the continuum. Sex for these persons is an area of fear and dread. They may be the victims of early sexual abuse and have suppressed all of their sexual reality. Or they may have had little or no experience with sex and what they have had has been negative. It is difficult for them to talk about sex. Among this group are individuals who are in unfulfilling marriages and feel ashamed and guilty for their desires to find sexually gratifying experiences.

Deeply Ingrained and Longstanding Problems

Codependent traits start in early childhood and continue throughout life. These behaviors and patterns of thinking and feeling are not pathological episodes, but are unvarying and inflexible aspects of the individual's psychological makeup. They are therefore persistent and recurring aspects of the adult child's way of thinking.

Resistance to Change

Codependence is a part of the individual's fundamental constitution and as such is an automatic response of the individual to his or her environment. Codependent behaviors are a part of the individual's psychological life style. If severely codependent persons are to become whole, they must undergo a fundamental change in the structure of their personality. Such radical change is very difficult for a person. Adult children have developed many defenses to keep from dealing with the pain that life has created. They do not give up these defenses without a struggle. Also, family and friends of the adult child have a vested interest in keeping the codependent stuck in his or her problem. They will often conspire against any real and long-term change in the codependent.

TYPES OF CODEPENDENT PERSONALITIES

Now that we have these clinical features of codependence clearly in mind, let us turn to the various personality types that these traits produce. We may classify these special types of codependence with reference to the particular characteristic that is most prominent in each.

The characteristic that is the basis of each type of codependence results from an overemphasis of a normal trait. That is, the codependent takes a normal trait that is necessary for a well-adjusted and mature life and, by making it the focal point of life, turns it into an abnormality. For example, all people need acceptance and love from significant others. For some types of codependents, as we will see, the need for approval is so great that it takes precedence over all other aspects of life. When that occurs, what is a normal human need becomes a dysfunction. Gross (1974, p. 178) makes the point that the essence of personality disorder is in the extent to which an individual organizes the personality structure around a dysfunctional way of viewing life. In some cases, one type of codependence combines several of the traits.

We will consider six basic types of codependence (Table 1):

- Overresponsible
- Compulsive
- Schizoid/avoidant
- Paranoid
- Histrionic
- Antisocial/narcissistic

TABLE 1   CODEPENDENT PERSONALITY DISORDERS

Type of Codependence	Normal Trait	Internal Feelings	Outward Manifestation
Overresponsible codependence	Care of others, sensitivity	Self-doubt, enmeshed, need to be hero, inadequacy, shame	Overachievement, supersensitive, caring, never critical, always loving and understanding, always reliable
Compulsive codependence	Structure, need for organization	Self-doubt inadequacy, shame, guilt	Compulsive behaviors obsessive thoughts, perfectionistic, domineering
Schizoid/ avoidant codependence	Need for privacy	Unloved, need to escape, anger and loneliness	Withdrawn, aloof, independent with few friends, avoids stressful situations
Paranoid codependence	Self-defense	Inadequate, anger, nontrusting, loneliness, unloved	Suspicious, withdrawn, fearful, critical, complaining, and judgmental
Histrionic codependence	Need for attention, need to nurture	Anxiety, unwanted, fear, anger, rejection	Clowning, hyperactive, tries to please by serving and entertaining, supercute, immature, fearful
Antisocial/ Narcissistic codependence	Self-affirmation, assertiveness	Anger, rejection, insecure, not trustworthy	Defensive, competitive, sarcastic, need to belong to powerful groups, domineering, need to make and spend money, judgmental, overbearing, need to appear competent and in control

We must remember that each type can range from the very deep and serious to the relatively mild. All of these terms are subject to different meanings and variations in degree. It is best to think of these variations as a continuum. At one end is a fairly normal type of personality configuration that involves little internal distress and only slight functional impairment. At the other end are personality configurations that resemble the milder forms of psychosis. Most of the examples given in the following pages fall toward the more severe end of the continuum. That fact should not be construed to mean that the less severe forms are of less consequence and are not deserving of treatment.

As noted in Chapter Two, the DSM IIIR category of personality disorders is a helpful perspective from which to explain codependence. For that reason, this presentation of codependent personality types follows very closely the DSM IIIR description of personality disorders in general.

Overresponsible Codependence

Individuals who fall into this category of codependence show extreme dependence on the acceptance and approval of other people. They are called "people pleasers" and spend much energy trying to do what other people expect so as to ensure that they will receive approval. They build their lives around other persons and willingly sacrifice their needs to keep the other person involved with them. They are the classic rescuers and fixers. They have no self-confidence and do not work well alone. They feel helpless and may actually experience panic when threatened with the loss of the person on whom they depend.

They may be very dependent in some ways and may allow, and even encourage, others to make major decisions for them. They frequently marry physically abusive persons or individuals who are emotionally unresponsive and become major enablers of these persons. They may be extremely passive-aggressive as a way to cope with their anger at being so impotent. They appear to be selfless and may cloak their dependence in religious and unselfish language. They appear submissive and bland on the surface, but underneath they are rageful and retaliatory. They are sincerely convinced that they have no right to express even mild individuality.

Brenda was such a person. Fifty-one and the mother of three grown children, Brenda said that she continued to work as a secretary in order to "give to my kids." The oldest two were married and the youngest, at age twenty-two, still lived at home. Brenda and her husband continued to pay their car loans and bought them insurance and other expensive items. She cooked, baby-sat, and did other sacrificial things for them. "What's a mother for?" Brenda asked. Her question itself pointed out that Brenda believed that she had no value to her children other than serving them. For her, love and service were the same.

Brenda's mother was an alcoholic at seventy-two. An only child, Brenda felt total responsibility for her mother. She was able to admit that she was angry at her mother and that Brenda's behavior only enabled her mother to remain in her alcoholism. But she was unable to stop herself. "After all," she reasoned, "God requires that we honor our father and mother." Asked to talk about her feelings about her mother, Brenda related that she hated her and thought she was a "real loser." She also admitted that she wished her mother were dead. Still, she could not detach from either generation. She served both her mother and her children. When asked where her needs were being met, she responded, "I have no needs."

Compulsive Codependence

Compulsive codependence is very similar to overresponsible codependence. Many thinkers have likened the compulsive codependent to an addict. Schaef (1987, p. 18) defines an addiction as "any process over which we are powerless." We become progressively dependent on the process over time and become increasingly compulsive and obsessive about it. "A sure sign of an addiction," Schaef continues, "is the sudden need to deceive ourselves and others—to lie, deny, and cover up." Besides the various substances to which we may become addicted, Schaef adds the following: accumulating money, gambling, sex, work, religion, and worry. We may also become addicted to relationships and to particular people. We may even become addicted to certain rituals.

Adult children may, therefore, become compulsively dependent not only on people (as described in the "Overresponsible Codependence" section) but on other things like a job or even on a specific ritualized way of doing things. They need the order and structure, and they feel anxiety without it. These persons have little or no self-confidence and are overly inhibited, overly conscientious, and superresponsible. They also take themselves very seriously and lack a sense of humor.

They have difficulty relaxing and being playful and can easily become workaholics. They cannot do anything just for fun, and they are frequently excessively concerned with details. This person is incapable of flexibility and insists that everyone do things his or her way. They are, therefore, not only rigid in their expectations of themselves, but they are controlling toward others as well.

Marty, the wife of Ben in the story that introduced Chapter 3, was a compulsive codependent. Very insecure, Marty tried to control her behavior so that Ben would not be displeased with her. She tried to be perfect in every wifely way. A compulsive housekeeper and disciplinarian, she tried to keep their house and children as Ben wanted them. For her to feel comfortable, everything had to be in its place.

But Marty's inflexibility and compulsions did not end with herself. Because of her belief that she had no personal value, she feared Ben's relationship with his children and could not abide any comparison of herself with Ben's former wife. Thus, she tried to control not only Ben's behaviors but also his feelings toward his former family. She did not want him to talk on the phone with them and experienced near panic when she knew he was going to see them. She tried to show him how they only sought to use him and therefore did not love him as she did. She required that he tell her everything that happened in any conversation with them. She tried to regulate and structure the time and the content of any contact between him and his children.

Schizoid/Avoidant Codependency

Some adult children are so hypersensitive to rejection that they have difficulty forming attachments to other people. They are so apprehensive of derogation that they see ridicule and disparagement where none exists. They seem unable to develop social relationships and may even give the appearance of not wishing to do so. We call them "loners" or refer to them as "shy and bashful." They are "timid" and their problem is that they are "introverted."

These persons usually follow solitary occupations and interests that leave them isolated from others. They lead a life that is characterized by its barrenness in interpersonal experience despite their carefully hidden desire for affection and acceptance. We must not confuse them with genuine introverts who are individuals that, while they work in isolation and enjoy privacy and solitude, are fully capable of establishing and maintaining meaningful relationships.

Characteristically, schizoid/avoidant codependents originate in one of two kinds of families: 1. They were children of rigid but not necessarily overtly abusive parents. Parents who convey rigid religious requirements or parents who are emotionally distant can have this effect on their children. 2. The second type of family that this type of codependent comes from is the chaotic, disorganized, and overtly abusive family, especially the physically and sexually abusive family. Persons who grow up in one of these families are generally unsure of their own limitations. They suffer guilt and have difficulty expressing hostile or aggressive feelings appropriately. They sometimes react with excessive anger to trivial things. They have a difficult time with their own sexuality.

Extreme cases of schizoid codependency may approach the milder forms of schizophrenia. Leaff (1974, p. 1) refers to a type of personality disorder he calls "latent schizophrenia." According to Kolb (1981), individuals who suffer schizoid personality disorder sometimes ease the hurt of social isolation by taking refuge in autistic thoughts that are filled with fantasies of being powerful and vengeful. Cameron (1963, p. 648) explains that the schizoid has escaped full-blown schizophrenia by some social accident and that the extreme schizoid can decompensate into schizophrenia under conditions of overwhelming stress.

Ellen Ann is a drastic example of the schizoid codependent. Thirty-seven years old, she worked in a large firm as an accountant. Ellen Ann had taken the job when she graduated from college. She lived with her cats in the same apartment she had moved into when she left her parents' home at age twenty-four. Her only entertainment was her Sunday visits with her parents. She met them at the church she had attended with them as a child. After worship, they all went to the parents' home. They sat around with virtually no conversation until about six in the evening, when Ellen Ann returned to her apartment.

Ellen Ann was a physically attractive woman. She wanted to meet men and have a relationship but was too afraid to try. Even to consider breaking the routine of her life was overwhelming to her. She attended group therapy for six sessions without saying more than her name. Finally, she began to tell her story. She reported rather matter-of-factly that she had a hard time making friends and didn't know what to say in a conversation. She had never heard her parents fight. Neither had she ever witnessed a single spontaneous act of affection between them. After nearly a year of individual therapy, she began to express the rage that was stored away inside. She was able to stop the meaningless Sunday visits. She left her childhood church, a monumental change for her, and began to attend a Sunday School class for single persons.

Paranoid Codependency

Individuals who suffer from paranoid codependency are suspicious, hyper-sensitive, rigid, and envious of the accomplishments of others. They have perfectionistic expectations and can never accomplish enough to experience satisfaction with themselves. Others always seem to accomplish more than they, and they attribute that person's success to luck. The other person always has some "secret" advantage over them. They are always comparing themselves to others in all areas of life. They expect trickery and find it hard to trust anyone. Other people are either enemies to be carefully guarded, or they are tools for the codependent to use to accomplish his or her purposes. Their life is characterized by chronic jealousy, pessimism, and dissatisfaction. They feel discriminated against and refuse to take any responsibility for their failures. Many times, these people are very successful in their careers because, as Gallagher (1987, p. 124) indicates, they feel inferior and they try to counteract this feeling by performing difficult tasks.

Weintraub (1974, pp. 85–86) compares the paranoid personality disorder to the more troubled psychotic paranoid. The difference, he implies, is a matter of degree, and the paranoid personality is more stable. Individuals who suffer paranoid personality disorder, he asserts, are "known to therapists less often as patients than as interfering spouses and relatives." What this means is that the paranoid person does not come into therapy very frequently.

Barry was a paranoid codependent. He was a very successful and creative advertising account executive. He went to counseling with the presenting complaint that he was too pessimistic and could never enjoy his accomplishments. Barry had grown up in a home with a very religious mother and an emotionally disengaged father. The only affection that Barry ever got from his father was when they occasionally tossed a baseball back and forth. Barry was a good athlete in high school, and his father took some pride in that fact. Barry described his mother as an overprotective person who manipulated his father and him.

As Barry described his life, he found evidence that everybody took advantage of him. They used him financially and then threw him away. Others had gotten promotions that he deserved because they had used manipulation or had lied and cheated. His bosses, he insisted, had never cared about him. His wife didn't really love him. As he saw it, she stayed with him only because he made a lot of money. The more Barry talked, the more it became apparent that he felt about his life as an adult very much like he had felt about it when he was a child: He was there for the service of others and no one was there for him.

Barry's suspiciousness caused him to be constantly on guard. His mistrust of other people served as a barrier to close relationships. People found Barry to be cold and distant. They consequently moved away from him and thus confirmed in his mind that they never really cared for him. Thus Barry's paranoia set him up for a self-destructive pattern that only deepened as time went by.

Histrionic Codependence

Individuals who are histrionically codependent are highly excitable and engage in self-dramatization. These individuals use every occasion as an attention-getting device. They are immature emotionally and need to be the center of attention.

The histrionic codependent fluctuates between optimism and depression. In many ways, this individual is like the manic depressive in that he or she alternates between joy and despair. Contradictory traits like friendliness and rejection, prudishness and promiscuity, and religious faith and agnosticism coexist in the histrionic. Frequently, the individual seems unaware of the implications of his or her paradoxical behaviors and attitudes on others.

Despite being sexually maladjusted, the histrionic is often seductive and flirtatious. These individuals vacillate between helplessness and gullibility, on one hand, and caretaking and rescuing, on the other. Whatever behavior they engage in, they are sure to do it in such a way as to focus attention on themselves. They are always overly concerned with the approval of others. They are usually seen as self-centered, shallow, and insincere. Their relationships are likely to be chaotic and short lived.

Evelyn had been sexually abused by her father. She refused to tell me any of the details, but my impression was that it occurred frequently during her elementary school years. Her mother was not emotionally available to her. Evelyn cried a lot as a child and as a teenager. She was physically attractive as an adolescent and "made herself as pretty as possible." But she felt alone and afraid. She had no one to turn to.

At forty-two, Evelyn was a physically attractive woman. Married and with two teenagers, she still had the mannerisms of a little girl—wiggling shyly, glancing away, and having eyes filled with adoration. She frequently wore frilly, almost childlike clothes. Evelyn was very emotional and cried easily. She did everything very dramatically.

At work she required constant guidance from her supervisors to carry out her duties. She gave the impression of helplessness and dependence. However, when things did not go her way, she was capable of showing great irritation, even throwing temper tantrums. Evelyn was flirtatious and seductive at work. She stood too close to men and touched them in inappropriate ways. She gave "hugs" for rewards. Evelyn was largely unaware of her seductiveness. When men responded to her in a sexual way, she was "surprised" and "offended." After all, she was a married woman and a deeply religious person. She did not want an affair; she only intended to tease sexually.

At parties and other social gatherings, Evelyn scurried around taking care of everybody. Smiling brightly and encouragingly, Evelyn tried to nourish each person there, especially the shy and withdrawn. In therapy, Evelyn reported each week that she had made the "greatest breakthrough" during the previous session. She then described some inconsequential concept in exaggerated terms.

As Evelyn continued in therapy, she became increasingly aware of these self-destructive patterns of behavior. She wrote:

> I've always thought of myself as a warm and affectionate person who wanted closeness. I'm not. In reality, I avoid closeness, especially with men. In the past I always selected unavailable men as the focus of my desire—engaged or married men, priests, etc. I think I wanted the relationship without either the closeness or commitment.

> The last time I let someone get close to me and really win my heart was when I was sixteen. He was the typical boy next door. I think he was the only "man" I ever loved. He was twenty, extremely bright, religious, and really good looking. I had tremendous respect for him. One night our physical relationship got a little heavy and he pulled away. I blamed myself for this immoral behavior and decided I would never again allow such strong feelings to surface. They never did. I dated numerous wonderful men but never allowed one to get close. I was considered a challenge because as warm and bubbly as I came across, I let no one get close to my heart.

> I really don't see my worth and value yet. I feel worthless as an individual apart from anyone else. No wonder I shut the rest of the world off.

> I cried all the way home after counseling today. I couldn't stop. I cried out to God, "I hate me! I hate me! Why have you kept me alive? Why did you create me?" I have no idea why I felt so weepy or such pain.

Antisocial/Narcissistic Codependence

Individuals who exhibit antisocial or narcissistic codependence cover their negative self-feelings with aggressive and hostile behaviors. Leaff (1974, p. 1) points out that their destructiveness is focused outward rather than inward. They violate the rights of others without remorse. They are competitive and challenging in personal relationships and have no loyalty to anyone. Capable of manipulation, this type of codependent can use social charm to carry out a charade of warmth and friendliness. They are self-centered and take advantage of others with no regard for the other person's rights.

This person is a user in relationships. He or she cons their way into an affiliation and when finished, leaves without looking back. They take a utilitarian view toward other people. That is, others are instruments with which to accomplish their objectives. They may be very successful in collecting material things, but they never achieve inner serenity and peace. What Pasternack (1974, p. 51) says about the antisocial personality disorder in general applies to this kind of adult child:

> The Antisocial Personality wants what he wants, when he wants it. He usually has the intellectual and social skills to get what he seeks regardless of what he has to do to others. He is a master of manipulation and is mercilessly exploitative....Unfortunately, he lacks judgment and may undermine his own position in the process (of getting what he wants). He may engage in foolish, self-defeating projects, most often in response to an impulse which he enacts without thinking. He may appear to be incisive but over the long run the impulsivity shows itself. He remains the victim of ego immaturity which prevents him from building up any stable foundation for his life.

Antisocial/narcissistic codependents do not readily come into therapy, and when they do it is usually because a mate or child brings them in. As a rule, they do not respond well in therapy because they consider themselves to be normal, indeed superior. They think that everybody has the same outlook on life and the same goals as they. The major difference between them and others, in their estimation, is that they are better at it than others.

Ben, whose story began Chapter Three, is an example of an antisocial codependent. Extremely narcissistic, Ben could be openly abusive or manipulatively nice, as the occasion demanded. He expected favors from others, with no intention of reciprocation. He was exploitive of others and self-centered. Yet, he was himself very dependent on his mother and his children. He was manipulated and used by them in much the same way as he manipulated and used others.

We have now established what codependence is and what its clinical characteristics are. We have discussed the various types of adult children. We have looked carefully at the causes of codependence. Now let us turn to the question of diagnosis and assessment.

REFERENCES

Cameron, N. (1968). *Personality Development and Psychopathology: A Dynamic Approach*, Boston: Houghton Mifflin.

Cermak, T. (1986). *Diagnosing and Treating Co-dependence*, Minneapolis: Johnson Institute Books.

Fossum, M., and Mason, M. (1986). *Facing Shame: Families in Recovery*, New York: W. W. Norton.

Gallagher, B. (1987). *The Sociology of Mental Illness* (2nd ed.), Englewood Cliffs, N.J.: Prentice-Hall.

Gross, H. (1974). "Depressive and Sadomasochistic Personalities." in J. Lion, Ed., *Personality Disorders: Diagnosis and Management*, Baltimore: Williams & Wilkins.

Kolb, L. (1981). *Modern Clinical Psychiatry*, Philadelphia: W. B. Saunders.

Leaff, L. (1974). "Psychodynamic Aspects of Personality Disorders." in Lion, Ed., *Personality Disorders: Diagnosis and Management*, Baltimore: Williams & Wilkins.

Pasternack, S. (1974). "The Explosive, Antisocial, and Passive-Aggressive Personality," in J. Lion, Ed., *Personality Disorders: Diagnosis and Management*, Baltimore: Williams & Wilkins.

Schaef, A. (1987). *When Society Becomes an Addict*, San Francisco: Harper & Row.

Weintraub, W. (1974). "Obsessive-Compulsive and Paranoid Personalities," in J. Lion, Ed., *Personality Disorders: Diagnosis and Management*, Baltimore: Williams & Wilkins.

Whitfield, C. (1987). *Healing the Child Within*, Pompano Beach, Fla.: Health Communications.

Woititz, J. (1983). *Adult Children of Alcoholics*, Pompano Beach, Fla: Health Communications.

5

ASSESSMENT AND DIAGNOSIS OF CODEPENDENCE

Sometimes it is easy to detect codependence. Sometimes it is not. Clients come into therapy somewhere on the continuum between the two extremes. Some are like Karen. She was thirty pounds overweight. Divorced for the last seven years, Karen and her three teenage children lived with Karen's alcoholic father. Her mother had sexually abused her over a period of several years, starting when Karen was four years old. Her father had been lost in his alcoholism and was completely unavailable to her during all her growing years. Karen had become extremely shy to cover up her enormous fear of relationships. Sex had been her only way of having men in her life. Now, she confessed, she hated herself for being too afraid of life to move out of her father's home. She came to therapy to get help in establishing a life of her own. Karen wore her codependence on her sleeve.

Others are like Roger. He came for therapy at the insistence of Ruth, his wife of nine years. They were an attractive, middle-class, two-income family with no children. Ruth had wanted counseling because Roger had developed what she considered a "bad occupational habit." He could not keep a job for more than a few months. Also, he "wouldn't talk much about what was going on inside." A third thing Ruth mentioned as a problem was that he would not have anything to do with his father, who was in a local nursing home.

Roger was willing and open. He talked freely, volunteering information, and was interested in looking at what was happening in his life. He didn't seem to mind his wife's identification of him as the problem. He was a jovial man with a quick and easy smile. He also had a fiery temper that could show up without warning.

Roger had grown up in an alcoholic family, the middle child with two sisters. He ran away from home repeatedly because his parents "would not let him ride his motorcycle." Finally, he was sent to an Arkansas boy's home at age fifteen. Roger hated the rural atmosphere but finished high school. He returned to Dallas after a stint in the Navy, where he was trained in electronics. He learned about computers and got a job in a local electronics store. In the last ten years, he had worked for eight different companies in some form of selling.

Roger seemed to experience no problems with the past. He talked freely about his childhood and teenage years. He said that he felt that his father was just another human being, and Roger wanted nothing to do with him. His mother was dead and he didn't "like his sisters." He seemed to have no problem with putting the past in perspective. Roger appeared to be the kind of adult child of an alcoholic family who had worked through it all successfully. He said, "The past is not it. Other things are my problem." He seemed to feel no shame about himself.

For several weeks I worked with Roger and Ruth. I swung between two diagnostic conclusions: (1) Roger was severely codependent and was successfully denying it. The pain was so great that he was still running away from the family that had hurt him. (2) Roger had worked through the problems associated with growing up in a dysfunctional family and they now caused him no grief. He and Ruth needed some help in communications skills, and she was perhaps a little controlling of him. When they terminated therapy, I was still uncertain of Roger's degree of codependence. Also, I did not know if their therapy had helped or not.

Accurate assessment and diagnosis are critical components in effective treatment programs. Faulty procedures in assessment and diagnosis lead to poor treatment and are a waste of the client's time and effort. The client is not likely to make long-term changes when therapy has been based on incorrect diagnosis.

The purpose of this chapter is to present diagnostic and assessment suggestions for use by the therapist interested in working with codependent clients. Researchers are in the early stages of developing and testing assessment techniques and methods of diagnosis for working with adult children. There are some objective tests that are being standardized. This chapter includes a discussion of these tests. The therapist will need also to depend on his or her intuitive skills and some subjective methods of assessment and diagnosis. These methods will also be presented and explained.

PRELIMINARY STEPS IN ASSESSMENT AND DIAGNOSIS

Definitions

The words *assessment* and *diagnosis* mean roughly the same thing in counseling. They are procedures for determining the nature and causes of a situation that is a problem for an individual, a couple, or a family. When we do assessment and diagnosis, we determine the importance, size, or value of something. That is, how significant is this specific thing in this person's life? How severe is this problem? How much pain is it causing?

The whole procedure is a careful investigation of the facts to determine exactly what is going on in this family, between these two individuals, or in this person's life. It is a process to help us determine the exact nature of a predicament. Thus, in codependent asssessment and diagnosis, the counselor attempts to answer the following questions: Does this person (or these persons) suffer from codependence? In what ways has the dysfunctional family of origin affected this person? How severe is the problem?

Intake Form and Problem Checklist

Assessment and diagnosis is one of the primary goals in the first several sessions. The therapist collects data about the client in a number of different ways to assess the nature and severity of the problem. The therapist seeks to know about the client's background, problems in life, coping skills, current functioning, motivation for treatment, and general outlook on life. While that kind of information gathering goes on in the first several sessions, the initial interview is primary in the process.

Information gathering begins when the client fills out an intake form and a problem checklist.

Intake form. The intake form is a document that collects basic demographic data like age, sex, marital status, occupation, and address. These data are needed as a part of the client's permanent file. This form also allows the therapist to collect important information that may be used for assessment of the problem that has brought the client into therapy. Generally, the client fills out the form just prior to the first session. The following is a suggested intake form:

REALITY COUNSELING CENTER
Anytown, USA

Instructions: Please fill out the following as completely as possible.
1. Personal information
   Name _____
   Age _____
   Sex Male _____ Female_____
   Home address   _____
                    _____
           Phone   _____
   Business address _____
                    _____

```
              Phone        _____
       Occupation          _____
       Social Security number  ___  ___  ___
   2.  Marital status
          Married          _____
          Single           _____
          Divorced         _____
          Widowed          _____
          Never Married _____
   3.  Please give the age and sex of children, if any.  _____
       _____
       _____

   4.  How many years did you complete in school?
       High school graduate          _____
       College, number of years      _____
       Graduate degree               _____
   5.  Religious preference
       _____
       In your own words, how important is religion to you today?
       _____

       Does this answer reflect any significant change in your previous reli-
       gious outlook?  If so, please describe briefly.
       _____

   6.  Who referred you or how did you hear about this center?
       _____
   7.  Briefly describe yourself. _____
       _____
       _____
       _____
       What are your strengths? _____
       _____
       What are your weaknesses?_____
       _____
   8.  In your own words, why are you here? _____
       _____
```

Problem checklist.   In addition to this intake form, the therapist may wish to have the client fill out a problem checklist. The following might be used as such a checklist.

The intake form and the problem checklist are useful sources of necessary data for assessment and diagnosis. I look them over before I go into the first session with the client, and I take them with me into that session. I pay special attention to the questions about religion, the self-description, the client's depiction of his or her

REALITY COUNSELING CENTER
Problem Checklist

Please check any of the following areas that are currently problems for you and are reasons for your coming in for counseling.

_____ Feeling inferior to others
_____ Under too much pressure and feeling stressed
_____ Feeling down or unhappy
_____ Feeling nervous or anxious
_____ Feeling lonely
_____ Experiencing guilt feelings
_____ Suspicious feelings toward others
_____ Afraid of being on your own
_____ Angry feelings
_____ Can't feel anger
_____ Feeling down on yourself
_____ Feeling you don't belong
_____ Financial concerns
_____ Feeling cut off from your emotions
_____ Difficulty knowing your emotions
_____ Never being able to ask for what you want
_____ Difficulty expressing your emotions
_____ Concerns about physical health
_____ Concerns about emotional stability
_____ Lacking self-confidence
_____ Feeling fat
_____ Eating, then purging, to control weight
_____ Use of alcohol
_____ Use of other drugs (which drug(s) _____)
_____ Problems with someone else's use of drugs/alcohol
_____ Difficulty concentrating
_____ Starving yourself to control weight
_____ Feeling unappreciated at work or school
_____ Lacking assertiveness
_____ Not liking yourself
_____ Having difficulty being honest with others
_____ Difficulty communicating in close relationships
_____ Never being able to relax, always having to work
_____ Difficulties making friends
_____ Difficulties keeping friends
_____ Feeling pressured by other people's expectations
_____ Feeling controlled (manipulated) by others
_____ Thoughts of taking your own life
_____ Wondering "Who am I?"
_____ Disliking the shape or size of your own body
_____ Feeling confused about right and wrong

_____ Afraid that you are not competent to handle your problems
_____ Not knowing what is normal
_____ Difficulty with religious issues
_____ Difficulty making up mind
_____ Difficulties accepting getting older
_____ Confused about sexual issues
_____ Guilty about sexual behaviors or thoughts
_____ Confused about sexual feelings
_____ Sexual difficulties in intimate relationships
_____ Feeling sexually attracted to members of your own sex
_____ Feelings relating to having been sexually abused
_____ Feeling bad about your childhood

problem, and the items the client has marked on the problem checklist. With this information in mind, I begin the first session.

The Initial Interview

After the client or couple or family is seated comfortably, I begin with a statement like, "Let me get some preliminary information about you." I have a clipboard with a form that lists some basic questions that I want to ask. My plan is to ask the questions and record notes that I think are significant. Almost all clients are willing for me to take charge and ask these general questions. Sometimes, a client is not able to wait. This client interrupts my questions to begin telling what he or she sees going on. When this happens, I let them talk about what they wish. I can come back later in the interview or in another session to get what I need. Sometimes a client is so overwrought that I must spend the first session calming and stabilizing him or her.

The following is the form that I use to ask the questions in the first session. The nature and severity of the client's problems are the focus in this session, and all questions are designed to gather information for assessment and diagnosis.

1. Let me ask some questions about your physical health.
   What is your overall state of health? _____
   Have you had any serious health problems? If so, what?

   _____
   Are you presently taking any medication? If so , what?

   _____
   Name of family physician _____
2. I would like to ask about your social history.
   Are your parents still living? _____

Are (were) they divorced, separated? _____

Briefly describe your father._____
_____

Briefly describe your mother._____
_____

Briefly describe the nature of your family when you were a child.
_____
_____
_____

Do you consider your family to have been a mentally healthy family?
Please explain. _____
_____

How many brothers and sisters do you have? Stepbrothers or stepsisters? (List names and ages.)
_____
_____

Where do you come in this birth order?_____
Briefly describe the relationship you have with your siblings
now._____
_____

Briefly describe the relationship you had with your siblings when you
were a child. _____
_____

To whom do you feel closest in your family?_____
What makes you feel close to this person?_____
_____

3. Let me ask you a little more about religion.
   Do you believe in God? _____
   What place does religion have in your life?_____
   _____

   Do you come from a religious family? _____ Please explain briefly.
   _____
   _____

4. Tell me about your work.
   Where do you work? _____
   How long have you worked there? _____
   Do you like your job? _____ Please explain briefly.
   _____

   Do you plan any vocational change in the future? _____
   If yes, please explain briefly._____

5. Have you ever been in counseling before? _____ If yes, please explain._____
   _____

6. Now, what is it that you came to see me about? _____
   _____
   _____

If there is more than one person in the session, I collect the information about each one there. Usually, the first twenty to twenty-five minutes of the session are consumed answering the first five questions. The remainder of the session is spent dealing in various ways with Question 6. This question gives the client an opportunity to explain what he or she thinks the problem is. I pay close attention not only to what the client says, but the way he or she says it. I usually ask the client to reflect on what has made him or her choose now to begin working on the problem. As I move through the list of questions, I allow for diversions the client may want to take. I may expand on the list. The purpose is to give the client an opportunity to give information that will help me to assess what is going on in the client's life.

When the interview is ended, I add to the list several observations I made during the session. These observations are designed to help in diagnosis. I write the comments on a separate sheet of paper and attach it to the list of questions that I have just asked in the first session. I comment on the following:

- General appearance and behavior of the client
- Characteristics of speech
- Emotional state of client (mood, affect, and state of mind)
- Ritualistic behaviors and compulsions
- General intellectual evaluation
- Tentative assessment of the nature and severity of the problem
- Tentative treatment plan
- Other comments.

SUBJECTIVE METHODS OF ASSESSMENT AND DIAGNOSIS

Before looking at the more objective diagnostic and assessment tools, let us consider the subjective and unobtrusive methods that are available to the counselor. We must remember that paper-and-pencil tests as methods of assessment and diagnosis are not without limitations. Codependents can frequently sense how one should answer questions on a test, and they can successfully mask their problems, even from themselves. Seriously codependent individuals sometimes achieve very low scores because they deny a lot of negative things about themselves. For example, one of the questions invariably asked on these tests is, "Do you often lie?" Despite their proclivity to deceive and manipulate others, many codependents deny that they do not tell the truth all the time. For this reason, a low score does not always indicate the absence of codependence.

The counselor must, therefore, combine more subjective measures of codependency with these objective tests. The counselor must develop intuitive skills and some unobtrusive methods of spotting codependence. There are several behaviors, attitudes, ways of thinking, and beliefs that one may look for in the first several sessions with the individual or the family. These characteristics are important indicators of the presence of codependency.

Exploring the Problem

Careful exploration of the presenting problem as well as other problems that come up during therapy gives the counselor the opportunity to make assessment and diagnostic judgments. The therapist can ask about several aspects of the problem: how the client defines the problem, its frequency, its consequences, and the client's assumptions of cause.

Molineux (1985, pp. 94–95) suggests the following as pertinent questions which the counselor can ask about the presenting problem:

- How do you see the problem?
- What exactly happens?
- How often does it happen?
- What happens before? After?
- When did it start? What was happening in the family then?
- What brings you here now?
- What would you like to change about the problem or the family?
- How do you feel about coming to my office? Whose idea was it?
- Who in this family did not want to come?

Along with these questions, the counselor can probe about relationships inside and outside the family. These relationship questions can lead naturally to the client's family of origin. The simple inquiry, "What was it like for you when you were growing up?" may suffice to start the client talking. "How do you show love to others?" can be followed with the query, "Is that similar to the way your parents showed love?" The question, "How do you communicate what you want and need?" gives the client the opportunity to discuss issues that may reveal codependence. A similar question is, "Do people listen to you when you talk?"

Clients will often begin to deal with codependent issues when asked about how they would like to change their lives. "What would you like to see in your life one year from now?" or "What things would you like to work on in your life?" are good questions to start the client thinking in this area.

The counselor listens to the answers to these questions with an interpretive ear. They are diagnostic questions designed to help the therapist see what is going on in the client's life. These questions are designed to deal with what the problem *really* is and how severe it is. Let us look at some of the issues that are useful indicators of codependency.

Indicators of Codependency

Carey and coauthors (1984) developed what they call the "a priori method of assessment" in the field of substance abuse. Using this approach, the therapist generates a series of hypotheses in the initial interview about the nature and extent of the client's use of chemicals. He or she then proceeds to test these hypotheses in the next several sessions. According to Lewis, Dana, and Blevins (1988, p. 101), the a priori method of assessment involves four steps: (1) Conduct the initial interview; (2) draw hypotheses on the nature and severity of the problem; (3) test the hypotheses in subsequent sessions; and (4) develop a treatment plan based on validated hypotheses and other information gathered in interviews.

Following this method of assessment in codependent therapy, the counselor looks for certain indicators that help validate the suspicion of codependence. These indicators also help measure the severity of the problem. (You may want to refer back to the clinical features of codependency discussed in the previous chapter.) The following are some useful indicators.

Performance-based value. The individual equates performance with value. Conditional love in the family of origin leads the individual to the conclusion that he or she must perform in order to be accepted. Thus, the individual develops the core belief that he or she has no inherent value. This core belief may be shown in a number of small and seemingly inconsequential ways.

Ruby was an unusually attractive mother of two teenage boys. Her husband was an accountant. They were in my office to talk about their marriage because they "fought a lot." Ruby tearfully described the closing of her beauty salon. I asked, "Must your business succeed for you to feel good about yourself?" She talked for several minutes about how she longed for her beauty salon to grow and be successful. "It is my whole life," Ruby confessed with tears brimming in her eyes. She did not realize that she equated herself with her beauty salon. Her deep earnestness for her business to succeed was based on the low value Ruby placed on herself. Ruby lived with conditional acceptance and felt that she had to perform to be of value.

Service orientation. The individual takes a "service orientation" toward all of life. The individual does not matter or feel involved or relevant or loved unless he or she is taking care of others. The person feels responsible for the physical, emotional, or spiritual well-being of most of the people with whom he or she relates.

"My mother has no one else to turn to. If I turn my back on her, I don't know what she will do," Ron almost shouted at me. I had just asked him what kept him from taking the job he had been offered in another state.

Learned helplessness. Individuals feel that they have no control over what happens to them in life. Rather than having a sense of confidence and efficacy, they possess a defeated fatalism that says, "I am doomed to missing the good things of life. I will never have what I want."

Lynn's attractive face was sad. Her shoulders stooped, and she did not smile often. She whispered when she spoke. Sometimes her words trailed off in midsentence. "I can't meet guys," she murmured. "I can't think of anything to say and I just stand there and look dumb. I just...."

Grandiosity. The individual tries to feel more powerful and in control than he or she is in reality. He or she tries to be omnipotent. When this is the case, the codependency is coming out in the need to be invulnerable by being superhuman. The logic of such thinking is, I will perform above the ordinary person and then I will be recognized and loved.

Aaron was codependently grandiose. He was a perfectionist and a workaholic. He did a better-than-average job as an account executive in an advertising firm. At night he played guitar in small bars and wrote songs. His dream was to be discovered and go to Nashville. Aaron was forty-seven. His problem was not that he had a driving dream. Rather, Aaron's problem was that his dream was a shield from having to face his own humanness and vulnerability. He talked incessantly about his music plans because he was afraid to talk about himself.

Second generation problem. The simple fact that a client grows up in a dysfunctional family is not, as has been previously pointed out, sufficient to diagnose codependency. But if the individual has a long history with a dysfunctional family and in the sessions he or she mentions these problems frequently, there is reason to suspect that the individual has brought dysfunctional patterns of thought, emotion, and behavior from childhood into adulthood. So if an individual begins to refer to problems in the family of origin, it is time to stop and investigate.

Martha is an example. In her initial call for an appointment, I asked her what issues she wanted to discuss, and she said that she needed marriage counseling. She was not sure that her husband loved her. Almost as an aside, she added, "My father was mentally ill." In the first session, I asked her about that reference to her father. "He had spells and we just put him in a room and left him there," she said quietly. "But," she hurried on, "it was nothing to worry about." Exploration led to the discovery that her mother had used that very sentence to quiet Martha's concerns when her father had his "spells." The rule in Martha's family was, "You do not talk about this topic, in the family or out." Martha had never been allowed to process her feelings about her father's problems. Now, as an adult woman, she had some of the same feelings about her husband's emotional distance from her. The rule of silence was still in effect for Martha.

Need to protect parents. The individual still has a need to protect the family. He or she may become uncomfortable with any criticism of the family.

Whatever went on in the family remains something that must stay in the family, and the client's job is to protect the family, and especially the parents, from outside attack.

Sue's mother was dead. We had already established that Sue had trouble knowing and expressing her emotions. At this point, I suspected that Sue made herself an extension of her mother. I asked her if she would consider whether or not she felt some anger toward her mother. "Why should I?" she responded, "I dealt with that just before she died." I reasoned, "It is possible that your mother hurt you in a deeper way than you now realize." Sue replied, "I don't like it when you say that. It doesn't do me any good to come here and have you attack my mother. She did the best she could and I love her for it. Let's talk about something useful."

Overwhelming, unconscious anger. The individual has unexplained, overwhelming anger. Sometimes, this anger does not show up until the person has been in therapy for a period of time. It may come out in dreams of violence or in anxiety attacks. The individual may have difficulty being in a specific situation or with a particular person. There is great fear that the anger suddenly will spill out in a verbal or physical attack.

Karen was a kindergarten teacher. Unmarried at thirty, she came to talk about what kept her from falling in love and getting married. Several times in the first few sessions, she referred to a big knot in the pit of her stomach. She took prescribed antacids for it. The ache would come and go without warning. She avoided my efforts to consider the knot as anything but a physiological fact. As we worked on her relationship skills, she confided that she had never had a good relationship with her mother. Her mother, it turned out, was a bitchy person who was constantly nagging Karen's father. Subservient and passive, he never fought back openly. Karen felt responsible for caring for her father and defending him from her mother. Describing one agonizing episode that occurred on a trip in an automobile, Karen blurted out, "I hated them so much it made my stomach hurt!"

Stuck in relationships. The individual has problems getting out of relationships that are hurtful. Sometimes the person has extreme anxiety separating from the most destructive involvements. He or she can't end a destructive love relationship. Sometimes this separation anxiety appears when the person thinks about leaving a club or quitting a job. Codependents frequently continue to give loyalty long after they know that it is not deserved.

Perkins told me that he and Stan worked for the same company, and for seven years they jogged together every day. Perkins said that he didn't enjoy Stan for most of that time. Stan was a calculating and judgmental person. He frequently said things that seemed deliberately designed to hurt Perkins. Finally Stan was transferred and that is how the relationship was ended. "What kept you running with Stan when he hurt you?" I asked Perkins. "I just couldn't say the words 'I quit,'" Perkins admitted. "I would rather take his abuse than risk making him mad at me."

DIAGNOSING LEVELS OF INDIVIDUAL PROBLEMS

Codependent clients come into therapy for a variety of reasons. They also exhibit a wide range of problems that vary not only by content but also in degree of severity. Several different approaches are available to help us understand these differences and to deal effectively with them.

Severity of Problems

We have noted in previous chapters that symptoms of codependence can range from mild to severe. In rare cases, individuals can grow up in severely dysfunctional families and become adults, with few or no negative effects. However, most individuals emerge from childhood trauma with some kind of psychic scars. These scars range from mild to severe. Ackerman (1983, p. 55) notes that children regard an alcoholic mother as being more detrimental than an alcoholic father. He further points out (p. 24) that children who are able to establish primary relationships outside the family can escape some of the negative consequences of the dysfunctional family. We do not now know all that we need to know about the variables that determine severity in the effect of the dysfunctional family. Nonetheless, effects on clients do vary, and we cannot always tell how deep the scars are when the client walks into our office.

For me, this fact means that I need to use humility and to deal gently with clients until I have established a very good idea of how deep the problems are with which I am dealing. For example, Loraine was an attractive forty-three-year-old who came in to discuss a relationship problem she was having at church. She was poised and confident. Well educated and very intelligent, she presented her problem clearly. She and Ralph, her husband, attended church with and were friends with Scott and Sally. They enjoyed each other's company for evenings out and went on vacations together. Loraine and Sally were friends away from the couples. Ralph and Scott were not as close as the wives, but they enjoyed each other and occasionally played golf together.

Loraine's problem was that she had recently become aware that Scott's interests in her were sexual. He had made a couple of veiled passes at her. "What," she wondered, "would be the mature thing to do about this?"

"What have you thought about doing?" I responded. "Oh," she said confidently, "I think I want to just ask him about it directly. That seems to me to be the mature thing to do and also the Christian thing to do. Don't you think?"

We had spent some time talking about her childhood, and she told me enough to know that she had come from a dysfunctional home. Her father had been verbally abusive (I later found that he had done a lot more than abuse her verbally), and her mother had been angry and unavailable emotionally. "Don't you think that I could just sit down and talk with Scott about it? I think our friendship means enough to him that we could do that without any real problems. Don't you think?"

Here was an adult child confidently saying that she wanted to speak directly to the individual about her feelings. She appeared strong and understanding. Almost absent-mindedly, I responded to her repeated question, "It sounds like you have thought it through very carefully." Loraine interpreted my words as, "Yes, go ahead and tell him." I did not correct her.

Loraine spoke to Scott about her perceptions. The result was calamitous. Scott exploded in fear and rage. He told Sally about what Loraine had said. Sally took it as a pass that Loraine was making at Scott. She and Scott told their children. Sally confronted Loraine angrily. Loraine was devastated. In subsequent sessions, I discovered that the person in my office was a much more troubled person than her outward appearance indicated. She was both a compulsive and paranoid codependent. She had been severely abused both physically and sexually in her childhood. Her confident demeanor was an act that covered up her painful insecurity. Her repeated question about what I thought she should do was an effort to find out what it would take to please me in this regard. Loraine was not nearly as prepared for a confrontation as she wanted me to think. She needed baby steps, and I had encouraged her to pole-vault.

I have discovered that it is a good idea to move cautiously in the first several sessions with individuals. Assessment of the severity of the problems with which the individual client is dealing is a subjective process at best. Rather than moving too quickly, the effective therapist probes carefully and gently to find how deep the codependent's scars are.

Assessing the Severity of Personality Disorders

We have repeatedly noted that codependency is a problem of self-perception that results in severe personality disorders. Codependence has to do with deeply ingrained and long-held patterns of thought, feeling, and behavior that have been reinforced by many years of repetition. These kinds of mental and behavioral patterns present specific problems that complicate assessment and treatment.

Diagnosis of personality disorders is problematic because such disorders are based on "normal" human traits which the individual has made inflexible and for that reason have become disorders. For example, Cermak (1986, p. 17) discusses the codependent's penchant for assuming the responsibility for "meeting other's needs to the exclusion of acknowledging one's own." This characteristic, which appears to be a classic symptom of codependence, is based on the socially necessary virtue of unselfishness. In the codependent, however, the denial of self is done *in order to be accepted by others*. The fear of being alone or abandoned is at its root. The codependent accepts this fundamental violation of the self to avoid the pain of this fear. Over the years, the codependent loses the ability to distinguish between his or her own needs and that of the other. The two become one, and the codependent loses contact with his or her own self.

The normality of many of the traits associated with codependence make diagnosis and treatment difficult. The skill of codependent clients in denying and masking their problems further complicates the problems of diagnosis. They are likely to define what they do as desirable, even superior, behavior. These are, after all, patterns of self-thought and behavior that they have practiced since childhood. These patterns may be dysfunctional and cause inner distress, but they are integrated into the very identity of the codependent person. Furthermore, their family and friends, who generally benefit from the self-destructive behavior of the codependent, may resist any changes. They may argue for the "normality" of the status quo.

As an example, consider Abe, a father who wanted to teach athletic skills to his ten-year-old son. Abe had been a star baseball player in high school. When he was growing up, he got a lot of attention from his father for his athletic abilities and for little else. Now, as any normal father, Abe wanted his son, Josh, to love and respect him. To accomplish this goal, Abe sought every opportunity to play ball with Josh. Abe was proud of his interest in Josh.

Two things became evident in therapy with Abe: First, without recognizing it, Abe did not think that he had anything to offer Josh other than his abilities as a "coach." Second, Abe was putting Josh in a double bind. He said that he loved him and wanted him to be happy. At the same time, he sent signals that Josh's athletic performance was the standard by which he would determine whether Josh was acceptable.

Abe felt that the only way he could have Josh's love was to *make* him be a successful athlete. He felt that he was under scrutiny by Josh and that he had nothing else to offer with which to ensure that Josh would love him. Josh, on the other hand, felt judged by his father and that nothing short of perfection would get him acceptance by his father.

When I suggested these emotional and behavioral characteristics of the relationship for Abe to consider, he at first professed not to understand. Then he remonstrated. In Abe's view, it was I who did not understand. "Hey," Abe rejoined, "I love my son and just want him to be happy. I'm a good coach and my son wants me to attend all his games and offer criticism." Josh would tell me as much if he were present, Abe added.

Abe was motivated by normal desires and in some ways was following acceptable methods of father-son relationship in our culture: He wanted to talk sports with his son. Yet, in Abe's case, this one element constituted the entire relationship. And what was worse, because of his own largely unconscious needs and fears, Abe was unwilling to consider changing.

I have found it advantageous not to move too quickly to dismantle the defense systems of the codependent. He or she has spent a lifetime using these defenses as protection against some source of personal annihilation. At the same time, the effective therapist must develop methods of helping the codependent deal with his or her individual issues as they learn new and more healthy ways of surviving in the world.

Labeling and Diagnosis: A Warning

One further word of caution is necessary. Rowan (1983, pp. 11–13) warns about the dangers of diagnosis in general. Labels, including psychological and mental health labels, can become self-fulfilling prophecies. That is, what happens in a specific situation depends on the expectations we have in that situation. And the expectations we have are, in turn, dependent on the labels we give ourselves and others in that situation. Thus, what we see happening and how we define our own behavior and that of others is a function largely of the labels we use in the situation. Noting that diagnosis is far from a precise discipline in psychotherapy, Rowan agrees with the suggestions of Walkenstein (1975). She gives labels that describe the individual's behavior. That is, the diagnosis is the symptom: Your diagnosis is "excessive politeness," and the only cure is to practice some "excessive rudeness." You are a "zombie." You are a "marshmallow." For her, the symptoms of the problem represent a shield, not the personality of the person. Rowan concludes: "The diagnosis then becomes not a life sentence but rather something to be put aside when the person is ready to do so. She looks on the symptoms as a message, a plea for attention and the diagnosis as a method of giving that attention, in a temporary and nonhurtful way."

This gentle warning represents a useful recommendation to those of us who deal with the codependent. That word itself, as well as the roles that individuals choose to play, is no more than a description of symptoms. It is a useful shorthand description by which we try to understand what is going on and then map out a strategy to deal with it. We create the map because it is helpful to us. But the map is an abstraction; it is not the reality. Thus, codependence should not be construed as a lifelong aspect of the individual's character, but rather as something the individual can surrender when he or she so chooses.

ASSESSMENT AND DIAGNOSTIC DEVICES

Researchers from a variety of disciplines are involved in developing several paper-and-pencil instruments that promise to be useful in assessing codependence. When applied in conjunction with other methods, they offer valuable objective measurement of codependence. This section presents four of these tests. As would be expected, there is some similarity and some repetition between them. The therapist may want to try all four and pick one or more that seem to serve best.

The Friel Codependent Assessment Inventory

The first test was developed by Friel (1985, p. 21). It is a true-false test, and all odd-numbered answers must be reflected—that is, reversed—before summing up for a total score. Thus, if the answer to item 1 is "True," it should be reversed to "False" before adding up the total. Reflection is done because half of the items are worded in the codependent direction, while the other half are not, to control for acquiescent response sets. The total score is then the sum of all "True" answers after reflection. According to Friel, scores below 20 indicate few codependent concerns; scores between 21 and 30 indicate mild to moderate codependence; scores between 31 and 45 indicate moderate to severe codependence; and scores over 46 indicate severe codependence.

Friel Codependent Assessment Inventory

Below are a number of questions dealing with how you feel about yourself, your life, and those around you. As you answer each question, be sure to answer honestly, but do not spend too much time dwelling on any one question. There are no right or wrong answers. Take each question as it comes.

1. I make enough time to do things just for myself each week.
2. I spend lots of time criticizing myself after an interaction with someone.
3. I would not be embarrassed if people knew certain things about me.
4. Sometimes I feel like I just waste a lot of time and don't get anywhere.
5. I take good enough care of myself.
6. It is usually best not to tell someone they bother you; it only causes fights and gets everyone upset.
7. I am happy about the way my family communicated when I was growing up.
8. Sometimes I don't know how I really feel.
9. I am very satisfied with my intimate love life.
10. I've been feeling tired lately.
11. When I was growing up, my family liked to talk openly about problems.
12. I often look happy when I am sad or angry.
13. I am satisfied with the number and kind of relationships I have in my life.
14. Even if I had the time and money to do it, I would feel uncomfortable taking a vacation by myself.
15. I have enough help with everything I must do each day.
16. I wish that I could accomplish a lot more than I do now.
17. My family taught me to express feelings and affection openly when I was growing up.
18. It is hard for me to talk to someone in authority (boss, teachers, etc.).
19. When I am in a relationship that becomes too confusing and complicated, I have no trouble getting out of it.
20. I sometimes feel pretty confused about who I am and where I want to go with my life.
21. I am satisfied about the way I take care of my own needs.
22. I am not satisfied with my career.

23. I usually handle my problems calmly and directly.
24. I hold back my feelings much of the time because I do not want to hurt other people or have them think less of me.
25. I don't feel like I'm "in a rut" very often.
26. I am not satisfied with my friendships.
27. When someone hurts my feelings or does something I don't like, I have little difficulty telling them about it.
28. When a close friend or relative asks for my help more than I'd like, I usually say yes anyway.
29. I love to face new problems and am good at finding solutions to them.
30. I do not feel good about my childhood.
31. I am not concerned about my health a lot.
32. I often feel like no one really knows me.
33. I feel calm and peaceful most of the time.
34. I find it difficult to ask for what I want.
35. I don't let people take advantage of me more than I'd like.
36. I am dissatisfied with at least one of my close relationships.
37. I make major decisions quite easily.
38. I don't trust myself in new situations as much as I'd like to.
39. I am very good at knowing when to speak up and when to go along with other's wishes.
40. I wish I had more time away from my work.
41. I am as spontaneous as I'd like to be.
42. Being alone is a problem for me.
43. When someone I love is bothering me, I have no problem telling them so.
44. I often have so many things going on at once that I'm really not doing justice to any one of them.
45. I am very comfortable letting others into my life and revealing "the real me" to them.
46. I apologize to others too much for what I do or say.
47. I have no problems telling people when I am angry with them.
48. There's so much to do and not enough time. Sometimes I'd like to leave it all behind me.
49. I have few regrets about what I have done with my life.
50. I tend to think of others more than I do of myself.
51. More often than not, my life has gone the way that I wanted it to.
52. People admire me because I'm so understanding of others, even when they do something that annoys me.
53. I'm comfortable with my own sexuality.
54. I sometimes feel embarrassed by behaviors of those close to me.
55. The important people in my life know "the real me," and I am okay with them knowing.
56. I do my share of work, and often do quite a bit more.
57. I do not feel that everything would fall apart without my efforts and attention.
58. I do too much for other people and then later wonder why I did so.

59. I am happy about the way my family coped with problems when I was growing up.
60. I wish that I had more people to do things with.

Codependency Assesment and Inventory

I developed the following codependency assessment inventory at the University of North Texas and I use it as a part of the diagnostic phase of all codependent therapy I do.

A Codependence Test

Please circle the response that is usually true for you. When you have completed the test, please total your score by adding together the responses to all questions using the following values:

Never   0
Seldom   1
Occasionally 2
Often   3
Usually   4

I take myself very seriously. For me, life is hard work.
    Never   Seldom   Occasionally   Often   Usually
I have trouble being at ease even in close relationships.
    Never   Seldom   Occasionally   Often   Usually
I avoid confrontation.
    Never   Seldom   Occasionally   Often   Usually
I seek approval and affirmation from others because I cannot give them to myself.
    Never   Seldom   Occasionally   Often   Usually
I overreact to things over which I have no control.
    Never   Seldom   Occasionally   Often   Usually
I am extremely loyal even in the face of evidence that the loyalty isn't deserved.
    Never   Seldom   Occasionally   Often   Usually
I keep my anger in.
    Never   Seldom   Occasionally   Often   Usually
I feel isolated and afraid of people, especially authority figures.
    Never   Seldom   Occasionally   Often   Usually
Once committed to a course of action I cannot walk away, even if I know I have made a mistake.
    Never   Seldom   Occasionally   Often   Usually

I cannot stand to fail because when I fail, I think I am worthless.
   Never   Seldom   Occasionally   Often   Usually
I am frightened by angry people and by any personal criticism.
   Never   Seldom   Occasionally   Often   Usually
I avoid conflict.
   Never   Seldom   Occasionally   Often   Usually
I do not feel that I have a right to walk away from people who put me down or hurt me.
   Never   Seldom   Occasionally   Often   Usually
I feel as if I don't have much control over my life.
   Never   Seldom   Occasionally   Often   Usually
I feel guilty when I stand up for myself.
   Never   Seldom   Occasionally   Often   Usually
I seem to have lost the ability to feel or to express my own feelings.
   Never   Seldom   Occasionally   Often   Usually
I am my own most harsh critic.
   Never   Seldom   Occasionally   Often   Usually
I fear rejection, yet I reject others.
   Never   Seldom   Occasionally   Often   Usually
I have difficulty with intimate sexual relationships.
   Never   Seldom   Occasionally   Often   Usually
I fail to tell the truth frequently.
   Never   Seldom   Occasionally   Often   Usually
I have difficulty having fun, and playing makes me feel wrong or guilty.
   Never   Seldom   Occasionally   Often   Usually
I can't say no without feeling guilty.
   Never   Seldom   Occasionally   Often   Usually
I feel absolutely terrible when I "make mistakes," "mess up," or " blow it."
   Never   Seldom   Occasionally   Often   Usually
I do not like myself.
   Never   Seldom   Occasionally   Often   Usually
I do not trust my feelings.
   Never   Seldom   Occasionally   Often   Usually

Score Interpretation:
   0–25   Healthy
   26–50   Mild codependence
   51–74   Serious codependence
   75–100   Severe codependence

Recovery Potential Survey

The following is an assessment inventory which I adapted from Whitfield (1987, pp. 2–4).

Recovery Potential Survey

Circle or check the word that most applies to how you *truly* feel. When
you have completed the test, please add your score by giving yourself
0 for each "Never," 1 for each "Seldom," 2 for each "Occasionally," 3
for each "Often," and 4 for each "Usually."

1. Do you seek approval and affirmation?
    Never   Seldom   Occasionally   Often   Usually
2. Do you fail to recognize your accomplishments?
    Never   Seldom   Occasionally   Often   Usually
3. Do you fear criticism and conflict?
    Never   Seldom   Occasionally   Often   Usually
4. Do you overextend yourself?
    Never   Seldom   Occasionally   Often   Usually
5. Have you had problems with your own compulsive behavior?
    Never   Seldom   Occasionally   Often   Usually
6. Do you have a need for perfection?
    Never   Seldom   Occasionally   Often   Usually
7. Are you uneasy when your life is going smoothly?
    Never   Seldom   Occasionally   Often   Usually
8. Do you continually anticipate problems?
    Never   Seldom   Occasionally   Often   Usually
9. Do you care for others easily, yet find it difficult to care for yourself?
    Never   Seldom   Occasionally   Often   Usually
10. Do you isolate yourself from other people?
    Never   Seldom   Occasionally   Often   Usually
11. Do you respond with anxiety to authority figures and angry people?
    Never   Seldom   Occasionally   Often   Usually
12. Do you feel that individuals and society in general are taking advan-
    tage of you?
    Never   Seldom   Occasionally   Often   Usually
13. Do you have trouble with intimate relationships?
    Never   Seldom   Occasionally   Often   Usually
14. Do you attract and seek people who tend to be compulsive?
    Never   Seldom   Occasionally   Often   Usually
15. Do you cling to relationships because you are afraid of being alone?
    Never   Seldom   Occasionally   Often   Usually
16. Do you often mistrust your own feelings and the feelings expressed by
    others?
    Never   Seldom   Occasionally   Often   Usually
17. Do you find it difficult to express your emotions?
    Never   Seldom   Occasionally   Often   Usually
18. Is it difficult for you to relax and have fun?
    Never   Seldom   Occasionally   Often   Usually

19. Do you find yourself compulsively eating, working, drinking, using drugs, or seeking excitement?
    Never   Seldom   Occasionally   Often   Usually
20. Are you afraid of being rejected and abandoned?
    Never   Seldom   Occasionally   Often   Usually
21. Are you afraid of being a failure?
    Never   Seldom   Occasionally   Often   Usually
22. Is it hard for you to trust?
    Never   Seldom   Occasionally   Often   Usually
23. Do you have an overdeveloped sense of responsibility?
    Never   Seldom   Occasionally   Often   Usually
24. Do you have feelings of guilt, inadequacy, or low self-esteem?
    Never   Seldom   Occasionally   Often   Usually
25. Do you have difficulty asking for what you want from others?
    Never   Seldom   Occasionally   Often   Usually

Scoring interpretation: 0–25 Healthy
   26–50   Codependent
   51–75   Serious Codependence
   76–100 Severe Codependence

(Questions adapted from Charles Whitfield: *Healing the Child Within,* 1987)

The ISFAD Orientation to Life Inventory

Gossett (1988), along with other students and staff at the Institute for the Study of the Family and Addictive Disorders (ISFAD) at the University of North Texas, developed an extensive assessment and diagnostic test. Gossett says that the test has three functions:

Function 1. The test measures codependence in much the same way as the other tests developed for that purpose.

Function 2. The test contains fifty statements (actually two sets of twenty-five statements). One set makes the statements in a positive direction, and the other makes them in a negative direction. For example, the test contains the following statements: "If someone has something I want or need, I ask for it" and "I find it difficult to ask for what I want." These two statements measure the same phenomenon—the first from a positive perspective and the second from a negative perspective.

Gossett suggests that the test may be scored to determine the difference in these two subsets of statements. This score measures the difference in internal consistency in responding to the statements. Gossett maintains that the difference is a function of the degree to which the individual refuses to allow himself or herself to become consciously aware of the codependence in his or her life. Thus, according to Gossett, this score measures the individual's own lack of internal consistency, or what he calls *denial*.

Function 3.   The third function of the instrument is that it measures three different aspects of codependence that Gossett labels cognitive rigidity, emotional disintegrity, and normative expectations: (1) *Cognitive Rigidity*: Specific questions are designed to measure the degree of rigidity or flexibility the individual exhibits in thinking and solving problems. (2) *Emotional Disintegrity*: For Gossett, this term refers to the degree to which the individual possesses an integrated sense of self. (3) *Extreme Normative Expectations*:   This term connotes the extent to which the individual is aware of and comfortable with his or her own emotions. Also, the term refers to the way the individual has integrated his or her "primary socialization," or "early family background" into a functional and healthy life style as an adult.

Orientation to Life Inventory

Please indicate how often you engage in the following behaviors and feelings. Use the following scale to rate your response.

Always   5
Often   4
Occasionally 3
Seldom   2
Never   1

_____   1. When I am upset, I find it best to let others know how I feel.
_____   2. Even during a busy week I manage to find time for myself.
_____   3. I have difficulty making major decisions.
_____   4. I have no trouble getting out of dysfunctional relationships.
_____   5. When I am meeting a new person, I know just the right thing to say or do.
_____   6. I am frequently embarrassed by the behaviors of those close to me.
_____   7. I find it difficult to ask for what I want.
_____   8. I find the truth is best.
_____   9. I fear rejection and abandonment, yet I reject others.
_____   10. I feel that everything would fall apart without my constant attention.
_____   11. I fear failure, but I have difficulty handling success.
_____   12. I love to face new problems because I am good at finding solutions to them.
_____   13. I am satisfied when life is uncomplicated.
_____   14. I am uncomfortable when I must speak to someone who has authority over me.
_____   15. I am either super responsible or irresponsible.

_____ 16. I lie when it would be just as easy to tell the truth.

_____ 17. I don't trust myself in new situations as much as I would like.

_____ 18. If someone has something I want or need, I ask for it.

_____ 19. When I am confronted by a difficult situation, I carefully consider my alternatives before taking any action.

_____ 20. I fear criticism and judgment, yet I criticize others.

_____ 21. When it comes to those close to me, I feel that live and let live is the best policy.

_____ 22. It does not embarrass me to be praised for a job well done.

_____ 23. I am satisfied with my intimate love life.

_____ 24. I lock myself into a course of action without serious consideration to alternate choices or consequences.

_____ 25. When others criticize me for what I say or do, I feel it's their problem and not mine.

_____ 26. I am neither overly responsible nor unresponsible.

_____ 27. I manage my time poorly because I don't set my priorities in a way that works well for me.

_____ 28. When I have problems with someone, I sit down and honestly talk it out with them.

_____ 29. I am reluctant to do anything for someone which they can do for themselves.

_____ 30. I am good at smoothing out the wrinkles in complicated relationships.

_____ 31. I judge myself without mercy.

_____ 32. I easily care for others, yet find it difficult to care for myself.

_____ 33. When I have to, I am comfortable asking an authority for permission to do something.

_____ 34. I am extremely loyal even in the face of evidence that my loyalty is undeserved.

_____ 35. I handle important decisions calmly and directly.

_____ 36. I am comfortable to live my life within my limitations.

_____ 37. I look happy when I am not.

_____ 38. I enjoy praising others when they have finished a job well done.

_____ 39. I seek tension and crisis and then complain.

_____ 40. When someone I love is bothering me, I have no problem telling them so.

_____ 41. When I do a favor for someone and they show no gratitude, I think twice before helping them again.

_____ 42. I guess at what is normal.

_____ 43. I am uneasy when my life is going smoothly because I continually anticipate problems.

_____ 44. I do too much for people and later wonder why I did so.

_____ 45. I find it easy to relax and have fun.

_____ 46. I am pleased with my sex life.

_____ 47. When someone I care about annoys me, I just keep it to myself.

_____ 48. When nothing much is going on, I am content just to relax.

_____ 49. I have time to do what I want because I am good at arranging my priorities.
_____ 50. I constantly seek approval and affirmation.

Scoring:

FUNCTION 1—Codependence score

After completing the test, please write in the numbers which you assigned to each of the following statements.

"A" Statements:

1. ____	21. ____	35. ____
2. ____	22. ____	36. ____
5. ____	25. ____	38. ____
8. ____	26. ____	40. ____
12. ____	28. ____	41. ____
13. ____	29. ____	45. ____
18. ____	30. ____	46. ____
19. ____	33. ____	48. ____
		49. ____

TOTAL **A** SCORE _____

"B" Statements:

Please write in the score which you gave each of the following statements. After you have recorded the number which you assigned to each, please *change the score* using the following code and place the changed score in the second column:
5 = 1
4 = 2
3 = 3
2 = 4
1 = 5

3. ____ ____	16. ____ ____	37. ____ ____
4. ____ ____	17. ____ ____	39. ____ ____
6. ____ ____	20. ____ ____	42. ____ ____
7. ____ ____	23. ____ ____	43. ____ ____
9. ____ ____	24. ____ ____	44. ____ ____
10. ____ ____	27. ____ ____	47. ____ ____
11. ____ ____	31. ____ ____	50. ____ ____
14. ____ ____	32. ____ ____	
15. ____ ____	34. ____ ____	

TOTAL **B** SCORE _____
TOTAL *CHANGED* SCORE _____

Please add Total **A** and Total *CHANGED* Score. This number is your Codependence score.

Interpretation of score:
200–250	Healthy
160–199	Mild codependence
120–159	Serious codependence
Below 119	Severe codependence

FUNCTION 2—Denial/Inconsistency

To determine your Denial/Inconsistency Score, please subtract whichever is smaller of TOTAL **A** and TOTAL **B** from whichever is larger. If your score is 10 or less, you have little or no denial. Serious denial is indicated above that number.

FUNCTION 3—Aspects of Codependency

As indicated above, this test measures three different aspects of codependency. Please write in your scores on each of the following statements. Change the "B" column scores using the following code before totaling:
5 = 1
4 = 2
3 = 3
2 = 4
1 = 5

Cognitive Rigidity

A Statements		**B** Statements		
19 ____		24 ____	____	
49 ____		27 ____	____	
30 ____		4 ____	____	
35 ____		3 ____	____	
12 ____		17 ____	____	
45 ____		10 ____	____	
Total ____		Total ____		

Please add the two totals.
Cognitive Rigidity Score ____

Interpretation:
49–60	Healthy
37–48	Mild codependence
28–36	Serious codependence
Below 27	Severe codependence

Emotional Disintegrity

A Statements	**B** Statements
26 _____	15 _____ _____
48 _____	39 _____ _____
28 _____	9 _____ _____
8 _____	16 _____ _____
38 _____	20 _____ _____
22 _____	11 _____ _____
13 _____	43 _____ _____
2 _____	32 _____ _____
1 _____	37 _____ _____
Total _____	Total _____

Please add the two totals.
Emotional Disintegrity score _____

Interpretation:
    75–90   Healthy
    55–74   Mild codependence
    35–54   Serious codependence
    Below 34   Severe codependence

Extreme Normative Expectations

A Statements	**B** Statements
41 _____	34 _____ _____
25 _____	50 _____ _____
18 _____	7 _____ _____
36 _____	31 _____ _____
29 _____	44 _____ _____
5 _____	42 _____ _____
21 _____	6 _____ _____
46 _____	23 _____ _____
33 _____	14 _____ _____
47 _____	40 _____ _____
Total _____	Total _____

Please add the two totals.
Extreme Normative Expectation Score _____

Score Interpretation:
    80–100   Healthy
    60–79   Mild codependence
    40–59   Serious codependence
    Below 39   Severe codependence

REFERENCES

Ackerman, Robert J. (1983). *Children of Alcoholics: A Guide for Parents, Educators, and Therapists* (2nd ed.), New York: Simon & Schuster.

Friel, J. (1985). "Co-dependency Assessment Inventory: A Preliminary Research Tool," *Focus on Family*, May/June, pp. 20–21.

Carey, M., Flasher, L., Maisto, S., and Turkat, I. (1984). "The A Priori Approach to Psychological Assessement," *Professional Psychology: Research and Practice*, 15, 515–527.

Cermak, T. (1986). *Diagnosing and Treating Co-dependence*, Minneapolis: Johnson Institute Books.

Gossett, G. (1988). Unpublished seminar report, March, 1988, Denton, Tex.: University of North Texas.

Lewis, J., Dana, R., and Blevins, G. (1988). *Substance Abuse Counseling: An Individualized Approach*, Pacific Grove, Calif.: Brooks/Cole.

Molineux, J. (1985). *Family Therapy: Practical Manual*, Springfield, Ill.: Charles C. Thomas.

Rowan J. (1983). *The Reality Game: A Guide to Humanistic Counselling and Therapy*, London: Routledge & Kegan Paul.

Walkenstein, E. (1975). *Shrunk to Fit*, London: Coventure.

Whitfield, C. (1987). *Healing the Child Within*, Pompano Beach, Fla.: Health Communications.

6

THE ADULT CHILD IN GROUP THERAPY

Sheldon was a well-built, muscular twenty-five-year-old. His face was rugged and handsome. He was soft spoken and shy, with the manner of a little boy, yet he was intelligent. In group exercises, Sheldon was always the last to speak. He was satisfied to be passed over and he never pushed to be heard. In the second session, Sheldon told the group that he had never been intimate with a woman. "My father always made fun of girls," he explained. "When I would get home from school, my dad would ask me if I'd kissed any gals that day. He said other crude things about girls. I guess you could say that I'm afraid of girls. And you could say that I never understood my own sexuality." Asked to clarify, Sheldon quietly said, "I've never had a girlfriend. I've never even been on a date."

Sheldon's story, though severe, is not unique. Childhood abuse of any kind leads to trouble with intimacy. No codependent client can grow without dealing with social relationships. The groups in which we interact are our social support systems and as such do more than give us an environment in which to interact. They help us define who we are and they help us maintain a sense of self. Weiss (1969) has described the five important needs that can be met only through our relationships:

- The need for intimacy. Relationships give us someone with whom we can freely share our feelings.
- The need for social integration. Relationships provide someone with whom we can share our worries and concerns.

- The need to be nurturant. Relationships offer someone for whom we can care.
- The need for assistance. Relationships give us someone who will help us out when we need it.
- The need for reassurance of our own worth. Relationships provide us with someone who will tell us that we matter.

Brehm (1985, p. 5) says, "Ideally, in an intimate relationship, people disclose feelings, discuss practical concerns, help and take care of each other, and provide mutual reassurance." Edelson (1970, p. 6) makes the case that this kind of loving and accepting relationship is virtually absent in modern society. What ails the mental health patient, he says, is "too little connection with his fellows." That argument would not be debated by those who deal with the adult child. They realize that codependence affects every intimate relationship. Indeed, Woititz (1985, pp. 1–2) argues that dysfunctional families destroy one's capacity for intimacy. Coleman, Butcher, and Carson (1984, p. 236) argue that the most characteristic quality of individuals with disordered personalities is "the pattern of disrupted personal relationships."

We may, therefore, conclude that codependence affects all close relationships. It begins in our early relationships long before we are able to make rational responses and fend for ourselves. It shows up in our childhood and adolescent relationships and continues throughout our adult lives. For that reason, effective treatment of the adult child must include working with relationships both past and present. No place is better suited for doing this than in a group.

CODEPENDENT THERAPY IN GROUPS

Group therapy has several attributes that make it an attractive option in helping the adult child of a dysfunctional family. Reid (1983, pp. 187–199) explores group therapy as a method of treatment of all personality disorders and comes to the conclusion that insight-oriented, supportive groups are effective in working with individuals who suffer from these conditions.

The Advantages of Group Therapy

The following are some advantages of group therapy:

- The group therapy setting approximates interaction in real life. It provides group members with the opportunity to try out new behaviors in a safe environment. This nonthreatening climate encourages the adult child to experiment with new methods of interaction and to internalize a healthier way of relating to others.
- Group work allows feedback from others and can help the individual test the accuracy of perception and communication. The client must face false assump-

tions of both self and others. Distorted perceptions lose their value and can be discarded.

- Group therapy provides a supportive atmosphere and fosters a sense of psychological safety to encourage the elimination of self-defeating behaviors. Participants may unlearn old and deeply ingrained rules and replace old habits with new and healthy interaction skills.

- Group therapy allows a new type of social comparison. Through watching and hearing others, individuals learn that they share many problems they previously thought belonged uniquely to themselves. They begin to see their pain as a result of external processes, not so much the result of their own personal failings. Hearing the stories of others helps each individual understand his or her own story from a larger context.

- Interaction in a group can help codependent clients to give up some of their people-pleasing and manipulative behaviors in favor of a more genuinely empathic understanding of others. Intolerant and impatient behaviors may also be replaced with a deeper understanding and acceptance of individual differences.

- The group itself is a living, growing, and changing thing. It does not stay the same and it requires the individual to learn the process of relating to healthy change. Codependents especially need the experience of dealing with the fear and grief that accompany normal change.

- The group setting allows the individual to accept the risk of rejection and reveal his or her internal struggles and feelings. The client can see this behavior modeled by others and learn by their example.

These characteristics, as well as others associated with group therapy, are highly relevant to the issues faced by the codependent. I have found it to be the treatment of choice for most adult children. Other therapists in the field also recognize its effectiveness. Consider the work of Carnes (1983, pp. 133–160), Cermak (1986, pp. 65–66), and Lewis, Dana, and Blevins (1988, pp. 157–192).

Limitations of Group Therapy

Group therapy is not for everybody. Some people are largely unaware of their feelings. Others have great difficulty communicating their feelings. Both types of persons should work for a while in individual therapy before going into a group. Some clients are too immature for group therapy. Anyone who is in a very serious crisis may need to deal with the problem in individual treatment first. Some codependents are so introverted and anxious in the presence of others that the group would be overwhelming to them. For them, individual therapy may be necessary before entering the group.

Despite the obvious treatment advantages of group therapy, it is difficult to substantiate empirically what effect group therapy has on the individual. For example, Coleson and Horwitz (1983, pp. 304–311) surveyed the research literature from 1955 to 1983 on the effectiveness of group therapy. They cite the Bednar and Lawlis study, done in the early 1970s, that affirms the effectiveness of group therapy. They then turn to the 1975 study of Parloff and Dies that concludes the exact opposite. According to Parloff and Dies, there is no cumulative or compelling evidence that group therapy has any therapeutic effect. Acknowledging the difficulties in measurement, Coleson and Horwitz conclude: "The research in group therapy provides few conclusive answers about the efficacy of various types of therapists and groups in the treatment of different kinds of patients."

After years of work with addicts, I have found it to be an almost impossible task to find in the literature consistent, measurable benefits attributable to this method of treatment (Miller and Hester, 1985). In fact, the problems in evaluating any kind of psychotherapy are immense. It is an inexact process, at best. Perhaps Coleman, Butcher, and Carson's (1984, p. 669) conclusion on the effectiveness of any therapy is the best we can say for group therapy. After surveying the literature on evaluating the effectiveness of therapy of any kind, they sum up: "Most researchers today would agree that psychotherapy is more effective than no treatment."

So, despite its admitted limitations, group therapy remains an excellent treatment for the majority of codependents. They need to learn and practice new social skills, they have problems in interaction, and they have difficulty with trust and being vulnerable. They cannot share their feelings, they need feedback on their own self-defeating behaviors, and they have trouble with their own sense of omnipotence. They need to work on these and other issues at their own pace. Group therapy gives the adult child a unique opportunity to deal with these and other special problems.

STRUCTURE OF CODEPENDENT GROUP THERAPY

All therapy is based on the belief that individuals with mental, emotional, or behavioral problems *can* change. Therapists assume that clients can learn more adaptive ways of thinking, feeling, and acting and that they can change their perceptions, evaluations, expectations, rules, coping skills, and communications styles. The therapist believes that these changes will overcome both inner stress and outward maladaptation in the client's life. The goal of therapy is for the client to make these changes a reality. Group therapy is based on this goal.

Codependent group therapy is a special kind of therapy. The overall goals of the group are no different from those of any other therapy group, but the needs of the codependent client are unique. The structure of the group and the methods used to meet those goals must be tailored to the needs of the codependent.

Types of Groups

Group therapy for the codependent must be differentiated from other classes of groups. There are five basic types.

Didactic group. The didactic group is a teaching group, and its purpose is to convey information from one person to another. The leader does the majority of the work, lecturing and giving examples. The group participant is mostly passive. He or she listens, occasionally asks a question, and perhaps writes down what the instructor says. Didactic groups fulfil an educational function and are cognitive in orientation.

Weiner (1983, p. 55) refers to this kind of group as repressive, because it actively suppresses material that emerges from the unconscious. This type of group deals with the present through practical suggestions by the leader and the other group members. Individuals in such groups are taught about their psychological dynamics and vulnerabilities.

Codependent groups must include some educational work, but groups that are exclusively didactic in character are not suited to the needs of the adult child.

Training group. This type of group is designed to convey special skills from one person to another. Both instruction and exercises are employed in training groups. The leader demonstrates the skill and then allows the participants to practice. The leader and sometimes the participants give feedback on performance. Practice drums the skill into the participant. For this reason, codependent groups need exercises that allow role playing and practice of skills. But groups that are exclusively designed to achieve training goals are not suited to the whole needs of the codependent.

Support group. Support groups are created to give emotional sustenance to the participants. They are powerful agents of help to individuals who are isolated and in a lot of pain. Primarily, they help the individual know that he or she is not alone. Cole (1983, pp. 145–146) points out that the support group is a self-help group and that it is effective because it validates the person's sense of self-worth. It also provides a powerful new reference group in which the individual can experience a sense of commonality and community.

Alcoholic Anonymous (AA) and all its spinoffs are examples of support groups. Groups of this type are very good for codependents, especially in combination with other kinds of therapy. They are limited, however, by the lack of a professional therapist who can help an individual over rough spots. Also, some thinkers, such as Fingarette (1988), are critical of the basic philosophy and therapeutic methods upon which AA is based. Nonetheless, support groups can frequently help the individual by providing the freedom to express the pain of their negative emotions. But both the group and the individual can get stuck and find it impossible to get beyond that point. Codependents need more than emotional support.

Interactive or process therapy group. This group is designed to help the individual experience personal growth. The participants do most of the work, and the leader is primarily a facilitator. He or she intervenes to interpret individual and group experiences and to keep the group involved in processing present emotions. Individual growth occurs when the client and the group are focused on what is going on in the group rather than avoiding the feelings they have about the present. Thus, the facilitator keeps them focused on what is happening currently. Codependents need large doses of this kind of activity, but they need more. Exclusive attention to the interactive process, as powerful and necessary as it is, omits several important aspects of therapy necessary for the adult child.

Codependent therapy group. Group therapy designed for the codependent must contain elements of each of the above types of groups. It must be educational and therefore contain a didactic element. It must convey skills and therefore contain explicit exercises to be done in the group and outside the group as homework. It must be emotionally sustaining and therefore emphasize support. And it must help the client to process emotions in the present. The codependent therapy group is a fifth type of group in a class by itself.

The codependent therapy group would be what Weiner (1983, p. 55) calls an *ego-supportive group*. The basic interventions are in the present, but attention is paid to "preconscious attitudes and emotions, such as fear of authority or unexpressed anger, which motivate the behavior." In such a group, Weiner says, there is direct feedback on self-defeating behaviors, there is modeling by group members of healthy behaviors, and there is intellectual stimulation by the therapist in explaining the psychological processes that the individual experiences. Effective group therapy for the codependent, then, combines the best of all the approaches.

Codependent Therapy Group Content

The following is a suggested agenda for a sixteen-week group therapy experience for adult children. I developed this program in the groups I facilitated at the Relationship Enrichment Counseling Center in Dallas, Texas. Groups meet for two hours, and membership runs between ten and fifteen persons in each. I allow and encourage couples to participate in the groups together. On some occasions I have even had adult participants and their middle-aged parents in the same group.

This suggested content has been through several revisions. Every group is different and the structure and content that is suggested in this detailed outline is never written in stone. If a group needs to stay with a subject over several weeks, I make no effort to hurry them on to the next assigned task. After all, it is for the good of the group that we meet, not for the purpose of covering a predetermined agenda.

Week 1: Introduction

Week 1 is for accomplishing three main tasks: (1) To introduce the concept of the group and to describe its basic goals; (2) to let group members introduce themselves and speak briefly about why they are there and what they hope to gain; and (3) to give an assessment test to allow group members to determine the extent of their codependence.

This session is designed to begin the process of putting group participants at ease and helping them begin to trust that the group is a safe place. Group members are asked to commit themselves to the following: They will try to be honest and tell the truth; they will try to deal with the present and be willing to look at the past in order to understand the present; they will promise strict confidentiality; and they will commit themselves to attend the entire sixteen weeks. This latter commitment means that they will not quit, no matter how hard the going gets. I explain that when they just quit and do not show up for a scheduled meeting, the other members feel rejected. If for some reason they cannot honor this commitment, I ask that they come to a group meeting and share their reasons with us.

Exercise 1. At this point, I give the group members a brief assessment instrument and ask that they take a few minutes to answer the questions. The instrument I normally use is the Codependence Test, described in Chapter Five (p. 89).

At the conclusion of this meeting, I give the following homework. I ask that during the week each person think about their past and select a specific event or series of events from their childhood that is an example of abuse they received. I give them a brief example from my own childhood that models the kind of thing I am interested in and also allows me to be self-disclosing.

Week 2: Getting in Touch with Our Past

The purpose of the Week 2 session is to let participants begin the process of looking at and sharing their past. This session is conducted entirely as an interactive group. I begin by asking if there is anything that anyone wants to say to any other person in the group. Sometimes one or even several people will say something like, "I thought about what Bill said and it helped me a lot." Or, "What did you do about your problem, Suzi?" Frequently, two or three persons will describe the feelings they had about the group or even me during the week. Usually these comments are about how hard it was for them to come back. Sometimes someone will even admit that they would not have returned had they not promised to continue the entire sixteen weeks.

After several minutes of this activity, I remind them of the homework and say, "I wonder if anyone would share the event they have selected?" We wait. Sometimes it can seem like an eternity until someone speaks. I *never* break the silence, realizing the truth of the cliché "Nothing is never happening in a group." At last, someone will begin to speak and the relief of group members is almost visible. (There will be many more such periods of silence in the weeks ahead, but none will produce the pressure of this first one.) I let each person talk. Usually my only intervention is to ask, "How does it feel to be talking about this now to this group?" I sometimes will guess at what they felt in the past ("That must have made you angry") or how they feel as they are talking in the group now ("You seem to enjoy talking about that" or "You are still feeling something deep about that"). Sometimes I express my own feelings about what they are saying: "I feel anger for you when I hear you describe that experience."

I always thank the person for sharing when they conclude. I never evaluate them or what they say. Comments like, "Boy, that took a lot of courage" are out of place. Such statements evaluate the person and may be taken to mean, "How in the world did you find the courage to admit such an outrageous thing?" It is enough to say simply, "Thank you for sharing that with us."

Sometimes a group will come along that is made up of individuals who are all very introverted. Sharing in that group will be hard, and this session will be tense and difficult. When that happens, I share something about my own codependency. If I have had a recent event in my own life that has been especially revealing about my problems, I share it. Or I may talk about some aspect of my childhood that I have come to see as relevant in the pain I feel as an adult. I am always free to disclose my experiences at any time. It is a good modeling technique, especially when the group does not yet know much about sharing.

When everyone has had a turn, I ask if any one wants to say anything to any other person the group. Frequently, a brief discussion will emerge. When about five minutes are left in the session, I start to create closure. I begin by saying, "The thing that is abusive about abuse is that it *shames* us. That is, we come to think of ourselves as defective. When abused, the child responds by thinking, 'Something is wrong with me because I am being treated like this.'" I enlarge briefly on these ideas using the concepts of Fossum and Mason (1986) to talk about shame.

If the session goes as planned three important things will take place: (1) Participants get a sense of sharing and dealing openly with inner issues. It usually feels good to them to unload some of these things. Some individuals have a hard time opening up. But even these persons have the healthy experience of seeing it modeled for them. From this point onward, it is easier for everyone to get in touch with their emotions and talk about them. (2) Individuals begin the process of identifying events of the past as abusive. It continually amazes me that group members will describe a parent slapping them in the face or humiliating them in some public place and not recognize this experience as abuse. This exercise helps everyone to see that there are events in our past that we have taken for granted as our parents' or others' rights, when they are in fact abusive events. (3) This session lays the groundwork for participants to learn about their present by looking at the past. The closing comments are designed to produce that effect in them. We feel defective and incompetent and deformed *now* because we were abused *then*.

Week 3: Codependence: Definitions and Descriptions

The primary purpose for the Week 3 session is to convey information and allow participants time to process some of what they learn. To carry out this goal, three activities are done. First, we go through Exercise 2, which is designed to help each person see how the past has influenced the present through the development of codependent patterns of thinking and behavior. The exercise helps each participant see himself or herself as the precious child which he or she was at birth and to conceptualize how childhood experiences impaired the natural growth of the child. The exercise is built on the concepts of Mellody and coworkers (1989, pp. 62–113). Each participant has a copy of the exercise, and I merely explain what the chart means. I encourage questions and discussion as I go through the materials. The following is the exercise.

Exercise 2.   The Precious Child.   All children, grown up or otherwise, are precious, vulnerable, needy, conflictual, immature, and imperfect. Yet when the childlike qualities of the person are abused at any age, the symptomatic traits listed below in the left and right columns will result and generally develop to an extreme. Recovery is the process of redeveloping the childlike qualities and growing toward the characteristics listed in the center column.

Codependency	Traits of Recovery	Codependency
1. Self-loathing (Low self-esteem)	Self-valuing (Appropriate esteem)	Arrogance Grandiosity
2. Too vulnerable (No boundaries)	Vulnerable with Protection	Invulnerable (Solid walls)
3. Dependent (Too needy)	Interdependence (Interrelated needs)	Independent (Needless)
4. Uncontrolled (Chaotic life)	Moderation (Control from within)	Controlled (Overorganized)
5. Superimmature	Mature at own level (Accountable for self)	Supermature
6. No Confidence	Confidence from within	Overconfident
7. Full of Shame (Shameful)	Accepting of own Faults	Lack of Shame (Shameless)

The second activity of Week 3 is to present the codependent compulsions as a "Cycle of Shame." The chart in Figure 5 is useful in this regard.

I accompany this chart with a brief explanation. Pointing to the top rectangle, "Pain," I talk about early feelings of rejection and abandonment that come with growing up in a dysfunctional family. Moving on to the next rectangle marked "Behavior That Relieves Pain," I explain that the child or teenager finds a behavior that covers over the pain. It may be a chemical or food or sex or some other substance or activity. Or it may be some socially approved behavior like rigid religion or being a "good boy." The point is that the individual finds in the self-destructive behavior relief for the pain that he or she feels. The individual makes a habit or compulsion of the behavior. I point to the next rectangle called "Compulsive Behavior" and explain the nature of addiction briefly. I then move to the final rectangle, "More Pain." The behavior originally brought relief from shame, but now, as an addiction, it contributes to the pain and starts the cycle over again. Round and round the codependent goes through the cycle that only deepens the shame.

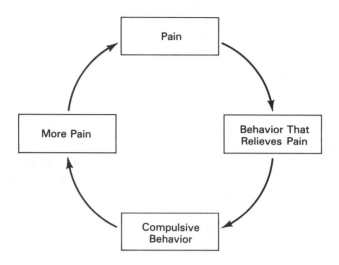

Figure 5: THE CYCLE OF SHAME

This exercise helps the group understand the nature and purpose of our codependent compulsions. They are presented as "addictive" patterns of thinking, feeling, and acting that we learned in our childhood as methods of avoiding the pain that comes from our dysfunctional families. These ideas are offered as the definition of codependence.

These first two exercises are presented in about thirty or forty minutes, including discussion. The remaining hour and twenty or thirty minutes is given to processing these ideas by helping the group members apply them to their individual lives. I begin this section by asking, "Would someone like to share how these concepts help you to understand your childhood?" My interventions are limited to helping them to discover and reveal both past and present feelings and to interpret their meaning. By this point in the group, several members usually have caught on and are making these kinds of interventions with other group members. This is what we want to happen and when it does, I remove myself from the conversation and allow it to happen on its own.

The following occurred in a recent group session and illustrates the kind of exchange that is therapeutic:

MARY: I am always strong and people depend upon me for everything. They sense that I am strong and happy. And I am. (Mary's voice was too loud for the room we were in. Her fists were clenched.)

GREG (in a soft voice and with sensitivity): I don't know if I really believe you, Mary. I hear the words you say and I feel an intensity about you. You seem to need us to believe you.

STAN: I kinda see that same thing. You confuse me.

MARY: Well, I feel confused myself. I'm supposed to be strong for everybody. (Mary talked on about how people always expect her to be happy and strong.)

GREG: Sounds like you have a rule going there. How does it feel for everybody to expect you to be what they want and not let you be what you are?

MARY: Like hell.

Week 4: Knowing Your Broken Child

Week 4 is intended to bring the group members into contact with their past in an unusually powerful manner. After giving a few minutes for them to process any material from the preceding week, I move directly into a visual imagery exercise. Usually I preface the exercise with a brief explanation about meditation. I do this because some people have meditation confused with hypnosis and are a little frightened about it. My comments are intended to calm their fears. I conclude the introduction by telling them that the exercise we are about to do will last no more than five minutes.

I then ask the group members to sit straight in their chairs with both feet on the floor and their hands resting in their laps. I ask them to close their eyes and concentrate on breathing by becoming aware of the air as it enters their nostrils and goes into their lungs. I keep my voice soft and I proceed slowly. This part of the exercise is done to relax them. I stop speaking at this point and concentrate on my own breathing. This latter calms me and it also makes sure that I give them time to carry out my instructions.

After this moment of relaxation, I continue:

Now, I want you to get an image of the house you lived in when you were a child. Picture yourself as a grown-up standing on the street facing the front of the house. Take a moment to look up and down the street and then look slowly at the front of the house and the front yard. (Pause briefly.) Now, picture yourself walking up to the front door and opening it. Step inside. Look around at the room you are standing in. (Pause briefly.) Try to smell the room. Be aware of how you feel standing there. Reach out and touch the wall or a piece of the furniture. Be aware of how it feels. (Pause briefly.)

Now, walk slowly toward the back of the house. Concentrate on the smells and sights of each room as you go through it. (Pause briefly.) Now, go to the room that was yours when you lived there. Go into that room. Look around you. Is it light or dark in the room? Are there toys there? Is the room neat or scattered? How do you feel being in this room? (Pause briefly.)

See yourself as a child sitting on the bed. Walk over to that child and sit down on the bed. Reach out your hand and touch the child. Put your arm around the child and hug him or her. Kiss the child on the cheek. (Pause briefly.) Say these words to the child, 'I love you,_____, and I will take care of you. I will be here for you and you will never be alone again.' (Pause briefly.) Now, say to the child, 'You may come with me, _____, if you wish. I will take you out of here.' Take your child by the hand and walk slowly back through the house. Go out the front door and stand facing away from the house. (Pause briefly.) Breath deeply, and when you are ready, open your eyes.

When the exercise is over, I let the group sit quietly for a moment. Sometimes someone will begin to speak about the meditation. If no one volunteers after a couple of minutes, I ask if someone would share their response during the exercise. The remainder of the session is spent processing the feelings that the experience has raised.

This session is meant to get the group members in touch with very deep feelings about themselves. Responses vary, but largely people do a lot of grieving in response to the experience. Sometimes, the grief does not start until the next day. Sometimes, an individual will have a response of distaste for the child they encounter. They will report that they felt uncomfortable or even repulsed by the child. They refuse to touch or kiss the child.

There is usually an intensity in this session. The feelings that this exercise brings to the surface are frequently both painful and relieving. Many times it puts the client in touch with the very feelings that his or her compulsions are designed to hide. Sometimes individuals feel anger at the therapist for putting them through these experiences.

I conclude the session by talking about the child and the therapeutic value of getting in touch with him or her. We can go back and give that child the love and care and nurturing that was not given when he or she so desperately needed it years ago. I leave them with the adage, "It is never too late to have a happy childhood."

Week 5: Truth in Relationships

By this time in the group, we have had many opportunities to talk about how codependents avoid revealing how they really feel and what they really think. They lie a lot, both by telling things that are not true and by not telling things that are true. This session is dedicated to truth-telling.

I begin by asking them to fill out as honestly as possible the answers to the questions on Exercise 3, *To Tell the Truth...*, which follows:

Exercise 3. To Tell The Truth...

Please complete all the following questions. Your answers are confidential, but you will be encouraged to share them with the group when finished.

1. How did you feel about the group at the first meeting? How do you feel right now?
2. Who in this group do you feel most positive about right now? Describe what makes you feel good about that person.
3. Toward whom in this group do you feel most negative right now? Describe what produces this negative feeling.
4. What prevents you from being more open and honest in this group?
5. Which person in this group do you think feels most positively toward you right now? Why do you think this person experiences positive feelings about you?
6. Which person in this group do you think feels most negatively about you right now? Why do you think this person experiences negative feelings about you?

When they are finished (usually in about ten to fifteen minutes), I say, "I would like to request that we share our responses with each other. Who would like to begin?" I have found that it is better to let everybody answer Question 1 and then move on to Question 2 rather than letting each person answer all questions and then moving on to the next person.

This session can be a difficult one. Codependents do have a hard time sharing their true feelings. Exercise 3 is designed to get people to deal with their true feelings about specific members of the group in the present. Some people will avoid doing so and will even refuse to do it. I have found that it is best to let the group deal with these persons. Again, my interventions are intended to keep the group on course. I conclude the group with no effort to get closure for them.

Week 6: Confrontation: Knowing and Expressing Your Feelings

I begin Week 6 by letting the group process any material that is left over from the previous week. When they are finished, I introduce the concept of confrontation by noting that we all seem to have trouble with it. I talk briefly about the derivation of the word. It comes from two Latin words. The first, *con*, means "together" or "with." The second, *frons*, means "forehead." *Confrontation* is, then, "the process of putting our heads together." I point out that we can put our heads together in three ways: We can knock heads, which is what we normally think of when confrontation comes to mind. But kissing is also a method of putting our heads together. (The mention of kissing as confrontation usually brings a smile or comments like, "God, help me to confront!") Finally, we can put our heads together in open and simple talking. This type of confrontation is close to the old Biblical idea, "Come, let us reason together." These comments take no more than five minutes. When I am finished, I divide the group into pairs. I then ask each person to complete Exercise 4, *The Gentle and Healthy Art of Confrontation.*

Exercise 4.   The Gentle and Healthy Art of Confrontation

---

1. When I first met you, overall I thought you were: (Write out a brief description of your first impressions of the other person.)

   _____
   _____
   _____
   _____

2. The most positive trait I saw in you during that first meeting was:

   _____

3. The most negative trait I saw in you during that first meeting was:

   _____

4. After knowing you for a while, I see the following things about you:
   a. Your strongest and most positive traits are:
      (1.) _____
      (2.) _____
      (3.) _____
   b. Your weakest and most negative traits are:
      (1.) _____
      (2.) _____
      (3.) _____

5. I want to thank you for being in my life because you have helped me in the following ways:

   _____
   _____
   _____

They are to answer each question with reference to the individual with whom they are paired. I give them about ten minutes to write out their answers, and then I ask them to share their responses with each other. I give them about twenty minutes. If I am working with a cotherapist, I pair up with that person and we do the exercise with one another.

When they are finished, I bring them back into the group and we share our experiences together. Most people dread and fear confrontation. This is especially true of codependents. There is relief when they see that the pleasant exercise they have just finished is *confrontation.*

Frequently, several persons will want to talk about how they can do this kind of confronting with people in their lives. Martha is an example. A small and frail forty-year-old, she had two unruly teenagers that she felt she could not control. Her husband, Rick, was an accountant who was also a mild and introverted person. He, too, was a member of the group. One bone of contention between Martha and Rick was Rick's mother, who was a dominant person. For example, Martha's anger simmered beneath her quiet exterior about her mother-in-law's constant instruction on child rearing. "How can I use this to confront her?" she asked. Her eyes darted to Rick's face to see if he was angry. An understanding grin spread across his face. "Start with 4b," he said quietly. There was no hesitation in his voice. All eyes in the group went back to the page to see that Rick had advised his wife to begin the process of confrontation with his mother with the statement, "Your weakest and most negative traits are...."

I conclude by pointing out that what we have done is to experience the principles of healthy confrontation. I ask them to practice these principles during the coming week with at least one person.

Week 7: Open Session, No Assigned Topic

I begin Week 7 by saying something like, "Who would like to begin?" The session is handled as an interactive therapy period during which group members process their own feelings. Some want to report on their confrontational experiences of the preceding week and how they integrated the exercise into them. Others want to talk about the group. Anything can come up. My interventions are usually expressed by the following questions: "How does that make you feel?" "What are you feeling now as you relate this to the group?" and "I wonder how the group responds to what you are saying." The entire session is given to this kind of exchange.

Week 8: Playing: Learning to Let the Child Out

Week 8 is one of the most satisfying sessions of all for me. We play. Before the meeting begins, I place an empty soft-drink bottle in the middle of the circle of chairs where the group sits. As they arrive, they are aware of the bottle and they make comments like, "Are we going to play 'spin the bottle'?" When everyone is in their place and it is time to begin, I say, "Yes, we are going to play 'spin the bottle'!" I talk a little about playing as a characteristic of children and that many adult children were denied their childhood by having to be responsible and mature from an early age. "Tonight," I say, "we are going to be children and learn to play."

The rules of the game are simple. When you spin the bottle, you may respond to the person at which it points in one of four ways:

- You may ask the person any question you wish.

- You may ask the person to do anything you wish.
- You may ask the person to let you do anything you wish.
- You may tell the person anything you wish.

I usually write these statements on a blackboard so they will be at ready reference during the game. I also point out that no one is to feel that he or she has to do anything they do not want to do.

At this point, the fun begins. If the bottle points at me, I join in and take my turn. Otherwise, I remain silent. About halfway through, I begin to watch that no one is left out. Bottles have a way of returning to the same few persons repeatedly. If there is a person or two that the bottle is overlooking, I will ask to be allowed to intervene and will deliberately point the bottle at those persons. However, I do not take over asking the questions.

It is a game, but I find that serious therapy takes place in the playing. People usually ask questions about each other or make comments to each other. A lot of truth comes to the surface. "What makes you happy?" they ask and people talk about their joy and sorrow. "Tell us about your most embarrassing moment," they ask and people tell stories that are sometimes funny and sometimes sad. They laugh and they cry, but they always enjoy talking about themselves.

Before leaving this session, I give an assignment for the next week. I request that each person write a letter to their child. That is, each individual is to write a letter to themselves as a child. I ask them to speak as an adult to that child and to tell her or him what they think that child needed to hear back then. I ask that they bring the letter in a stamped, self-addressed, sealed envelope to our next session. I do not tell them what I will do with the letter.

Week 9: Dealing with Anger

I begin Session 9 with comments similar to the following: "Both fear and anger are God-given emotions. In their proper context, and understood correctly, they are both healthy and constructive. Allowed to be disordered or immature, they are overwhelming and destructive."

"Both help us deal in a healthy way with those things that would hurt us. Fear is a defensive emotion. It helps us draw back when attacked. Anger is an offensive weapon. It helps us keep going in the face of attack. Both are a part of courage. If you have no fear, you need no courage. If you have no anger, your courage is without stamina. Fear makes courage admirable, and anger energizes and ennobles courage."

I allow time for questions and comments on these emotions. Then I say, "When something occurs that may potentially hurt you, there are four possible responses available to you. I call these responses the 'ladder of fear and anger.'" (I developed these ideas after reading Grant, Thompson, and Clarke [1983], pp. 96–98.) I draw a ladder with four rungs on the blackboard and write the word *Submission* on the bottom rung. I talk briefly about submission, noting that it means that I put my needs down and put the needs of the other up. I give the following example. If I bring my wet dog into your house, submission means that even though you may not want me to, you do nothing and let my dog drip on your furniture. Submission can occasionally be a noble thing, but most of the time it is not. In fact, I comment, it is self-destructive.

Next, I write the words *Passive-aggressive* on the second rung from the bottom. I give a brief explanation of the concept and end with the wet dog example. A passive-aggressive response, I point out, would not deal with the dog at all. Instead, you would say something like, "Hey, you seem to have put on a few pounds," or "You've got a few more gray hairs." Passive aggression puts my interest down along with your own, I note in explaining the concept. Also, you are protected from my anger by being able to deny responsibility for your aggressiveness. If I comment on your statements, you can respond by saying that you were only joking. There is no healthy way to deal with your anger or my own in such a conversation.

On the next rung of the ladder I write *Aggressive Hostility.* I explain that this response is very much to be desired over the two previous responses. It is what we usually think about when we think of anger. Returning to my wet dog analogy, I point out that you would throw me and my dog out of your house while dumping all your hostility on me. You not only feel anger, you act angrily. Aggressive hostility, I explain, puts your well-being up and puts mine down.

The top rung is reserved for the word *Self-affirmation,* which I write on the board. I explain that when you are self-affirming, you simply ask for what you want and need or you report accurately what you feel. A self-affirming response to my wet dog would be, "Your dog is wet and is soiling my furniture. Please put him outside." Such a response affirms you and also affirms me. Neither one of us is put down, I note.

Anger and fear are very difficult emotions for the codependent to understand, accept, and express. For that reason, I am slow and deliberate in this educational exercise. I give them time to reflect and comment as I go through these materials. When I am finished, I let them ask questions and discuss what I've said. This all takes about twenty or thirty minutes. The remainder of the session is a time for processing their experiences of dealing with their own fear and anger both in the present and in the past.

This session is usually hard. Anger makes codependents anxious. Most of the group will have lived their lives on the first two rungs of that ladder, and they don't want to take the responsibility to move up. Much denial comes out in this session. Frequently, they will want to intellectualize about anger and affirmation. They ask, "But this sounds selfish." Sometimes religious discussions will come up as people try to put it all into perspective. I do not engage them in debate, religious or otherwise. To do so is to miss the opportunity for growth. My interventions are designed to help them focus on their feelings in the present. That is because it is *those feelings* that give them a hard time about anger in the real world.

I conclude the session by collecting the letters I asked them to write in the previous session.

Weeks 10–13: Open Session: No Assigned Topic

These sessions are conducted in the same manner as those in Week 7.

Week 14: Accepting and Expressing Your Sexuality

At the beginning of this session, I divide the group into two sections made up of all the men in one section, and all the women in the other. I request that they discuss the following topics and that one person be designated to keep notes on the discussion:

1. List the ideas you had about the opposite sex when you were a teenager. For example, answer the questions, What did they think of sex? What turned them on? What did they want in sex?
2. List some of the slang words and descriptive phrases your sex had for the members of the opposite sex.
3. When you were a teenager, how did other teens think pregnancy occurred?
4. When you were a teenager, what did your sex think about:

   a. masturbation?

   b. oral sex?
5. When you were a teenager, how did you think your sexual experiences would be like when you were married?

I give about twenty-five minutes for this discussion to take place. Then the group is called back together, and we talk about their answers. I conduct this session more as a didactic group. But I leave room to deal with emotions that can surface.

The day after Session 14, I mail the letters that participants have written and brought in earlier. I make no mention that I am planning to do so.

Week 15: Open Session: No Assigned Topic

This session is conducted as an interactive session and usually deals with sexual issues left over from the previous session. If no one brings it up, I will ask toward the end of the session if they got their letters in the mail. We spend a little time processing the feelings they had when they read what they had written to themselves as a child.

Week 16: Closing

I begin this group with a "stemming" exercise. I give group members the first few words of a sentence (the stem) and they finish it. We go around the room, and then I give another stem and they complete the sentence. We do several like the following:

- One thing that is changing about me is _____
- One thing I wish I could do is _____
- The most important thing I'm learning about me is _____
- The thing I've enjoyed most about this group is _____

The group will want to stop and discuss these things and individuals will make comments to others as this exercise is going on. After about thirty or forty minutes, I ask that the group members close their eyes and picture every other person in the group. I say, "Imagine yourself saying something to each person." I give a few minutes for them to complete these instructions and then ask them to open their eyes. I ask, "I wonder if anyone would like to share what you imagined yourself saying." Some very emotional things occur as members of the group talk about their feelings toward each other. I give them forty-five minutes or so. Then I say, "I would like each of you to say an appreciative word to yourself. Tell us what you are coming to like most about you."

I conclude by reminding them that this is a beginning, not an end. It is like a commencement and I request that they continue to practice the things they have learned in the group.

This chapter has introduced the subject of therapy for adult children in groups. We have looked at the advantages and limitations of group as therapy for codependents and at the different kinds of groups. The major task of the chapter has been to present a suggested structure for group therapy with adult children. Now we will turn to some special concerns that the therapist must keep in mind to make group therapy an effective method of treatment for the problems of the adult child.

REFERENCES

Brehm, S. (1985). *Intimate Relationships*, New York: Random House.

Carnes, P. (1983). *Out of the Shadows: Understanding Sexual Addiction*, Minneapolis: CompCare.

Cermak, T. (1986). *Diagnosing and Treating Co-dependence*, Minneapolis: Johnson Institute Books.

Cole, S. (1983). "Self-help Groups" in H. Kaplan and B. Sadock, Eds., *Comprehensive Group Psychotherapy*, Baltimore: Williams & Wilkins.

Coleman, J., Butcher, J., and Carson, R., (1984). *Abnormal Psychology and Modern Life* (7th ed.), Glenview, Ill.: Scott Foresman.

Coleson, D. and Horwitz, L. (1983). "Research in Group Therapy" in H. Kaplan and B. Sadock, Eds., *Comprehensive Group Psychotherapy*, Baltimore: Williams & Wilkins.

Edelson, M. (1970). *The Practice of Sociotherapy: A Case Study*, New Haven: Yale University Press.

Fingarette, H. (1988). *Heavy Drinking: The Myth of Alcoholism As a Disease*, Berkeley: University of California Press.

Fossum, M. and Mason, M. (1986). *Facing Shame: Families in Recovery*, New York: W. W. Norton.

Grant, W., Thompson, M., and Clarke, T. (1983). *From Image to Likeness: A Jungian Path in the Gospel Journey*, New York: Paulist.

Lewis, J., Dana, R., and Blevins, G. (1988). *Substance Abuse Counseling: An Individualized Approach*, Pacific Grove, Calif.: Brooks/Cole.

Mellody, P., Miller, A., and Miller, K. (1989). *Facing Codependence: What It Is, Where It Comes From, How It Sabotages Our Lives*, San Francisco: Harper & Row.

Miller, W., and Hester, R. (1985). "The Effectiveness of Treatment Techniques: What Works and What Doesn't," in W. Miller, Ed., *Alcoholism: Theory, Research, and Treatment*. Lexington, Mass.: Ginn Press.

Reid, H. (1983). *Treatment of the DSM-III Psychiatric Disorders*, New York: Brunner/Mazel.

Weiner, M. (1983). "The Role of the Leader in Group Psychotherapy," in H. Kaplan and B. Saddock, Eds. *Comprehensive Group Psychotherapy* (2nd ed.), Baltimore: Williams & Wilkins.

Weiss, R. S. (1969). "The Fund of Sociability," *Transaction*, 7, 36–43.

Woititz, J. (1985). *Struggle For Intimacy*, Pompano Beach, Fla.: Health Communications.

7

SPECIAL ISSUES FOR CODEPENDENT GROUP THERAPY

The therapist who has never facilitated codependent groups will need to consider a number of special points. Some of these concerns are associated with the nature of groups in general and would arise no matter what kind of group therapy one is doing. Others are related to the particular problems of codependence. The purpose of this chapter is to raise these issues and to look in depth at their resolution.

GETTING THE GROUP STARTED

Many of the individuals who come into group therapy conceive of it as a support group where people offer each other attentive and nonconfrontive encouragement. Or they see the group as a place where people listen to other people's problems and try to help them find solutions by offering advice and guidance. These persons think the therapist is there to keep group members from giving bad advice. Some see the group much like a class, where they come to listen and learn. They wait for the therapist to say something that they may apply to their lives. They are prepared to ask questions and expect the therapist to answer in a practical and efficient manner. The therapist must deal with these and other misconceptions early in the group's experience. The first meeting of the group is important in setting the tone for the rest of the sessions.

The following are some suggestions that I have found helpful in setting a therapeutic tone for the group.

Model Appropriate Sharing Early in the First Session

As noted in the previous chapter, I am comfortable with the therapist's making personal disclosure when it is done as a therapeutic tactic. Therefore, I talk about myself in the first session to model for the group the freedom to share that I hope they will all come to adopt. My opening up gives permission to others to do the same. "Let me tell you a little about me," I say after welcoming them to the group. I give a two-minute overview of my own dysfunctional family. Then I relate some recent experience that illustrates how this background is still affecting me in the present.

At the appropriate time later in the session, I ask them to share something about themselves and what they want from the group. I find that, as they talk about themselves, they use the model I have given to them. I encourage group members to respond by telling what they feel as they hear each person talk about themselves. "What do you feel as you hear Joyce talk about her experience?" I ask, adding, " Stay with your feelings and talk about you." I model this response by sharing my feelings after a person or two speak.

At the conclusion of the first session, I ask the group members to think during the next week about how their past has hurt them. I ask that they select a specific event or series of events which they think shows abuse in their childhood. Again, I model with a specific experience from my past. I pick some serious event in my life that I have been thinking about lately to show them how to do this assignment and to give them permission to deal with serious matters in the group. I take only about four minutes to relate my story.

I use this method whenever it seems appropriate in the group. To encourage them to process their present emotions about what is going on in the group, I try to get in touch with my own feelings about what is happening and share them. For example, if I am afraid, I may state that I am if I think that it would be useful to the group. I will sometimes share my feelings about what another person has said. For example, I may say, "I really felt anger for you when you told what Sue said to you." Or, "I was afraid for you when you were in that place. Did anyone else in the group feel that way?" I try to do this sparingly, and I stop when the group begins to practice this kind of sharing.

A useful intervention from time to time is to say something like, "I notice that every time the subject of religion comes up, the group gets very quiet. That makes me uncomfortable. I wonder if any one else has that response." This statement serves two purposes: (1) It models the appropriateness of getting in touch with feelings and sharing them; and (2) it helps focus the group on group processes.

Involving the Withdrawn

Many adult children are social isolates who have a hard time becoming vulnerable. Schizoid/avoidant, paranoid, and compulsive codependents especially prefer to remain as inconspicuous as possible. For that reason, in almost every group there will be at least three or four persons for whom speaking up in the group is very painful. How does the therapist deal with these withdrawn persons in a way that does not draw attention to their silence and discomfort?

Before looking at some effective ways of helping the insecure person begin to open up, let me first offer a reminder: All people are not alike in their need to talk. Some people process information by *talking* about it, and others process it more by *thinking* about it. We must not try to make extroverts out of everybody in our group. To do so is to ignore the rights of the genuine introvert and may perhaps contribute to his or her codependence. I try to be gentle in this regard and take those differences into account in dealing with the various members of the group.

However, when it becomes evident that someone wants to talk more and is struggling to do so, I try to encourage them to do so. I have found three methods to be useful in this regard. First, in some sessions, I use exercises that involve everyone. I trust these exercises to be effective in involving the person who has a hard time speaking up in the group. When this person is responding to the exercise in the group, I take special care to ask questions that are designed to lead the person out.

Second, in the third or fourth session I simply say at some point, "I wonder what Bill thinks about that. Would you mind sharing your feelings with us, Bill?" I find that even the most painfully shy individual appreciates being asked his or her opinion and will respond positively.

Finally, I have found that the group will try to bring the quiet and shy person into the discussion. Usually, they are gentle in this endeavor. They will say something like, "I want to hear from Bill more." Or, if Bill has said something, they will say, "I like your ideas, Bill. How about letting us hear from you more?" Sometimes, however, a client will say to the group, either by words or in some indirect way, "I really do not want to be pushed. I'm not ready yet." When that occurs, I ask the group to honor it by letting the person be wherever he or she is on the issue of sharing.

Healing Hurt Feelings

As noted in Chapter Six, adult children need to learn to deal with confrontation and conflict. If the group is to be therapeutic, it must involve group members in emotional exchanges that are sharp and sometimes disagreeable. The therapist must learn to walk an emotional tightrope. He or she must enable the group to process strong emotions in a healthy way. These feelings must come out, but sometimes the person who is the object of the emotions can feel overwhelmed. When this occurs, many group members may begin to see the group as an unsafe place.

Perhaps an example would help. Mary told the group that her stepfather performed oral sex with her on several occasions when she was in elementary and junior high school. He then gave her money in exchange for her silence. Mary's pain was evident as she spoke softly and hesitantly about these things. The tension was high in the group as this young woman "admitted" these facts about herself.

Through her tears she murmured, "I don't know why I did it." George, thinking perhaps to ease his own tension, said, "Maybe you needed the money." Mary squirmed and laughed softly. She continued her story.

The next session, Mary began with the words, "I am mad as hell." She turned fiercely on George and told him how shaming his statement the week before had been. The emotion in the room was high and I did not know where it would go. That Mary was dealing with her emotions in an open manner was, of course, a good thing for her. But how would George respond? Would this confrontation overwhelm him? As the exchange took place, I was able to encourage George to share his feelings about what was occurring.

The group is itself healing on these occasions. The therapist's task is to keep the group open so that the natural healing effects of the group can occur. No effort must be made by the leader or any group member to stop the flow of honest emotions. The therapist must not allow the group to sweep the powerful emotions under the rug. If the group seems unwilling to deal with what is going on, the therapist must encourage them to do so. For example, after Mary's sharp exchange with George, the group fell into silence. I gave them about two minutes to take in what had happened. Then I said, "In our dysfunctional families, we learned that confrontation is bad and that powerful emotions will kill us or others. We are here to learn that conflictual emotions are not that powerful. We cannot do so unless we are willing to talk about what is going on in us right now. Who will start?"

Nor must the group admonish the "offending" person to get control of himself. That kind of denial is what most of the group members have experienced in their families, and they are in the group to learn to deal in a more productive manner with these powerful feelings.

DEVELOPING TRUST IN THE GROUP

If therapy is to be effective, specific attention must be placed on creating an atmosphere that is not threatening. Making a group a safe place is primary in all group therapy and as such is not unique to codependents. Nonetheless, the therapist must address the special needs of the adult child in creating an environment of safety. The very nature of codependency is such that adult children have spent the greater part of their existence avoiding all risks of rejection and abandonment.

Their intentions in every interaction have been to keep themselves and their feelings, thoughts, needs, and motivations concealed. They develop a number of tactics to accomplish this end. For example, the overresponsible codependent may serve others. In this mode, they become rescuers or people pleasers. Or, the schizoid/avoidant and the paranoid codependent may stay hidden. No one knows what is going on inside them, because they never let it show. The histrionic codependent may try to be the entertainer and keep everybody laughing and happy. The compulsive codependent may become superserious and want long and involved intellectual discussions. These people, along with other types, may ask for more teaching in group and complain about the lack of direction in the group. They ask for more "crowd control" and wonder out loud what good it does to come here and listen to other people's problems. The antisocial/narcissistic codependent may hide behind caustic and cutting words and behaviors. These are the persons who "always say what they think," regardless of other's reactions. Their bitterness is their guiding force, and they can create chaos in the group. Turning loose their anger on others is justified with a snappish, "Well, you said we were supposed to share how we were feeling!" Creating safety in a room filled with codependents is no easy task.

Davenport (1983, p. 282) reminds us that "In an interactional therapy group the most important work for members' growth is that which is oriented to the here and now in their struggles to find satisfaction with one another in the room." To arrive at this kind of growth, group members must be willing to reveal themselves and thus risk rejection, the codependent anathema. The therapist must work to create the environment for this kind of exchange to occur. Peck (1987, pp. 46–47) defines safety as a condition in which we are completely free to be ourselves. He says, "When we are safe, there is a natural tendency for us to heal and convert ourselves." A number of suggestions can be made for how to create safety in the group.

Attempt to Reduce Advice Giving

In the beginning stages of the group, participants frequently bring up problems, and others in the group attempt to find solutions for them. For example, Harold and Betty, who were married to each other, came to the group fighting about buying a new car. They continued their conflict in the group. Betty wanted a new car and Harold had agreed. After reflection, he now thought it was not a good idea because of the expense. Nathan began to work with them on their budget. His approach was that the fight would be over if enough money could be found in their bank account. Sara began to scold Harold for his inconsistency. If Harold would only make up his mind and be consistent, life would go easy for them. Bill took another tack. Betty expected too much. He reasoned that if she would lower her expectations the pressure would ease and the fight would be over.

Problem-solving conversations will be filled with shoulds and oughts. Whitfield (1987, p. 82; 1990, p. 35-39) states that people who immediately try to give us advice are not "safe," and it may not be wise to continue to share our feelings with them. To counter this type of exchange and to foster a safe environment, the sensitive therapist may want to say, "Nathan, I am aware that you are trying to solve Betty's problem for her. I wonder, Betty, what that makes you feel?"

Another intervention that may be useful in reducing the "I'll tell you my problems and you tell me what to do" syndrome is to bring the person back to the group with the following: "Jan, I notice that you are describing a problem in relating to other people. With whom in this group would you most likely have this problem?" The therapist will encourage Jan to explore the relational process rather than the content of her response. Both Jan and the other members of the group learn the necessary skills of dealing openly with inner processes.

Or the therapist may wish to ask the rescuer, "What are you feeling now as you say those words, Jan?" For example, Dorothy had just told the group that her mother had told her that she was ugly when she was growing up. She still felt ugly, no matter what she looked like and what others said to her. Katherine, a combination compulsive and histrionic codependent, responded by telling Dorothy that she could do a lot more with herself. She mentioned makeup and was going into colors when I asked her, "What are you feeling now as you say those words to Dorothy?" She paused a long moment and then said, "Anger. I'm pissed off at the people who told me that I was fat...." Katherine and Dorothy engaged in several minutes of therapeutic discussion of their present and past feelings about how they looked.

Comment on Processes in the Group Rather Than Individual Processes

If individuals in the group seem to be floundering or if an unpleasant exchange occurs between individuals, let that be an opportunity to make a group intervention. For example, the therapist might say, "We seem to be testing our relations with each other." Or, "The group seems to get stuck at this point often. Any ideas?" The group may respond to these statements in a number of ways. They may challenge them, ignore them, or agree with them. The important thing is that the group gain a sense of itself.

Peck (1987, p. 89) suggests a number of group interventions: "The group seems to be acting as if everyone has the same religious faith," or, "It looks to me as if the younger and the older members are dividing themselves into different factions," or, "The group seems to change the subject every time someone says something painful, as if we didn't want to hear of one another's suffering." He concludes, "The general rule, therefore, is that leaders should restrict their interventions to interpretations of group rather than individual behavior. And the purpose of all such interventions is not to *tell* the group what to do or not to do but to awaken it to awareness of its behavior."

Make Individual Interventions as Personal as Possible

Codependents attempt to hide their feelings by depersonalizing them. We can help them by being aware of this tactic and countering it. Rather than asking, "How does *it* feel to do so and so," ask, "How do *you* feel doing so and so?" If a member has been talking about grief and expresses some anger, do not say, "People sometimes feel angry when they are grieving." Instead, say, "You seem to be feeling some anger." Encourage group participants not to generalize their feelings. For example, in a recent group, Fred said, "When I sit here and listen to you people talk, I realize how hopeless we all feel." I responded, "Fred, I wonder if you would restate that and say, 'When I sit here and listen to you people talk, I realize how hopeless I feel.'" Fred talked about his feelings of hopelessness. The next week Suzi brought him a rose.

In personalizing interventions, it is best to stay in the realm of feelings. It is not good to say, "You are angry." This statement is an evaluation of the person. A better comment would be, "You seem to feel angry." Referring to feelings in a nonjudgmental manner is helpful feedback. Putting people in a category can be threatening and counterproductive.

Be Willing to Guess at Feelings

It is permissible to ask the question, "How are you feeling?" This question keeps the person dealing with process rather than content, and that is always therapeutic. There is, however, one disadvantage to that question. We run the risk of getting the individual out of his or her emotions and into their cognitive processes. That is, the question, "What are you feeling?" moves the awareness from the emotions being felt and into a rational consideration of the emotions. A better method is simply to guess at the feelings. The comment, "You seem to be feeling some sadness," allows the person to deal with the emotion without stopping the emotion.

Another important consideration at this point is to use all possible cues to determine what you think the other person is feeling. The therapist must listen to more than words. Nonverbal messages are important here. For example, you may say, "Jeff, I'm aware that you are saying angry things about your wife. But you are smiling and you are very animated as you speak. You seem to me to be feeling happy and sense yourself as in control when you are saying angry things."

Encourage the Group to Communicate Directly

Do not let members of the group talk about one another. Instead, encourage them to speak directly to one another. For example, you might say, "Steve, you are saying that bossy women make you angry. I notice that you are looking at Sue when you say that. Would you like to tell Sue that you feel bossed by her?" If Joan says, "I think Laura really helps the group by being a good listener," I say, "Joan, I thank you for saying such a nice thing about Laura. I wonder if you would like to tell her that directly?" I then encourage Joan to turn to Laura and make her comment *to* her rather than *about* her. Also, I find it helpful to encourage group members to address each other by name rather than by the pronoun "you."

Model Nondefensive Attitudes and Behavior

One of the most important elements in creating a safe atmosphere for group members is the ability of the group leader to take criticism in a nondefensive manner. Participants learn by observing the leader's interaction within the group. We must be careful not to take ourselves so seriously that we resent criticism or think that our leadership is never in need of correction and improvement. Too many codependents have been reared in families that communicated the rule, "You may never criticize the parent." What damage do we do if we communicate the same rule to them in the group? Davenport (1983, p. 284) reminds us that "a group, like any other human enterprise, will falter, regress, require redirection, and threaten to destroy itself with aberrant behavior. At such times, the influence of firm but patient and graceful leadership will be a needed corrective....The impatient, threatened leader will be anti-therapeutic here as in so many other critical times in working with people."

Expressing honest feelings about the group or about the leader of the group is often evidence of growth on the part of the adult child. They do not need to be confronted with defensiveness on the part of the leader. When someone in the group says, "I am not getting my needs met by you," I almost always try to use it as an opportunity to help them open up more. At the end of the exchange, I carefully commend them for what they have done. After all, that is one of the things adult children need to learn to do.

There are two possible exceptions to this rule: (1) The first is in dealing with the antisocial/narcissistic codependent. Sometimes it is necessary to directly confront the sarcasm and surliness of this type of codependent. I attempt to do so in a nondefensive manner. (2) There are times, especially at the beginning of the group, when a struggle for control of the group occurs. Some members want to assert their authority and take command of the group. They express a desire for more direction, or they complain that too much time is taken up in matters that have no relevance. Some even explain how it was done in other groups in which they have participated. I respond to these concerns out of my firm conviction that the therapist must control the structure of the group. Without becoming defensive, I deal with their complaints in a straightforward manner. But I leave no doubt that, while I am open to their suggestions, the overall structure of the group is in my hands.

DANGERS OF GROUP THERAPY WITH CODEPENDENTS

Group therapy is an excellent method of healing for codependents. Nonetheless, it is a good idea to consider some of the pitfalls that a group can have for the adult child. Because of the nature of the problems that codependents have, if group therapy takes too narrow a focus, it can be counterproductive. The following are some of the dangers the therapist should look for in groups of codependents.

Overemphasis on Verbal Confrontation

Because work with codependency originated in the chemical dependency field, there is much borrowing of both method and vocabulary. Lewis, Dana, and Blevins (1988, p. 181) are critical of group work with substance abusers because it can degenerate into semantic argument. They say, "Frequently, group sessions for substance abusers focus on confrontation, with leaders and members putting a great deal of effort into 'breaking through denial,' or convincing clients to accept the reality of their addiction. In these sessions the group process is considered successful only when the client verbalizes his or her acceptance of the label 'alcoholic' or 'addict.'" There is, they continue to argue, a difference between "correct" verbalization and behavior change. Clients can comply with coercion and accept labels that they do not in any way internalize.

Denial is a very significant defense for the addict, and the codependent uses it as a protection against giving up the compulsions he or she practices. Frequently, the feelings are so deeply suppressed that the codependent is unaware of them. He or she cannot pull them up to the conscious level. The therapist will serve no good purpose by allowing the group to engage in any confrontational tactic that is designed to overcome that denial. The group must give the individual time and patience. He or she needs space in which to work through the denial. Modeling in the group by other group members and the leader is much more effective than argument, no matter how rational or correct.

Fossum and Mason (1986, pp. 154–155) have an interesting suggestion about how the therapist may deal with a client's repeated denial. They discuss the subject under the topic "We don't accept the client's denial as our reality." Individuals who grow up in dysfunctional families, or what these authors call shame-bound families, have to learn to live with "affective shutdowns" and the "delusional myths" that emerge to survive in that system. "In order not to talk about real experience, the family creates myths to explain its reality and typically presents some delusional thinking about what is 'normal.'" To counteract this tendency in the client, they suggest that we therapists break family rules *by commenting on our reality*. We do this not to argue the client into our reality, but to give the client the opportunity to react to and talk about different realities. In fact, the client can talk about different-ness. The client may then begin to trust and allow his or her vulnerabilities to surface. In this context, the individual group member can begin to restructure his or her own cognitive and affective perceptions.

For example, Riley and his wife, Meryle, were participants together in a group. He was an overresponsible adult child and she was primarily a compulsive codependent. One evening, Meryle was describing how Riley's indifference and control had hurt her through the years of their marriage. Suddenly she jumped up from her chair and began hitting him with her coat. She was screaming, "How does this feel?" Her frenzy lasted less than a minute and she returned to her seat and began speaking in her soft voice. When she finished, I said to Riley, "What did you feel when Meryle jumped and began hitting you?" "Oh," he replied, "Nothing much. I didn't really feel anything." I persisted, "You must have been surprised and perhaps a little fearful." "No, not in the least," Riley said in an even voice. I was convinced that Riley was trying to control his emotions by denying a host of very powerful feelings. So, I said, "Would you object if I shared with you what my feelings were?" When he nodded, I shared how her action had made me afraid because I did not know what to do. I really wanted her to stop and sit down and go back to being a "good girl." I wondered what the rest of the group thought of me not being able to control this person and I was a little embarrassed. When I finished telling him what I had felt, I said, "I am guessing that you felt some of these things and don't know how to express them. Am I right?"

Thus, the danger is not confrontation. Codependents need to experience confrontation and learn it as a gentle and useful art. Most of them do not appreciate its benefits. They fear it and therefore have learned unhealthy methods to avoid it. The danger is in focusing the group on confrontation, especially confrontation that concludes with semantic correctness. There is great power in ending denial and seeing one's reality as it is. But that is an intrinsic process and we cannot verbally coerce the individual into it.

Lewis, Dana, and Blevins quote Kelman (1971, pp. 203–204) on a relevant point. He makes a useful distinction between *compliance* and *internalization*. According to Kelman, the former occurs "...when an individual accepts influence because he hopes to achieve a favorable reaction from another person or group. He adopts the induced behavior not because he believes in its content, but because he expects to gain specific rewards of approval and avoid specific punishments or disapproval by conforming." *Conforming* is the important word in that context. The individual *conforms* rather than *transforms*. He or she changes outwardly but inwardly remains the same. We should note that this outward conformity, or compliance, is what the codependent has been doing for most of his or her life and is one of the patterns that most stands in need of change.

Kelman's other word, *internalization*, is said to occur "...when an individual accepts influence because the content of the induced behavior–the ideas and actions of which it is composed–is intrinsically rewarding....Thus the satisfaction derived from internalization is due to the *content* of the new behavior." Compliance is no more than conforming behavior and as such represents the power of the group over the individual. Change based on compliance embodies no real or long-lasting internal change. According to Kelman, one "...tends to perform it only when under the conditions of surveillance by the influencing agent." Internalization takes place on the basis of the efficacy of the newly acquired behavior. It represents legitimate, inward change that is likely to be followed when the individual is away from the group. Verbal confrontation designed to get the client to accede to correct labeling is dangerous because it may result in no long-term influence on real-life behaviors in need of change.

Staying in the Pain

As noted in the preceding section, there is a danger based on the overemphasis of rationality and verbal argument. A second danger exists at the opposite end of the spectrum. It is based on an overemphasis on emotion.

Emotional catharsis is one goal of therapy with adult children. Often they do not know how to recognize and express their emotions. "Don't feel" is one of the important rules of the dysfunctional family. The codependent must learn experientially that his or her recovery begins when he or she can say, "When _____ occurs, I feel _____." Great relief comes when the client is able to get in touch with the pain and let it out. This relief is based on the very simple act of bringing long-repressed emotions and thoughts from the deep unconscious to the conscious level. It is the process of giving a label to the powerful emotions that surge around inside us. Relief comes in not having to hide them or deny them any longer. People cry as they tell their stories and their tears are of pain and relief. I have experienced this process personally and have witnessed it hundreds of times in private as well as in group sessions. It is an immense catharsis to let it out. But for the codependent, it must not stop there.

Adult children have difficulty trusting others, abandoning rigidity, identifying and expressing feelings, knowing and telling the truth, and relinquishing control. The counselor attempting to work with such a client must endeavor to get the client to face fear or express their anger or sadness or shame or guilt. But then that client must be helped to internalize new skills that are designed to replace the old patterns that he or she has followed most of the time. These skills are generally in the areas of self-affirmation, direct communication, dealing with conflict, relaxing, accepting praise, self-efficacy, and stress management.

Getting the client beyond the pain is what Fossum and Mason (1986, p. 176) call Phase II therapy. They divide therapy into two phases: (1) the initial phase and (2) the deepening phase. The initial phase lasts for only a few weeks and deals with a specific problem for which the client requires help. The client may not go beyond the initial phase. If he or she does, they enter with the counselor into a qualitatively different experience. Fossum and Mason (1986) say, "Now [in the deepening phase] clients need to examine many of the subtler aspects of their self-destructive or abusive behavior, identify the sources of traumatic and inherited shame, and take down the walls between their affect and their history. Most importantly, [clients] begin the long-term process of becoming self-affirming persons."

Ellen, a schizoid/avoidant and compulsive codependent, told the group that her husband called her dirty names when he became frustrated with her. She spoke with tears of shame in her eyes. "What names?" someone asked gently. With hesitation and with obvious pain, Ellen responded in a soft voice, "He calls me a dirty c-u-n-t." She spelled the last word in an almost inaudible whisper. "I wonder," I asked, "if you could tell us what there is about being called a dirty cunt that hurts you so much?" "It's degrading," she said, her voice getting stronger. "Of course," I persisted, "but I wonder what there is about that specific term that is so degrading to you." Ellen talked for a few minutes through tears about her memories of her father and mother fighting while she listened from a distance. Their words were angry, and Ellen felt very weak and vulnerable as her parents fought. She feared that they would kill each other. "My father often called my mother a dirty cunt," she concluded, still crying softly, "and when Ed calls me that, I guess I'm back to those feelings of my childhood."

An important connection had been made between Ellen's history and her present. And Ellen had made a real step in "taking down the walls between her affect and her history." But, as significant as this emotional event was for her, it was only the beginning. Now Ellen had to do the work of learning to let go of long-held dependencies and compulsions. These codependent behaviors do not change easily.

Once having broken through the prohibition to know and express feelings, many codependent clients find the relief so great and the support of the group so gratifying, that they want to return to the catharsis again and again. A new codependent compulsion can be developed, growth will stop, and the client will be stuck again.

Being Omnipotent and Rescuing

As noted earlier in this chapter in another connection, one danger that any group must confront is the temptation to degenerate into an advice-giving and problem-solving session. Giving in to that temptation appears to be in the nature of human beings. When someone begins to talk revealingly of the fears, problems, or trials of life, the rest of us try to tell him or her what to do about it. All therapists dealing with groups of any kind must guard against this tendency. Those working with codependents must be especially careful because of the great need of the codependent to be useful to other people.

As noted in Chapter Four, one of the most salient characteristics of codependence is the proclivity to please and serve other people. Becoming responsible for the other person is as natural and automatic for the codependent as breathing. One of their most important rules is to be unselfish and seek the good of the other person. Included in this rule is the obligation to do so without any regard for one's own personal needs. In fact, the service is of no real worth unless it is based on personal sacrifice; and the value of the codependent is based on this service to others. That is, the adult child's thought processes ensure that the codependent cannot be okay if there is anyone else around who is not okay. Thus, any individual with a significant problem in the immediate environment of the adult child is fair game for the problem-solving and advice-giving skills of the codependent. For this reason, group therapy with codependents can quickly become another game the adult child plays to continue his or her compulsion.

For example, John's need to take care of others came out in the second session of the group. He was a tall, slim, young man who had never been very successful with girls. His mother and father were divorced after a stormy marriage that had produced five children. John's father had been a Protestant minister who was very cool and distant in relating to his children. His mother had been manipulative and clinging with her husband and with her children after the divorce. John, the oldest child, was an overresponsible codependent.

Della was in the same group as John. At age fifty-five, she was an overweight lady whose mother was an alcoholic. Della was an angry, sullen person who covered her pain with a syrupy religion that proclaimed that since she has come to know God, all her problems had come to an end. By the middle of the second session, Della had explicitly told the group that she did not have the problems that they obviously suffered from and she felt sorry for them. She had begun her own advice-giving and rescuing by offering her religion as the solution to their problems. The group had not developed to the point that the members felt comfortable in revealing how Della's comments made them feel. Nonetheless, the discomfort in the room was evident. Everything stopped, several people squirmed uncomfortably, and everybody averted their eyes from Della. I allowed the silence for a long moment, and then said, "Della seems to feel that she is different from the rest of us. That makes me feel a little uncomfortable. I wonder if anyone else feels that way."

There was an immediate reaction. Several people responded with their feelings of being rejected and judged. After a few minutes, Della began to speak. Her words revealed that she was beginning to see how her attitudes and actions put a wall between herself and others. At this point, John came to the rescue. "Della," he said, "I want you to know that even though these people may not like you, I do. I like you just like you are. In fact, I wish I had someone as loving and spiritual as you for my mother." "Thank you," Della beamed, "it is good to know that someone understands. I wish I had a son like you." John's rescue was done and Della had stopped. I made an effort to bring the group back to the point of dealing with their feelings, but to no avail. Della felt vindicated and was enjoying John's favor. She was not about to go on looking at what was happening in the group. John felt great. He was getting his mother's approval. And the group felt intimidated and judged by John's rebuke that they did not like Della.

The therapist must observe special care in keeping rescuing and problem-solving out of the codependency group. Interventions designed to help the members process feelings and stay in the present are useful in redirecting well-meaning individuals who start giving advice. A useful rule for the group is that no one can use the words *should*, *ought to*, or *must*. Avoiding those terms can be very helpful in keeping the group away from rescuing. Also, a useful intervention is to say to the rescuer, "I am aware that you seem to have a need to solve So-and-so's problem. I wonder if you would be willing to share with the group what you are feeling right now." Finally, the therapist may inquire whether the advice giver has ever encountered a situation like the one he or she is giving advice about. All these interventions are designed to put rescuers and problem solvers back into themselves.

Development of Dependency on the Group Leader

Nothing stops a group from growth quicker than a leader who is an expert with all the answers. There is a dual problem involved at this point. First, adult children are particularly adept at putting the leader in this position. Second, those who are leaders may actually enjoy and seek this exalted position. The therapist must be aware of both of these concerns.

Peck (1987, pp. 87–88) suggests that the way to take care of both problems is to refuse to lead. He refers to this phenomenon as self-crucifixion and counsels those aspiring to be effective group leaders, "You must be willing to die for the group." In extremely poignant language, Peck describes the experience of not leading:

> The issue calls into question our very definitions of "strength" and "weakness" in leadership. To lead people into community a true leader must discourage their

dependency, and there may be no way to do this except to refuse to lead. Paradoxically, the strong leader in these instances is she or he who is willing to risk–even welcome–the accusation of failing to lead. The accusation is always made. Sometimes it is mild. Sometimes it is almost murderous.

An overemphasis on educational or didactic tactics can inadvertently contribute to the concept of the leader as expert. Lewis, Dana, and Blevins (1988, p. 182) are critical of any group that does no more than provide "cognitive information." That danger is great in a codependent group because some of the legitimate work of the group is in the educational area. As already indicated, some teaching must take place. However, the therapist must walk a tightrope between presenting information that is necessary for effective change and letting the group become dependent on him or her as an expert. No growth occurs when the therapist solves all problems with his or her reservoir of knowledge and experience. I find it a useful rule to divert to the group or reflect back to the individual every question that seeks an opinion from me.

Now let us look at a different kind of group therapy. The therapist may want to consider involving the whole family in counseling. Much of what has been said about group therapy is applicable to working with codependent families. But family therapy is a highly specialized discipline and has much to offer the counselor working with adult children.

REFERENCES

Davenport, R. (1983). "Pastoral Group Counseling," in B. Estadt, M. Blanchette, and J. Compton, Eds., *Pastoral Counseling*, Englewood Cliffs, N. J.: Prentice-Hall.

Fossum, M., and Mason, M. (1986). *Facing Shame: Families in Recovery*, New York: W. W. Norton.

Kelman, H. (1971). "Compliance, Identification, and Internalization: Three Processes of Attitude Change," in B. Hinton and H. Reitz, Eds., *Groups and Organizations: Integrated Readings in the Analyses of Social Behavior*, Belmont, Calif.: Wadsworth.

Lewis, J., Dana, R., and Blevins, G. (1988). *Substance Abuse Counseling: An Individualized Approach*, Pacific Grove, Calif.: Brooks/Cole.

Peck, M. (1987). *The Different Drum: Community Making and Peace*, New York: Simon & Schuster.

Whitfield, C. (1987). *Healing the Child Within*, Pompano Beach, Fla.: Health Communications.

Whitfield, C. (1990). *A Gift to Myself*, Deerfield Beach, Fla: Health Communication.

8

THE CODEPENDENT FAMILY

Family therapy is based on the belief that the family itself may be in need of healing. The family therapist attempts to recast the problems of individuals so that they are seen in a contextual framework. That is, the cause of the problem is located in the family, not in the individual. Rather than seeing the problem or its symptoms as coming from a single individual, the family therapist sees the family's problem as emanating from the system.

Adam's family is an example. When I first met them, their presenting complaint was that Sarah, the wife and mother, could not get along with Alex, the fourteen-year-old son of Adam by a previous marriage. There were no other children in the family. Alex was a shy youngster and a poor student. He was interested in animals and plants and had virtually no social skills. Adam was an overresponsible and compulsive codependent and felt that he was caught between his wife and his son, both of whom he loved. He was a passive person not able to express his feelings very well. Sarah was more of an activist, with leanings toward histrionic codependence. Her part in this triangle was to express everybody's feelings. When there was tension in the air, Sarah acted to deal with it. Both Adam and Alex used Sarah to deny their anger at each other. Sarah acted out the family's anger and got the blame for it. When the family saw what was happening and Sarah stopped allowing Adam and Alex to express their anger through her, the family began to heal. Adam and Alex had to confront their true feelings directly. Sarah was no longer enabling them to avoid each other.

133

In family systems theory, the individual is regarded as the symptom bearer. According to this view, a "problem teenager" is not so much a teenager with a problem as the expression of a problem that exists in the family. The therapist who works with a family from a systems perspective sees the family itself as the most fitting target for change. Individuals are helped by working with and changing the system in which they live.

CODEPENDENCE AND THE FAMILY

Codependent families are an appropriate arena in which the family therapist may work. Adult children grew up in a dysfunctional family and, more often than not, they create another dysfunctional family when they marry. The system itself becomes codependent, and individuals in the family are affected by the life in the system. The family ways, its rules and traditions and beliefs, are very powerful. Ackerman (1983, p. 148) refers to the family as a "habit cage." Wegscheider (1981, p. 84) has this same image in mind when she says that members become *trapped* in the dysfunctional family. In one of her articles (Wegscheider-Cruise, 1984, p. 1), she says, "Codependency is a primary disease and a disease within every member of….[the] family. It is what happens to family members when they try to adapt to a sick family system….Each family member enters into this collusion in his own individual way."

In the dysfunctional family, members are not aware of any healthy alternatives. To survive, they must hide their true feelings, try not to rock the boat, deny reality, become responsible for the feelings and well-being of everyone else, and strive for perfection. They feel shame and fear and thus have little self-esteem. They live behind this artificial behavioral and emotional smoke screen and hope that someone will finally love them. In this manner, children are trained to become symptom bearers of their family system. They grow up to become adult children and to perpetuate these behaviors and attitudes in the families they establish.

Such codependent patterns can run for generations. The family ways have great staying power even when they have no rational basis and are clearly dysfunctional. They are like the guru's cat, about which de Mello (1984, p. 63) wrote. The guru's cat disturbed him when he sat to worship each evening. So he ordered that the cat be tied while he prayed and meditated. After several years, the guru died and his followers continued to tie the cat as they said their daily prayers. After the cat died, they brought in a new cat to be tied during the worship. Centuries later, the guru's disciples continued to write scholarly treatises on the liturgical significance of having a tied-up cat present during worship.

Each family practices and passes on the rules for its behaviors and ways of thinking. In so doing, the system perpetuates itself. This chapter will help the family therapist deal with the special problems of the codependent family from a systems perspective so as to break into the vicious cycle and stop its continuation. The question is, How do we get families to see that they are tying up cats? Then how do we get them to stop? Family systems therapy has much to offer counselors who work with adult children. That fact is true even if we do not actually see families in our practice. Understanding the dynamics of the family from a systems perspective is essential if we are to deal effectively with codependence at any level. Therefore, before considering the dynamics of codependency in the family, let us look carefully at what the systems perspective entails.

APPROACHES TO FAMILY THERAPY

General Systems Theory

Family systems therapy evolved from general systems theory, developed first in the physical sciences and then in sociology and psychology (von Bertalanffy, 1968, pp. 3–28). A system is a configuration of units that are organized into an interrelated whole. The interrelationship is such that each unit is dependent on all others. In a system, a change in one unit brings about a commensurate change in every other unit. The total organization interacts so that the whole is greater than the sum of the parts.

Biological and physical systems. For example, biologists think of a living organism as a system. The body of a living animal is made up of component parts that are integrated into a functioning whole. Each separate part depends on all the other parts for its existence. Each part in turn has a specific function, and the whole is dependent on the parts doing their specialized tasks. In the early years of this century, biologists were writing about entire species as a system. They also applied this perspective to the delicate relationship of all species in a given boundary. Thus, they described the web of life found around a lake or in a river basin as an ecological system. Ultimately, they reasoned, all of life on the planet is interrelated in this profound way. Therefore, all life on the planet may be described as "the global ecosystem" (Commoner, 1971, p. 17).

Physicists, meanwhile, were writing about systems in the mechanical world. An automobile engine, they said, is a system. It is made up of component parts, all of which have a specific task to perform. The whole engine does its work by the functioning of each part in its interrelationships. Thus, each part is dependent on all the other parts, and the whole is dependent on all the parts together. If one part does not function, the entire system is shut down. No part exists in isolation from the others, nor can any part be considered extraneous. A change in one part affects all the others.

Social systems. It was but a short step from these biological and physical descriptions of systems to a perspective that applied these insights to social systems. In the 1950s, sociologists and social psychologists began to apply systems theory to human groups like the family. Parsons and Shils (1951, p. 104f) reasoned that families project the same interrelatedness and interdependence as biological and physical systems. They wrote, "The most general and fundamental property of a system is the interdependence of parts or variables." There is an emphasis on "self-maintenance" or equilibrium as the social system seeks to minimize change and maintain the status quo. Bertrand (1967, p. 25) said that four things were necessary for a group of people to be considered a social system:

1. There must be two or more people.
2. These people must be interacting to achieve a common goal.
3. Their behavior must be guided by symbols that they all share together. Among these symbols are beliefs, sentiments, rules, objectives, decision making, and communication.
4. The interaction and symbols must last over time, and one major goal of the system is self-preservation and equilibrium.

Family Systems Therapy

Norman Ackerman (1984, p. 1) traces the beginning of family therapy back to the fifties, with major development coming in the sixties and seventies. Noting that Freud and other early therapists treated some families as a whole, Nelson (1983, p. 1–27) describes in detail the founding of family therapy as a distinct approach to helping disturbed persons. "By the mid-1970s, most helping professionals had accepted family treatment as a legitimate practice method."

Before looking at how we can apply family systems theory to the codependent family, we will briefly survey how various schools of thought have developed and how they differ from one another. The following section gives a brief overview of family systems theory and some of its various proponents.

Psychodynamic Model. Early thinkers combined family systems theory with the psychoanalytic approach. Nathan Ackerman (1956), Murray Bowen (1966), and John Bell (1975) are among this group. They approached the family from the perspective of ego psychology. According to this perspective, individuals in the family are shaped by their past. They are frequently driven by emotions that may exist at the unconscious level. The goal of treatment is to help family members to think and act without being blocked by intrapsychic conflicts and to be able to relate in an age-appropriate manner. Therapists following this model attempt to get insight into intrapersonal and interpersonal functioning by a straightforward question-and-answer method. Their methods of assessment and treatment are very much like those of a psychodynamic therapist working with an individual. There is much exploration of feelings, thoughts, and reasons for behaviors.

Ackerman saw individuals as being shaped by roles. He was the first to refer to the "scapegoat" role. Bowen spoke of "undifferentiated ego mass." The family did not separate between the various members but fused them into one "ego." The family consisted of symbiotic functioning in which members unconsciously served each other's needs. He sought to separate family members emotionally and to help them cope with their feelings.

Communications Model.   The Mental Research Institute, established in 1958 in Palo Alto, California, made the second attempt to develop a coherent theory of family therapy. This group, along with Gregory Bateson (1955), emphasized the system maintaining functions of family communication. Besides Bateson, the Palo Alto Group included Jay Haley (1976), Don D. Jackson (1968), Virginia Satir (1972, 1983), and Paul Watzlawick (1976). Having recently studied schizophrenic families, they noticed how communication in the family can become dysfunctional. Schizophrenic families practice "double-bind" communication, they said. The schizophrenic, who is the family's symptom bearer, and members of his family are trapped in self-reinforcing, dysfunctional interaction cycles when they give contradictory messages no one in the family is allowed to clarify. These communications become patterned in the family, and a trained outsider can detect the patterns. Patterns reflect rules, they reasoned. Members implicitly agreed with the norms by accommodating their behavior to them.

Communication patterns are protected from change. Family members will work together to maintain their present equilibrium, even against the therapist. To counteract this tendency, the Palo Alto group came up with the innovative therapeutic tactic of "prescribing the symptom." This tactic is also called *therapeutic paradox*. Using it, the therapist directs the family not to change but to perpetuate the problem behavior. In so doing, the therapist creates a paradox. The family must either obey, thus allowing the therapist to influence them, or change as the therapist hopes.

Virginia Satir (1972, 1983) was the first to emphasize the impact of self-esteem on how individuals behave in the family. The family rules are designed to enable parents to maintain their own self-esteem. Parents who learned to think poorly of themselves in their family of orientation communicate their own lack of esteem to their children. Satir's therapy focused on teaching the family better communication skills, such as how to listen and how to ask questions. She sought to reinforce whatever strengths they might have and in so doing foster self-esteem. She helped parents see how they had learned destructive patterns from their parents and to change them in more positive directions.

The Structural Model.   Salvador Minuchin (1974) came into prominence in the late 1960s. Earlier theories in psychodynamic-based and communication-based family therapy clearly influenced him. He developed a systems-oriented approach that he referred to as "structural family therapy." Structure, according to Umbarger (1983, p. 13), is "enduring interactional patterns that serve to arrange or organize a family's component subunits into somewhat constant relationships." In other words, structure is the patterns of behaviors that people practice in their relationships in the family. It is made up of the rules and roles that people carry out as they interact over time in their family.

Family systems practitioners who take a structural approach consider the life-cycle stage of the family in understanding the stresses and challenges of the family. The structure of the family changes as the family moves through the various stages of development in the normal life course. Young married couples with a new baby, for example, are struggling with an entirely different set of problems than the family with adolescent and young adult children who are separating from home.

Minuchin's (1974) work has been with lower-income, disorganized, urban families. Members of these families are not usually able to delay gratification and they usually follow their impulses into behavior. As a rule, they lack the conceptual and verbal skills to express themselves freely. For these reasons, Minuchin and his co-workers use treatment geared to help these clients communicate more effectively. To do so, the therapist joins the family group, sharing and imitating the communication style of the family. The therapist often uses enactive or nonverbal means to demonstrate effective communication patterns. For example, the therapist may ask family members to act out specific messages. Sometimes he or she may ask family members to leave the room or to reseat themselves in the therapy room. Minuchin insists that we understand families in an organizational or structural way. He wants to know, Who sides with whom? Who is dominant? Who is too close, and who is too distant? Treatment is designed to change this structure by revealing and altering power relations, alignments, and closeness and distance.

Family therapists using the structural model look for and attempt to help the family change dysfunctional structures. Some of these structures are inappropriate coalitions, enmeshment, and disengagement. They may ask families to "restructure" by enacting or demonstrating their problematic interactions. Acting out the problems in the session helps enhance the family's awareness of the patterns involved. The therapist may try to reduce enmeshment by having family members speak for themselves. They may attempt to reduce disengagement by seeing nonaligned members together, without other family members being present. Sometimes they may attempt to restructure by adding to the family tension—a somewhat controversial method that must be used with codependent families with extreme care. Andolfi, and co-workers (1983, p. 54) call this tactic "provocative intervention" or "therapeutic chaos." Using this technique, a therapist might side with one family member against others for an extended period. Or, the therapist might exclude one family member by asking that person to sit with his back turned to the group.

DYNAMICS OF THE CODEPENDENT FAMILY

Codependent families suffer from all the "normal" stresses and strains that other families experience. Many of the characteristics that make the codependent family dysfunctional are no more than normal traits that have been elevated to the dysfunctional level. That is, a "normal" problem becomes unmanageable in the codependent family because the family does not have the mechanisms to handle the problem. Or the problem may be a problem simply because the family cannot deal with it or refuses to deal with it.

For example, expectations are a part of all normal families. In the dysfunctional family, expectations can become unreasonable. When this condition exists, the family loses the ability to deal with the failure of any member to live up to the expectations. Failure, however, is a fact of normal life in all families. In the dysfunctional family, failure (or even the potential for failure) may represent such a threat that the family does not even have a method of dealing with it. When a family member fails, a vicious cycle goes into action. Massive structures must be mobilized in the family to deny or to redefine the event of failure. What starts as a simple quarrel over Jane's bad grades is in reality a complex and powerful set of emotional links and unwritten rules that affect all aspects of the family. In such a family, the threat of failure is so overwhelming that the entire structure of the family is organized so as to protect against its occurrence. The avoidance of the problem becomes the center of the family structure. The avoidance is more important than the family itself or any of its members. Everything and everyone else must be relegated to second consideration.

In this manner, the dysfunctionality becomes the center of the family. The problem itself becomes the "system-maintaining and system-maintained device" (Kaufman, 1985, p. 37). This destructive pattern affects every member of the family, especially the children. Children entering this addictive and destructive system must figure out how to adapt and survive in this atmosphere. The main dynamic is how to deal with the problem. The child's needs are not met. The child has no sense of safety and security. That is, he or she never has the feeling, "I belong here; I'm safe." Instead, the children perceive that they are there to serve the system and that their interests are second to the needs of the parents and the system itself.

Effective therapy is based on understanding the particular problems that are associated with the codependent family. These families have trouble predominantly in the areas of flexibility, boundaries, parent-child coalitions, blaming, poor communicating, discounting, and unhealthy rules.

Inflexibility

The need for stability. All systems seek constancy. The term used to refer to this tendency is *homeostasis*. There is no doubt that families devote considerable energy to maintaining order and stability. These characteristics are necessary if members are to experience security and predictability. If realities change daily, no one in the family can ever achieve a comfortable state.

Homeostasis provides balance in the relationships. According to Satir (1983, p. 2), all members need the balance in their relationships that homeostasis provides. All members contribute to this balance, and when it is threatened, all members exert considerable effort to maintain it.

The homeostatic need for order and stability, then, appears in all families. The codependent family has problems with homeostasis in two different ways: (1) It overemphasizes order and becomes rigid, or, at the other extreme; (2) it loses all stability and becomes chaotically unpredictable. If the family moves toward rigidity, the rule is balance at whatever cost. If it moves toward chaos, no rules apply in any situation. In either case, positive change, or what systems thinkers call *morphogenesis*, becomes impossible.

In a healthy family, a member's deviation from the usual pattern is considered an opportunity for positive growth. If the change is functional, it may be incorporated as an acceptable pattern into the family's behaviors and attitudes. Consider a family for which religious belief and practice is a significant part of family life. John, at fourteen, tells the family one day that he is having problems believing in God. In the healthy family, this statement is regarded as a normal part of John's religious growth. His questioning attitude is encouraged. The family believes that he will come to a mature and useful religious faith only as he is open to the experience of God in his own life. Therefore, John is supported and encouraged by the healthy family in his quest. The dysfunctional family, contrarily, rushes in to ensure that John conforms to the family's understanding of God. Or it communicates to John that his questions are of no significance. In either case, John's needs as a person are not validated, and it is questionable that morphogenesis will occur.

The inevitability of change.   Healthy families welcome change as they move through the developmental stages of normal family life. This is the way morphogenesis takes place and the way people grow and families change. If the need for stability is placed above the need for change, the family becomes dysfunctional because change is necessary in healthy human growth. Bernard and Corrales (1979, p. 15) make the point nicely when they comment, "If the family rules that applied to Johnny when he was five still apply when he is twenty-five, Johnny is probably showing some maladaptive symptoms."

The healthy family needs both stability and flexibility. Neither extreme rigidity nor chaotic unpredictability contributes to healthy human functioning. In general, codependent families fall into one or the other extreme and thus cannot handle change. Bernard and Corrales (1979, p. 15) say, "How much homeostasis and how much morphogenesis is optimum probably varies from family to family and the environment in which they function."

In the rigid atmosphere, there is criticism, blaming, and authoritarian discipline. Domineering communication patterns persist along with a pessimistic view of human nature. There is always a top dog-underdog perspective. Children learn unquestioned obedience but develop poor decision-making skills. They have little resourcefulness and depend on others for validation. They become timid and evasive. They may lie and steal and become fanatical. They become ultrasensitive and lose their spontaneity, creativity, and playfulness. They may become sarcastic and cynical. They usually have black-or-white values and see the world in terms of good and bad.

In the chaotic atmosphere, on the other hand, there is either erratic discipline or none at all. Routines are inconsistent and there is a crisis orientation in which every problem has the potential of being turned into a catastrophe. Children experience this environment as unstable and in it fail to develop self-control. They become self-centered ("I've got to look out for me") and insecure at the same time ("I'll never get what I want.") They become addicted to chaos and do not feel loved unless a crisis is going on. They have a sense of confusion and craziness and they mistrust their own sense of reality.

Boundary Confusion

Emotional space. From the beginning, systems theorists have been aware of the question of social space in the family. How the family divides up its emotional territory is a significant question. Andolfi and co-workers (1983, p. 7) note the necessity of each family member's learning to "share his personal space with the others without feeling forced to exist only as a function of them." They point out that everyone needs a sense of unity within the group over time (they call this *cohesion*) and the freedom for self-expression of individuality (which they call *differentiation*). In their view, how this question is resolved is the most important variable in family dynamics.

In this context, Bernard and Corrales (1979, p. 21) talk about dyadic spatial patterns—that is, the spatial patterns that may occur within two-person subsystems in the family. They may exist between any two members of the family and are not limited to husband and wife. Dyadic spatial patterns may be diagrammed in the following way:

Dyadic Spatial Patterns

Person A	Person B
⟶	⟵
⟵	⟵
⟶	⟶
⟵	⟶

A healthy relationship is one that satisfactorily combines the first and fourth sets of arrows. In such a relationship, the two persons enjoy the quality of togetherness and meaningful interaction (the first arrow set) and at the same time enjoy leaving the relationship space temporarily to peruse independent activity. In other words, the healthy relationship provides for both closeness and distance. The unhealthy or dysfunctional relationship, on the other hand, does not. That relationship involves the middle two arrow sets.

Enmeshment and disengagement.   A number of terms have been used across the years to describe these dysfunctional, dyadic, spatial arrangements. Ackerman (1956) spoke of them as "interlocking" relationships. Bowen (1966) referred to a family with no boundaries as an "undifferentiated family ego mass." He said that family members were fused and needed to become differentiated. By *fused*, he meant that the self of one becomes emotionally merged with that of a significant other. Minuchin (1974) used the terms *enmeshment* and *disengagement* to refer to roughly the same phenomenon. According to Minuchin, *enmeshment* refers to the tendency to emphasize togetherness, belongingness, and conformity at the relative expense of separateness and a sense of personal autonomy. *Disengagement*, on the other hand, means that boundaries are really walls, and no real communication or other meaningful interaction between two subsystems is possible.

The need for personal boundaries.   The opposite of enmeshment and fusion is clarity of boundaries. Having boundaries means that one is not the extension of the other. Boundaries do not represent unavailability. Rather, when there are clear boundaries, open communication may flow in both directions. The existence of boundaries also means that one subsystem may close ranks and reduce or temporarily shut off interaction from the other. For example, in the healthy family, father and mother are available to their children for play, talk, support, and understanding. However, when they need time for themselves, they are able to create the social space necessary to meet their needs and shut out the demands of their children.

In the enmeshed family, the members are overly involved with one another. They experience a false mutuality that says, "We always agree on everything." There is also a false intimacy that is evidenced by statements like, "We never fight. We are always loving. We stick together and everyone out there is our enemy."

The invasiveness of such a family produces individuals who do not feel entitled to their own thoughts, feelings, or activities. They do not know their own needs and if they do, they do not feel that they have a right to have them met. Children in such a family feel guilty unless they are taking care of someone else's problems. Intimacy and smothering get confused, and love is defined as caretaking. Thus develops the attitude, "I do not love you unless I am taking care of you and you do not love me unless you are taking care of me." Fear of engulfment can lead to trouble with intimacy. No one is allowed to be different or to have any space.

Parent-Child Coalitions

In discussing the problems involved in parenting, Lidz (1968, p. 454) refers to "the child-centered home." He correctly notes that this kind of family is "considered one of the outstanding [negative] characteristics of American society." The child-centered family is defined by Lidz as "a home in which the ultimate welfare of the children takes precedence over the convenience and comforts of the parents." When the whims and wishes of the children supercede the genuine needs of the parents, trouble is imminent for everyone involved. This kind of trouble is especially characteristic of the codependent family.

In an earlier work, Lidz and his associates (1965) had noted the need for the husband and wife to create a "parental coalition." Such a coalition recognizes that the spousal relationship is the primary one in the family. It calls on the parents to form a solid husband-wife subsystem within the family. By so doing, the parents create a clear generational boundary that allows the children to build and maintain their own identities. Lidz concludes, "Few things are as important to a child as a parent's self-assurance and security."

When parents do not create this husband-wife subsystem in the family, two related problems are likely to appear. The first is that the parents will form parent-child coalitions. Mother may, as a example, join with children against Father. She draws their allegiance away from him in an effort to get love and support from them. Or, their coalition may give her the balance of power, and with it a sense of being "right" or at least the illusion of control. Or, Father may coalesce with one child and Mother with another. This insidious enmeshment pits one parent-child coalition against another. Of course, the battle lines are never explicitly and openly drawn. They remain masked sometimes under parental "love and concern for the children." That they are unconscious and justified with loving motivations makes them all the more powerful and thus all the more destructive.

The second result of the failure of parents to develop a solid subsystem is role reversal. That is, the adults become the children and the children take on adult responsibility. A parent who cannot enter into a mature, loving relationship with another adult will replace the spouse with a child. The child is expected to give the support and care to the parent that would be expected from the spouse.

Families, then, can become fused into an amoebalike mass, with no clear boundaries between parents and children. When this condition exists, a number of negative consequences result. Among them are the following: The authority figures are not held accountable for their legitimate responsibilities in the family. Children irretrievably lose their childhood. In this environment that has no clear-cut perimeters between individuals, it is difficult for the child to learn assertiveness skills. Parents project family tensions onto the children, and the family environment is characterized by irrationality and the lack of a meaningful basis for communication. The children in this context cannot make sense of their environment and thus of their own identities.

Scapegoating

When a couple is troubled, they frequently look for a third point. Bernard and Corrales (1979, p. 24) state that bringing a third person into a troubled relationship is based on one of two motives: It can diffuse the intensity when one individual is being emotionally suffocated, or it can substitute for the lack of intensity when one partner is withdrawing emotionally. "If, for example, the intensity in the husband-wife relationship diminishes to a dissatisfactory level, the wife may seek emotional companionship from the daughter. This lets the husband off the emotional hook; he does not have to be fully responsive to his wife's relationship needs. A triangle is born."

The term by which family therapists have referred to this condition is *triangulation*, or *scapegoating*. The logic is that when a two-person system is under stress, the person who first feels the strain (or who is least able to deal with it) attempts to shift the tension from the dyad to some other person. Or, as Fogarty (1972, p. 43) points out, the third point can be an issue such as drinking, sex, religion, or a number of other similar things. By the process of triangulation or scapegoating, the pair may continue to relate and yet avoid each other at the same time. They talk (or fight) about the third point without dealing with each other. When there are more than three persons in the system, a series of interlocking triangles can emerge.

Triangulation takes a number of forms. Communication becomes indirect. That is, if Father wants Mother to know that he is angry, he tells Daughter and it is her job to tell Mother. She serves as a go-between, but primarily she is used to keep the parents from having to face and deal honestly with their emotions. The marital bond is preserved but at a tremendous price to everyone involved.

Genuine intimacy is impossible in any of these relationships. The daughter in this case is faced with enormous pressure to serve as a pseudospouse to her father and as a pseudoparent to her mother. She may begin some acting-out behavior in response to the pressure and thus become the scapegoat in another sense: She becomes the identified patient and the symptom bearer of the family. As such, she becomes responsible for the family homeostasis. If she begins to get well, another child may be substituted to take her place.

Bernard and Corrales (1979, p. 28) cite research that demonstrates the power of the negative effects of triangulation. They note that in the families of schizophrenic patients, when the parents are developing closeness, the schizophrenic improves. However, when *either* parent becomes more emotionally invested in the patient than in the other parent, the patient immediately and automatically regresses.

Inadequate Communication

Nonverbal communications. Communication takes place at two levels. The first is the verbal or literal level. This level involves the content of the words used to convey the message. The second level is nonverbal. Michener and associates (1986, pp. 147–148) describe nonverbal communication as occurring in three ways:

1. Paralanguage. This category of nonverbal language involves all the vocal aspects of speech other than words. It includes vocal behavior such as loudness, pitch, speed, inflection, breathiness, stretching or clipping of words, and pauses.

2. Body language. Body language is all the silent motion of the body: scowls, smiles, nods, gazing, gestures, leg movements, postural shifts, caressing, and slapping. The face is one of the most important instruments in body language. They quote Birdwhistell (1970) to the effect that the human face is capable of 250,000 different expressions. All of these, along with other body movements, combine to give visual cues of meaning in human communication.

3. Interpersonal spacing. Where and how people position themselves when they are talking, the varying distances and angles they take, is a powerful element of communication. Individuals can use their postures as well as other physical objects to create or to remove barriers. Whether or not we touch another person as well as how we touch carries an important communication.

In families today, we have a tendency to overlook the significance and power of the nonverbal level of communication. Words are much less important in conveying meaning than are all the messages of our silent prose. The wife who says to her husband, "This is the worst cake I have ever baked," does not mean to convey what her words literally mean. The father who says to his son, "You think you are so perfect," does not intend to give a compliment.

Metamessages.   Bateson (1955) was the first to refer to this second level of communication as *metacommunication.* According to him, metacommunication has to do with the tones, expressions, posture, and gestures one person uses to get a message across. Metamessages tell *how the words are to be taken.* It is the communication about the communication and is more important than the words themselves in getting messages from one person to another.

For example, let us say that my wife said to me this morning, "I appreciate your concern." In themselves, the words convey a positive message. But, let us say that she spoke these words with her hand on my arm looking up into my face and followed the words with a soft kiss on my cheek. She conveyed her message of warmth and love more clearly with her metamessage than with her words. On the other hand, suppose she spoke the words in a perfunctory manner as she hurried past me, busy with some other task. In the context of that set of nonverbal messages, her words lose some of their positive meaning. Or, imagine that she spoke them with a coldness in her voice and a stern and unyielding look in her eye. No inflection in the words flattened them into a sarcastic tone. The metamessage here is the exact opposite of the words she spoke. In all three instances, my wife used the same words, but they meant something different in each case because the nonverbal communication was different.

Dysfunctional families have trouble in the area of metacommunication. They send mixed or double messages, an action that means two things: First, what they say verbally is not what they say nonverbally. Family members are confused by the mutually exclusive signals they get in such a context. For example, a teenager hears his father say on his graduation night, "Congratulations, I'm proud of you." But the words are spoken in such a way as to communicate signals that say, "I am not proud of you. You have much left to prove to me." Or a husband commits the family to an event without first consulting with the wife. When he tells her about the occasion, her words say that it is okay. But her metamessage is that it is not. Everyone is confused by these mixed messages, and no one knows what to do about the confusion.

Double binds. Mixed messages lead to double binds. In a double-bind situation, one person sends two messages that are mutually exclusive. That is, if the receiver of the messages does one thing, he or she cannot do the other. For example, a mother may say to her daughter, "Take a bath before you go to bed." Two minutes later, the mother says, "What are you doing? It is past your bedtime. Go to bed!" Later, the mother enters the daughter's room and shouts, "Why didn't you take a bath like I told you!"

According to Annis (1987), a double bind can occur under four conditions:

1. There must be two or more persons. One is the designated victim of the double bind. Usually, neither party to the double bind is conscious of what is occurring.
2. The double bind is a part of the relationship and is repetitious. That is, it is not a one-time event. Rather, it is a part of the typical, ongoing interaction of the people involved.
3. The situation occurs in such a manner that no escape route is made available to the victim. Despite the mutual exclusivity of the two choices, the victim is forced to choose. Annis calls these "conflicting negative injunctions." The first injunction says, in effect, "Do." The second says, "Don't." The third says, "You have to choose."
4. Any injunction that one fails to follow brings punishment. Thus, one is always set up to fail and to be punished.

Mixed messages have a very detrimental effect in the dysfunctional family. It is hard to trust in this environment. The messages are coming from people on whom we depend. We need them. What does it mean, then, when they say simultaneously to us, "I love you—go away"? We know that something is missing or not right in this situation. It is our job to find it, and we believe that it is our fault that we cannot. We cannot trust them, and, in our confusion, we cannot trust or even like ourselves.

Children who grow up in this context frequently become very rule bound. Their first question becomes, What is expected of me? If I am to avoid punishment, I must get it right and do what is demanded of me. I will do nothing until I am clear on what is expected of me. A rigid perfectionism results. These children live with the belief that life can never be expected to make any sense. The world is a crazy place. Things will never work out, so why try?

Discounting Feelings

Whitfield (1987, p. 79; 1990, pp. 59–79) describes the individual who grows up in a dysfunctional family as living in a "feeling armamentarium." He means by this term that the adult child has so circumscribed his or her feelings that he or she lives in an emotional fort. Their defenses are so entrenched as they try to protect themselves from revealing their emotions that they may be described as living in an armory.

The child growing up in a dysfunctional family learns that emotions are not to be experienced and certainly not expressed. The child learns not to tell the truth about what he or she is feeling or about what he or she thinks others are feeling. Fossum and Mason (1986, p. 97) tell about one family in which a teenage son came home drunk every Saturday night. He threatened to beat up the other members of the family. The father and another son would wrestle him to the floor and hold him down until he fell into a drunken sleep. On Sunday, no one acknowledged the events of the previous evening, nor did they acknowledge there was anything to acknowledge.

Fossum and Mason say that, while feelings are basic and natural to all human beings, having and sharing deep and strong feelings must be *developed* in the family. In some families, the feelings are "familiar and comfortable" while in others they are "denied, naive, and primitive." Comfortably experiencing feelings and acknowledging them openly is "learned with practice and increasing maturity *when that is allowed into the family climate*" (italics added). The dysfunctional family simply does not permit open acknowledgment of feelings. In the dysfunctional family, feelings are denied, especially those feelings ordinarily considered negative, like anxiety, fear, grief, loneliness, rejection, neediness, and anger.

Hastings and Typpo (1984) graphically illustrate the denial of reality and human feelings in a book designed for use by people working with children in alcoholic families. They say:

Imagine an ordinary living room...chairs, couch, coffee table, a TV set and in the middle, a

LARGE GREY ELEPHANT.

The ELEPHANT stands there, shifting from one foot to another and slowly swaying from side to side.

Imagine also the people that live in this house; you, along with your mother and father and maybe some sisters and brothers. People have to go through the living room many times a day, [they] go through it very carefully...around...the...ELEPHANT. No one ever says anything about the ELEPHANT. They avoid the swinging trunk and just walk around it. Since no one ever talks about the ELEPHANT, you know that you're not supposed to talk about it either. And you don't.

But sometimes you wonder why nobody is saying anything or why no one is doing anything to move the ELEPHANT. After all, it's a very big elephant and it's very hard to keep walking around it all the time and people are getting very tired. You wonder if maybe there is something wrong with *you*. But you just keep wondering, keep walking around it, keep worrying and wishing that there was somebody to talk to about the ELEPHANT.

In therapy, families that deny feelings may appear very task oriented and practical. They may be very logical and businesslike. They seem to be saying, "We are here to get a job done; get on with it." This is how they live their entire lives. For them, feelings have no relevance or validity. They normally exhibit great control and rely on the effective performance of roles to carry out family interaction. They define themselves in terms of proper roles and expectations. If they are following the rules, they are safe. So they seek to know what is expected in the relationship. Fossum and Mason (1986, pp. 97–98) note that individuals who come from this kind of family do well in task-oriented and impersonal environments such as school and work. They are, however, disasters in places where personal uniqueness, spontaneity, and feelings are required. For that reason, they usually fail in intimate situations.

One repercussion of growing up in such a family can be massive denial. People do not know their honest feelings. The excessive secrecy leads to the inability even to *identify* feelings. People come to distrust their own perceptions and they mask real emotions. They lose the ability to perceive reality, and they learn to depend on projection and unrealistic fantasy to help them define what is going on. In such a way, they discount the whole realm of feelings. For them, life becomes a process of defense against feeling.

Unhealthy Rules

Family rules are the forces that dictate family behavior. They are necessary to give a family balance and to maintain order and stability. Some rules are explicit and are openly acknowledged in the family. Most are not. They exist in an unwritten form and are not transmitted verbally. For example, few people ever say, "In this family you do not talk about money." Everyone is simply expected to know that money is a taboo subject. And no one breaks that rule. Normally, no one knows where the rules come from. Usually there has been no family conference to decide where each person will sit at the table. But each one has his or her designated place.

All families have rules. In some families, the rules are healthy and contribute to the well-being of the group and all members of it. In others, the rules are unhealthy. According to Annis (1987), healthy rules have the following characteristics:

1. Healthy rules tend to be human. That is, it is possible for human beings to carry them out. Unhealthy rules are inhuman. They are double binds from the start, because they cannot be followed by normal people. Take the well-known rule

that children should be seen and not heard. This rule is inhumane when applied to most normal, small children. It is especially inhumane when applied rigidly to a child who is active and outgoing by nature.

Wegscheider (1981, p. 50) gives the following as examples of *inhumane* rules:

Be nice to everyone.

Always look on the bright side of things.

Control your feelings.

If you can't say something nice, don't say anything at all.

Wegscheider points out that inhumane rules encourage the individual to be dishonest with others to avoid punishment and rejection, and to be dishonest with oneself to avoid guilt.

2. Healthy rules are flexible and unhealthy rules are rigid. In healthy families, the rules are *not* the same from one situation to another. And they are *not* applied equally to everyone in the family. Rules are consistent but flexible. In the healthy system, the person matters more than the rule. In the unhealthy system, no allowances are made for individual differences. In that family, the rule says, "Everyone in this family is interested in sports," or "Everyone makes top grades."

One family that I know, had a rule that everybody in the family played golf. On weekends and every day during the summer, all three adolescent children were forced to play eighteen holes. One of the children was a girl, and at this vulnerable time in her feminine development, her father forced her to take on what she considered a masculine role. There was no flexibility in the rules, and she had to play golf with her brothers. She became unruly and resentful but got no relief from the uncompromising rules. She was defined as unreasonable and uncooperative and the source of the family problems. All along, it was the rigidity of the rule that was the problem.

3. Rules in a healthy environment encourage openness. The rules help the family members to share, talk, and communicate openly. In the unhealthy family, the rules enforce a closed system. Secrets are very important in that atmosphere.

4. In the healthy family, there is unconditional acceptance. In the dysfunctional family, rules contribute to a conditional atmosphere. Each person has to fit the mold, and anyone who does not is not accepted.

5. The healthy system provides rules that validate the person's natural and inherent worth. The rules are not used to put people down, including people who are not members of the family. No one is made to feel unworthy. On the other hand, no one's self-esteem is enhanced in an unhealthy system. In this

system, the rules are designed to control people and are therefore often used to make people feel bad about themselves.

6. Healthy rules encourage change and growth. Unhealthy rules do not. They encourage self-deceit and lying. They reward dishonesty and manipulative behavior. They discourage change and growth.

7. Healthy rules tend to benefit everyone. Everybody gets some protection from them. No one is left out and made to feel more at risk than anyone else. In the dysfunctional system, the rules generally benefit the rule maker.

Annis points out one other consequence of the unhealthy rules in the dysfunctional family. She says that in all families, at least initially, children try to follow the rules. People want to belong and following the rules is the only way to fit into the family. But in the dysfunctional family, everyone breaks the rules. They are, after all, unhealthy. But one can never admit that one has broken the rules or talk about why. Neither can one suggest new ways of doing things. Not talking about the rules is one of the cardinal rules of the dysfunctional family. So a vicious cycle emerges that is sustained by the dysfunctionality of the rules and in turn sustains that same destructiveness.

Subby and Friel (1984) have isolated eight rules that are a part of every codependent family:

1. It's not okay to talk about problems.
2. Feelings should not be expressed openly.
3. Communication is best if indirect, with one person acting as messenger between two others (triangulation).
4. There are unrealistic expectations—Be strong. Be good. Be right. Be perfect. Make us proud.
5. Don't be "selfish."
6. Do as I say, not as I do.
7. It's not okay to play or be playful.
8. Don't rock the boat.

Children who grow up in a family in which these are the rules have a hard time feeling loved or accepted. The bond between parent and child is damaged. The child has a difficult time developing an adequate sense of identity. Self-esteem is negatively affected. The child feels, "It is not okay to be me," and the resulting sense of shame makes it difficult to love one's self or others.

In summary, then, the codependent family is clearly an appropriate target for therapy from a systems theory perspective. How does the therapist intervene in this area? That is the subject of the next chapter.

REFERENCES

Ackerman, Norman J. (1984). *A Theory of Family Systems*, New York: Gardner Press.

Ackerman, Nathan W. (1956). "Interlocking Pathologies in Family Relationships," in S. Rado, and G. Daniels, Eds., *Changing Concepts in Psychoanalytic Medicine*, New York: Grune & Stratton.

Ackerman, Robert, J. (1983). *Children of Alcoholics: A Guide for Parents, Educators and Therapists* (2nd ed.), New York: Simon & Shuster.

Andolfi, M. et al. (1983). *Behind the Family Mask: Therapeutic Change In Rigid Family Systems*, New York: Brunner/Mazel.

Annis, B. (1987). Unpublished workshop presentation at Advantage Health Services Seminar, Dallas, Tex.

Bateson, G. (1955). "A Theory of Play and Fantasy," *Psychiatric Research Reports*, 2: 39–51.

Bell, J. (1975). *Family Therapy*, New York: Aronson, Inc.

Bernard, C., and Corrales, R. (1979). *The Theory and Technique of Family Therapy*, Springfield, Ill.: Charles C Thomas.

Bertrand, A. (1967). *Basic Sociology: An Introduction to Theory and Method*, New York: Appleton-Century-Crofts.

Birdwhistell, R. (1970). *Kinesics in Context: Essays on Body Motion Communications*, Philadelphia: University of Pennsylvania Press.

Bowen, M. (1966). "The Use of Family Theory in Clinical Practice," *Comprehensive Psychiatry*, 7: 345–374.

Commoner, B. (1971). *The Closing Circle: Nature, Man, and Technology*, New York: Alfred A. Knopf.

de Mello, A. (1984). *The Song of the Bird*, Garden City, N.Y.: Image Books.

Fogarty, T. (1972). "Family Structure in Terms of Triangles," in J. Bradt and C. Moynihan, Eds., *Systems Therapy*, Washington, D.C.: Groome Child Guidence Center.

Fossum, M., and Mason, M. (1986). *Facing Shame: Families in Recovery*, New York: W. W. Norton.

Haley, J., (1976). *Problem-Solving Therapy: New Strategies for Effective Family Therapy*, San Francisco: Josey Bass, Inc.

Hastings, J., and Typpo, M. (1984). *An Elephant in the Living Room*, Minneapolis: Compcare.

Jackson, D., (1968). *Human Communication Volume I*, Palo Alto, California: Science & Behavior Books.

Kaufman, E. (1985). *Substance Abuse and Family Therapy*, Orlando, Fla.: Grune & Stratton.

Lewis, J., Dana, R., and Blevins, G. (1988). *Substance Abuse Counseling: An Individualized Approach*, Pacific Grove, Calif.: Brooks/Cole.

Lidz, T. (1968). *The Person: His Development Through the Life Cycle*, New York: Basic Books.

Lidz, T., Fleck, S., and Cornelison A. (1965). *Schizophrenia and the Family*, New York: International Universities Press.

Michener, H., Delamater, J., and Schwartz, S. (1986). *Social Psychology*, New York: Harcourt Brace Jovanovich.

Minuchin, S. (1974). *Families and Family Therapy*, Cambridge, Mass.: Harvard University Press.

Nelson, J. (1983). *Family Treatment: An Integrative Approach*, Englewood Cliffs, N.J.: Prentice-Hall.

Parsons, T., and Shils, E., (Eds.), (1951). *Toward a General Theory of Action*, Cambridge, Mass.: Harvard University Press.

Satir, V. (1983). *Conjoint Family Therapy* (3rd ed.), Palo Alto, Calif.: Science and Behavior Books.

Satir, V. (1972). *Peoplemaking*, Palo Alto, Calif.: Science and Behavior Books.

Subby, R., and Friel, J. (1984). "Co-dependency—A Paradoxical Dependency," in *Co-dependency; An Emerging Issue*, Pompano Beach, Fla.: Health Communications, Inc.

Umbarger, C. (1983). *Structural Family Therapy*, New York: Grune & Stratton.

von Bertalanffy, L. (1968). *General Systems Theory: Foundations, Development, Applications*, New York: George Braziller.

Watzlawick, P., (1976). *How Real is Real? Confusion-Disinformation-Communication.* New York: Random House.

Wegscheider, S. (1981). *Another Chance: Hope and Health for the Alcoholic Family*, Palo Alto, Calif.: Science and Behavior Books.

Wegscheider-Cruise, S. (1984). "Co-dependency—The Therapeutic Void" in *Co-dependency: An Emerging Issue*, Pompano Beach, Fla.: Health Communications.

Whitfield, C. (1987). *Healing the Child Within: Discovery and Recovery for Adult Children of Dysfunctional Families*, Pompano Beach, Fla.: Health Communications.

Whitfield, C. (1990). *A Gift to Myself*, Deerfield Beach, Fla.: Health Communications.

9

TECHNIQUES FOR COUNSELING THE CODEPENDENT FAMILY

Philip and Carol brought their nine-year-old daughter, Melody, to see me because she was a "discipline problem." Philip explained in the first interview that Melody had always been very obedient. She had always seemed like a happy child and had been very well adjusted in life. She was extremely intelligent, he explained, and did well in school. She had lots of friends. What bothered the parents was her attitude at home. The problem was that she had become surly and irritable and was no longer the "sweet and lovable little girl" that she had always been.

Carol said little as Philip described Melody's problems. "How do you see what is happening, Carol?" I asked when Phillip gave a pause in his overlong presentation. "He expects too much of her and is always criticizing her," Carol responded. Her voice had a critical edge. "Would you talk about that?" I asked.

Carol began to illustrate Philip's overbearing parenting style. Philip interrupted to reinterpret for me the incorrect impressions his wife was giving of him. He spoke with forced pleasantness in his voice. The problem, he went on to explain, was his wife's lack of interest in parenting. She was more interested in her job as a professional photographer than in their daughter. His voice took on a sharpness. "That's not fair," Carol remonstrated. "If you made enough money I would not have to work so much and I could be home with Melody." Carol's voice was sarcastic and cutting. Philip, when he responded, had regained control and spoke with a faked sweetness in his voice. They continued to debate each other with alternate sweetness and bitterness on their relative merits as parents and human beings.

After about ten minutes of this "discussion," I turned to Melody and asked, "What do you think about this?" She looked at me with a slight smile, "I think they both need a good spanking."

Philip and Carol and Melody are a codependent family. They are a family system that has, for whatever reason, gotten off balance. Neither Carol nor Philip can deal with their problems in a direct and open manner. They are both controlled and controlling with each other. They do not feel good about what is happening in their lives. And they are triangulating on Melody. Her job in the family is to act out the anger that both parents feel and cannot express.

The question this chapter addresses is, What can we do to help codependent families? How does the therapist intervene so as to help a family heal?

PRELIMINARY CONSIDERATIONS

Before looking at specific intervention tactics, let us investigate three overall considerations the therapist will want to keep in mind throughout family therapy. These considerations are among the factors that present unique challenges to the family therapist working with the codependent family.

Not All Family Members Are There for the Same Reasons

The therapist may assume that most of the people who are present in a group session are there because they chose to be. That is not a sure assumption in family therapy. Most frequently in family therapy, there is at least one person, and usually more, who have been coerced into coming. Family members who are there under duress present unique challenges in therapy.

Furthermore, it is a safe bet that in codependent family therapy, there are some who come with ambivalent feelings. Usually one family member has pushed for the session. The other family members respond with reactions ranging from disinterest to fear. They are hurting and they very much want the pain to go away. Yet they are afraid of the changes that may be required to remove the pain. They have secrets they do not want to share. In fact, as pointed out in the previous section, one of the salient factors in their dysfunctionality is a rule that prohibits the very thing they must do to get help. They fear that recovery may cost them the little they have in terms of identity and security. The compulsions of behavior and emotion they have developed for survival in their crazy world will be lost, and they will have to face themselves and the others without their defenses.

The Family Needs to Assume Proper Responsibility

The therapist working with the codependent family must start by helping the family to assume appropriate responsibility. Each family member will need to become responsible for his or her own behavior, feelings, and thoughts. To be responsible for oneself necessitates giving up responsibility for others. Bernard and Corrales (1979, p. 111) make the point that control is very important in the first sessions. They state that it is necessary for the therapist to control *structure* and for the family to control *initiative*.

The question of structure revolves around who controls the process of therapy. Families attempting to avoid change and to protect the status quo will seek to bring the therapist into their normal interaction and make him a part of it. The dominant person may attempt to call the shots so as to establish for the family and therapist that nothing is different in the session from outside. Conversely, the weaker member may attempt to demonstrate weakness to win the therapist's protection. If this happens, no change will occur and the family's usual way of doing things will go on in the session, with the therapist simply being the family's newest participant.

Initiative, on the other hand, is concerned with who controls the lives of family members. At this point, the family will attempt to put the therapist in control. If they succeed, they can sit back and say, "Heal me." No change will occur if the therapist allows this to happen. Bernard and Corrales (1979, p. 110) conclude that the family's willingness to assume responsibility for their lives is the "heart of change."

The Family Needs to Face Reality

The codependent family needs help in seeing and dealing with reality. They must learn to distinguish between their needs and their wants and to recognize that they must deal with the things that are real and not with the things they wish were real. They must come to grips with the dynamics of their own system and the part that each person plays in the family.

The big problem is that the codependent family avoids reality. They discount feelings. Individual family members pretend to feel things they do not feel. They act as if they like things which they do not. They are responsible for making the family appear happy to all outsiders. Each family member must seem secure and well adjusted. In no way is any family member allowed to let any person outside the family see anything but positive facts about the family. These are unwritten and are even sometimes unconscious rules, but they are very powerful in the family. They ensure that denial remains a way of life in the family.

When they come into therapy, these families bring with them their patterns of seeing "reality" and a history of dealing with whatever occurs from that perspective of reality. Codependent families do not have a lot of trust in each other. They interpret things that happen in the session from the perception that the others are not trustworthy. The therapist's task is simultaneously to allow them to own their perception of what is happening and to develop the awareness of potential change. The therapist has two apparently mutually exclusive objectives: He or she must somehow get all family members to the point where they affirm their reality and talk about it openly in the family. And at the same time the therapist must help them realize that how they perceive reality and what is real may be two different things.

A daughter who has always perceived her father as a domineering and insensitive jerk is not likly to believe him when he says to her, "I've changed and I really want to be a good father to you." Her retort may very well be, "Where were you all those years that I wanted and needed your love? How do I know I can trust you?" The daughter needs to express her feelings of mistrust and at the same time to be open to her father's change.

The Fullertons are an example of all three of these preliminary considerations. They were a family of six persons who came into therapy to deal with an impending divorce. As we will see, they were not all there for the same reasons. Nor were they assuming proper responsibility for themselves. And they were not dealing with reality.

Bob and Mary Anne had been married for twenty-three years. They had four children: twenty-one-year-old Cindy, eighteen-year-old Morris, fifteen-year-old Mary Lynn, and ten-year-old Ben. The parents were separated and Mary Anne had filed for divorce. Bob had requested that they meet with me as a family to help heal the wounds that had accrued through two decades of life as a dysfunctional family. His desire was not to put the family back together but to help the family deal with the past and prepare for the future. Mary Anne agreed with great reluctance and Morris, the oldest son, refused to attend at all. The other children came, but with a sense of dread.

The family projected a classic image of a dysfunctiuonal family. When they entered the room, the mother sat on one couch, which was situated at a right angle to another couch. Mary Lynn and Ben sat on either side of her. Cindy, the oldest child, sat on the end of the couch closest to her mother. Had there been room, she would have sat on the couch with the mother. Bob sat on the end of the couch farthest from the family. These seating arrangements proved to be prophetic of the family's problems. The father was emotionally disengaged from the family. He was an outsider. It turned out that his job in the family play was to figure out what needed to be done and to "force" the family to do it. The session we were having was a perfect example of the game this family played. The whole idea was his, and the rest of them were there under duress.

The mother was totally enmeshed with the children. There were no boundaries between her and them. They spoke for her, and she spoke for them. The fifteen-year-old, Mary Lynn, performed as the parental child, giving directions to the others and comforting them when they cried or had a hard time articulating an idea or feeling. All the females banded together to protect Ben from my questions and later in the interview from their father's influence. All the children were very protective of their mother during the session. Mother must be thought right and blameless in every sense. All responsibility for the failure of the marriage was shifted to the father.

The session proved to be fruitless. I began with a brief period of conversation that I hoped would make us all feel comfortable. All family members answered my questions politely. However, their metamessages were that they did not want to be there. They would talk, they seemed to be saying, but they would say nothing that did not conform to the established patterns. And they were surely not going to help their father or give him what he wanted. I asked the family to rearrange their seating, with the parents on one couch and the children on the other. That arrangement only seemed to confirm their coalitions.

The family had never discussed the divorce as a group. I asked that we talk about it. "Let's talk about what went wrong and how we feel about it," I suggested. "Okay," their lips said. But the real message I got was, "Oh, no! I can't do this." "Lets start with Mom and Dad," I suggested. "Would you begin by telling what you did to make the marriage fail?"

Father led off with no hesitation. He described what he had done wrong over the years as a father and as a husband. He had it figured out and spoke fluently and convincingly. When Mom spoke, she hesitated. She looked to Mary Lynn for confirmation. Mary Lynn smiled and nodded approvingly. Mom's voice grew stronger and more confident. "I don't think I did anything wrong," she said. "I always tried to save our marriage. Bob was never *there*, and all I ever wanted was to be loved by him and for him to love the children." She continued relating stories of how he went away emotionally or physically and she worked to get him back in the family. I interrupted her after a moment to have her deal with her feelings about the divorce. The chidren began at this point to correct her and clarify the story as she left out details and forgot her feelings.

I asked the children to talk about their feelings about their parents' comments. "What they said was true," the two daughters responded quickly. I encouraged them to talk further about the divorce and their parents. Cindy cried and so did Ben. Mary Lynn did not shed a tear. They did not deviate from the story their parents had established in their comments.

Toward the end of the two-hour session, I asked the children if they had a request for their parents that would make the situation more bearable for them. Ben said nothing. He shrugged and tried not to cry. The daughters said that what their mother was doing was good and they could suggest no changes in her behavior. Both of them said that they would prefer that their father leave them alone. They would get back to him to reestablish the relationship when they got ready.

At the end of the session, I attempted to discuss briefly what I had seen of the structure and dynamics of the family. When I suggested that the father was disengaged, all other members of the family nodded in agreement. However, when I tried to describe the enmeshment of the mother and children, the daughters and then the mother responded angrily. What I called *enmeshment*, they saw as genuine love, and they were incensed that I would be so insensitive as to describe it in negative terms. The session ended and the Fullertons left. They never came back.

To help in this process, the therapist must observe, question, challenge, and test the family's behaviors, attitudes, assumptions, and feelings. The therapist must watch as a member of an audience watches an ongoing play. Sometimes, she must climb on the stage and join the play by acting out a part for the others to observe. At times, she must stand in the wings as a vigilant director and give instructions for alterations. At other times, she must educate the performers on the skills of acting, even as the play goes on. Or, she may have to stop the performance and join the family as a playwright to restructure the script. And, at other times, she must applaud as a member of an appreciative audience.

STAGES OF CODEPENDENT FAMILY THERAPY

We may divide codependent family therapy into three stages: The initial, intermediate, and final stages.

Initial Stage

The crucial issues during the first two or three sessions are trust and awareness. Trust is hard because codependent individuals have learned that vulnerability leads to pain, and they do not open up easily. It is important for the therapist to do all that he or she can to establish trust.

Because codependent families do not trust easily, I feel that these opening sessions should have little or no confrontation. During this time, therapists do not need to destroy defense systems. Family members must be given time to develop new coping techniques before we ask them to tear down the old defenses. Not all therapeutic approaches are based on this gradual approach. Andolfi and co-workers (1983) have a perspective based on immediate confrontation of family defenses. They have a largely enactive technique that in many ways is reminiscent of the approach of Minuchin (1974) and his associates.

Awareness is reached when each person admits that what is happening in the family is a *family* problem. In such an admission, each member realizes that he or she has a hand in causing the problem. Each begins to take responsibility for himself or herself. The family gives up scapegoating the scapegoat and begins to develop appropriate boundaries in this process.

There is a "honeymoon" period in family therapy that occurs at the end of the initial stage. The more effective the therapy, the greater is the temptation in the honeymoon. The therapy feels so good and the family is relating so well during the sessions that individuals are tempted to think that all their problems are solved. The family is now "cured" and in its euphoria the family may stop therapy.

Intermediate Stage

Typically, the initial phase ends with the third or fourth session. Some level of trust and awareness has been established and the family is now ready to do the hard work of change. The therapist seeks in the intermediate stage to do the following:

1. Increase and build on the trust and awareness established in the initial phase. The family must be encouraged to remain open and trusting, both during the sessions and outside.

2. Encourage open expression and exchange of information with each other. Codependent families must learn new methods of communication in which they recognize and avoid mixed messages. They need to learn to share feelings with each other. A reminder from Whitfield (1987, p. 82) is in order at this point. He says, "When we share our feelings, it is most appropriate to do so with safe and supportive people. Early in recovery people who grew up in troubled or dysfunctional families may want so much to share that they get rejected, betrayed or otherwise get into trouble by telling others, indiscriminately, about their feelings. They may find it difficult to learn that it is *not appropriate to share feelings with everyone.*" We must teach our codependent clients the "share-check-share" tactic of Gravitz and Bowden (1985), whereby we share a little of our feelings with selected people. Then we check their response. If they are safe (seem to listen to us, don't judge us, don't put a lot of "shoulds" on us, and don't solve our problems for us), then we share some more.

3. Break the old family traditions and rules. We help the family to become conscious of the incongruity of its normal ways of relating by deliberately breaking its rules for normal interaction. For example, we might ask the child who is withdrawn and fearful to be in charge of a particular exercise in the session. The family rule is that this child sits unobtrusively while someone else is always in charge. One therapist friend of mine asked the avoidant child in the family to keep the time in the session and to let the family know when the session was over. Or, we may wish to block the overresponsible child from playing the caretaker. Or, if it is apparent that one person is the family mouth, (that is, the one who answers for all persons in the family) we pay them no heed. These tactics are designed to reveal the irrationality of the family traditions by exposing their absurdity.

4. Develop healthy communication. The therapy is designed to bring the family to the point that fewer things are taboo. Secrets are now to be discussed openly. No feelings or thoughts or opinions are off limits. Indirect communication through other people is not permissible. In this manner, the family learns to talk about more subjects with more people, both within the family and outside it.

5. Restructure the family system. Questions like who is really in charge in this family, who communicates with whom, what coalitions exist and between whom, and who will and who will not change must be addressed.

6. In the course of family therapy, some attention must be paid to individual issues and issues of various subsystems. This is especially true of families in which there are previous marriages and children from more than one set of parents. The term used for this kind of family is *blended.* It might be necessary for the father and stepchildren, for instance, to meet with the therapist in the absence of the rest of the family. The therapist works with this subsystem in the same way and for the same goals that he or she works with the whole family.

Final Stage

The purpose of the final phase of family therapy is to continue the learning of tools that will help the family to continue growing. If the therapy has gone well, they will have found that change is not catastrophic. In fact, change is inevitable and can be pleasurable. The family should be prepared to recognize and deal with relapse.

The final phase, which may last for several sessions, may be a time for more enactive interventions and for more confrontive therapeutic methods. These tactics depend on the nature of the family, the codependent problems they face, and the nature of the therapist.

The ultimate goal of the final phase is, in fact, the ultimate goal of therapy: to bring the family to the point that they no longer need the therapist. The final phase prepares them for termination.

INTERVENTIONS IN CODEPENDENT FAMILY THERAPY

Types of Interventions

Three types of interventions are available to the therapist who works with the codependent family: information-oriented, action-oriented, and affective-oriented.

Information-oriented interventions. This type of intervention is cognitive and includes any type of education, exercise, and question-answer method that the therapist uses. We may ask questions for our own information or to cause the family to consider the answers and thus arrive at information or insights they previously did not have. We may offer positive or negative comments on their functioning. It is sometimes helpful to get family members to write out experiences and events of the past. Various exercises, both in the sessions and as homework (see the next section for suggested exercises), can be employed to get them thinking and to make them aware of family patterns. The objective of all these interventions is to convey greater understanding of the situation and to offer coping mechanisms they can learn and begin to practice.

Action-oriented interventions Using these intervention techniques, the therapist takes some action or asks the family to take some action. For instance, the counselor may ask for role modeling in which the family acts out in the session some troubling behavior. "Show me how your father speaks to you when he is angry" is a simple way of getting a family to enact a particular set of behaviors. Or we may move family members about in the session to make clear how seating arrangements demonstrate coalitions. The therapist may want to take some action to prevent a family member from enacting a particular role that he or she customarily performs. For example, a dominant member may be asked to leave the room or sit apart from the group for a while. To demonstrate power arrangements, it is sometimes helpful to ask someone to stand on a chair or perhaps to sit on the floor while others remain seated in a normal fashion. These tactics can demonstrate very effectively how power is distributed in the family and how the rearrangement of power can feel. The therapist may want to suggest exercises to do at home. The following section contains other examples of active exercises for codependent family therapy.

Affective-oriented interventions. All the methods that we can employ in group therapy to get clients in touch with their feelings are useful in family therapy. These include interventions that ask clients about how they feel when other family members do or say certain things. It is useful to deal with the present as well as the past. That is, the therapist may want to help the family process emotions as they occur in the session. The effort is to get individuals in touch with both positive and negative emotions. In such a manner, the entire family comes to see that feeling emotions and processing them openly in the family is a positive experience. Doing so in the session offers the therapist the opportunity to lead the family through the scary territory of dealing openly with emotions. The therapist may give positive or negative feedback on the family's experience.

Methods of Intervention

The purpose of this section is to suggest some specific things that the therapist may wish to employ in working with the codependent family. These exercises must be adapted to the specific needs of the family with which the therapist is working at any given time. Some are more useful for the earlier sessions, where less confrontive methods are usually required. Others are obviously more effective in later sessions, after trust and openness have been established. Some are designed to be used over and over in the therapy, whereas others are for one-time use only.

Reframing or relabeling. Therapists can help families when they attempt to redefine family members' behaviors and statements in a more positive fashion. Simply reframing some behaviors as normal brings enormous relief. For example, parents wrestling with the problems of their children can deal more effectively with them if they are relieved of the pressure of seeing them as pathological.

Jeffrey's parents brought him to me because he was lying. The ten-year-old son of a blue-collar family, Jeffrey was having difficulty in school. He had become lethargic and did not do his homework. As a result, he was failing several subjects. Jeffrey was a quiet and mild-mannered child, and was big for his age. He was repentant when disciplined by his parents but did no better. His father whipped him with a belt, and Jeffrey would sorrowfully promise to reform but then continue to perform poorly. His father would punish him more severely, because now Jeffrey had added lying to the list of his misbehaviors. Jeffrey would be more forceful in his ineffectual promises to do better. Nothing seemed to work and the family began to worry that Jeffrey had some deep moral defect. They spoke almost in a shameful whisper as they described Jeffrey's lying.

Clearly the first thing the family needed was to get out of the vicious cycle that had been established. I tried to help them by reframing what was occurring. First, a little probing proved that Jeffrey felt out of place in his school because he was new there; the family had moved into that school district about seven months earlier. Jeffrey also felt odd because he was so much bigger than the rest of the students. They made fun of him. I commented to Jeffrey that I could understand how he felt different from the other students because he was bigger than they were. I added that when I was in school, I looked up to the biggest boy. I wished that I were bigger than the rest of the kids in my grade. (My comments, which were true, were a reframe that I hoped would give Jeffrey some relief.)

Next, I redefined Jeffrey's behavior as normal for a child who does not feel like he belongs. His promises to do better were not lies, as his parents interpreted them. Rather, they were a sincere wish to do what they wanted because he loved them so much. Jeffrey was obviously a smart and capable youngster who wanted to do what his parents wanted. He was having a hard time in school because of some very normal needs of a ten-year-old.

Facilitative questions. When we ask facilitative questions, we ask questions that help the family to move deeper into what is going on. That is, the questions are designed more to help the family discover its own truth than for the therapist to point out what that truth is. For example, the family member's interpretation of what is occurring is often better than that of the therapist. Therefore, the therapist should ask questions like, What keeps you from sticking to your plans in your family? What are some things that keep your son from understanding what you say to him? These and similar questions encourage family members to explore within themselves for the truth.

With the proper use of facilitative questions, the therapist can involve all members of the family. We can ask, as examples, "Were you aware that the others felt that way when you did that?" "How do you respond to what your father is saying?" "How can it be that she did not know that about you?"

Pointing out family patterns. The therapist must always seek and be ready to point out typical and atypical family patterns. This may be done with statements like, "I'm aware that when the subject of money comes up, everyone falls into a kind of uncomfortable silence. Is anyone else aware of this?" Or the therapist may simply ask, "Does this happen often at home?" Or, "Is this the usual way the family responds in this situation?"

Sometimes it is necessary to confront patterned behaviors that damage one individual. For example, the therapist may have to say something like, "I'm not sure how Ruth feels, but I hurt for her when you two laughed at what she said." Or the therapist may have to ask individuals to personalize statements. For instance, a child may say, "People are usually unhappy in families where the father is gone a lot." A good response to this statement might be, "Do you mean to say that you are unhappy because your father is gone from home a lot?"

Sentence stemming.   Sentence stemming is an effective method of helping the family discover what is happening. This method is done by the therapist giving the start of a sentence (the stem) and letting each family member complete the sentence. A brief time is given to allow the family to process each person's response, if they wish to do so. Useful stems are

- "I feel loved when...."
- "The thing I like most about this family is...."
- "I wish I could tell my family...."
- "The thing I like least about my family is...."
- "When I'm with my family, I'm happiest when we...."
- "What I like about most other families is...."
- "The thing that is changing most about this family is...."

An effective variant of stemming is to give the family *feeling word lists* to fill out and then discuss in the session. These lists are designed to help family members identify and process their feelings. Examples of lists are the following:

1. "Right now I feel _____ because _____."
2. "When _____ occurs, I feel _____ and I want to _____ about it."
3. "When I feel _____, what I do is _____."
4. "When I feel _____, what I want from you is _____."

Developing listening skills.   Codependent families need help in communication. The reflexive listening exercise is helpful in this area. The therapist rehearses this exercise with the family in the session and then asks them to practice it at home. During the next session and in subsequent sessions, the therapist checks on how the family is doing with reflexive listening. The exercise involves the following:

1. The sender of the message sends it briefly and clearly.
2. The receiver *reflects* it back by repeating what he or she thinks the sender has said. This is done by the receiver rephrasing the message in his or her own words and feeding it back to the sender.
3. The sender responds by confirming that the receiver has understood the message. If the receiver has not understood, the sender further clarifies the message. The receiver again reflects the message. The shared-meaning pro-

cess is not complete until the sender is satisfied that the receiver understands the message. At that point, the sender says, "Thank you for listening to me."

The therapist can use this method of communication in the session. He or she may reflect what the client is saying and then ask whether or not the reflection is correct. Modeling healthy communication styles is important in therapy. Clear and open communication with the therapist may be the first that the family has experienced.

The therapist can watch for and point out metamessages that are incongruent with the words being spoken. Mom may say *yes* while shaking her head *no*. Or Dad may say that he really is in charge, while his tone and pitch say that he has no idea what is going on. In calling these mixed messages to the attention of the family, it is usually best to use facilitative questions. For example, the therapist may want to say, "I am aware of a mixed message as you speak, Frank. I wonder if anyone else is confused." If a family member points out what is occurring, an effective response might be, "How does that make you feel?" or "Is there something you would like to ask of Frank in this context?"

Careful listening, as Dorn (1983, p. 65) indicates, is a skill for which few of us have had any real training. Yet it is at least 50 percent of any communication. I point out that effective listening involves at least six things:

1. Willingness to hear. Too frequently, we do not *want* to hear what the other is saying. We do not listen, simply because we do not care about what the other is saying.
2. Positive listening environment. Careful listening necessitates full attention to what the speaker is saying, without distractions. Both speaker and listener must try to create a situation in which there is minimum interruption. The listener's job, then, is to give *undiluted consideration* to the speaker.
3. Attitude of support. Listeners show support by giving encouraging feedback. That may involve nothing more than eye contact and an occasional nod of the head. Or one may wish to be more active with a "That's interesting, tell me more" statement thrown in every once in a while. The most active feedback is to make positive reinforcing statements like, "I can see that you are really into this and I think you have every right to feel as you do."
4. Clarifying questions. If the listener does not really understand, he or she must ask for more information. As an example, the speaker sometimes asks, "You know what I mean?" If the listener does not know what the speaker means, an appropriate answer might be, "Not really, could you tell me more?"
5. Avoiding the *Why* question. Asking the speaker *why* she thinks or feels or did something may put her on the defensive. That is, asking *why* makes us feel that we have done something wrong and that we must justify it. Careful listeners frame Why questions as How or What questions. For example, instead of asking, "Why did you go over to John's house?" the careful

listener might ask, "What did you want to accomplish by going over to John's house?"

6. Not stealing the show. Careful listeners do not offer unsolicited advice or leap to conclusions. Their job is to *hear*, and they remember that hearing is done with the ears, not the mouth.

Developing talking skills.   We must remember that families that have problems in communication need to be taught *how* to talk. The following is an exercise designed to aid them in learning how to communicate. The exercise also helps to develop careful listening skills. Families with older children can use it as a family activity. Those families with small children will need to limit it to the parents only. The therapist provides a copy of the exercise to each family member who will participate in the process. The exercise is best done as homework. Each individual in the family writes out the answer to all questions in private. Then the family comes together and they go over the responses of each to the questions. Obviously, this exercise is designed to be used after the family has developed some trust and has learned some methods of open communication. To get the fullest effect, the therapist will ask family members to bring their completed forms back to the next session to process what happened when they went through the exercise.

TALKING POINTS

1. Here are five things I want to know about other people in this family. These things must be about others in your family. For example, "What are the things which you like most and least about your life?"

   _____
   _____
   _____
   _____
   _____

2. Here are five things I want to tell this family about me. For example, "I want to tell you the things I like about our home."

   _____
   _____
   _____
   _____
   _____

3. Here are two things I wish I could change about me.

   _____
   _____

4. Here are two things I wish I could change about this family.

5. Here is something I have never told you about me or that I have not told you in a long time.

6. I want to thank this family for being in my life because you have helped me in at least these two ways:

Emphasizing family strengths.   In working with the codependent family, the therapist must be constantly on guard to keep the family from becoming dependent on him. An effective method of doing so is for the therapist to remember that the solution to the family's problem is to be found in them and not in the therapist's skill or wisdom. Remembering this simple fact helps the therapist remind the family of its strengths. This can be done in a number of ways:

1. Always put the parents in charge. If a child needs to be controlled in a session, ask the parents to do it. Insofar as possible, attempt to involve the marginal parent. When family conferences must occur (to do exercises, etc.), put the responsibility for deciding when it is to occur in the parents' hands. This tactic is effective in helping parents to begin developing a strong parental subsystem and to break any parent-child coalition that may exist. However, special care is necessary where there is a domineering parent. In that case, the therapist must involve the disengaged parent or work to empower the children in the decision-making process.

2. Give praise sparingly. Rather than saying, "You are doing really well," the therapist might ask, "How do you think you are doing?" That the therapist would ask such a question means that he or she honors the family members' opinion and thinks that they are worthy of having one. The question also authenticates the feelings of the family members. That is, it says to them, "It is okay for you to feel the things you are feeling." It is also based on the belief that the family is able to monitor its own health and does not need the therapist to say how it is doing. Finally, the family's answer to the question allows family members to bring out and deal with issues that otherwise might not come to the surface. All of these things contribute to the family's becoming aware of its strength.

3. Talk about *strength* and *solutions*, not about *problems* and *weaknesses*. Therapists do too much labeling of individuals and categorizing of family problems. Clients want to have a name for what ails them. That seems to give them a

sense of direction and the feeling that, since we know what the problem is, we can come up with a solution. Their attitude is, "Tell me what is wrong with me and tell me what you plan to do to fix it."

Of greater profit to codependent families is the emphasis that the solution to the family's problem is in the family itself. Therapy is the search for that strength. The therapist, unlike the family doctor, does not administer a medicine that drives out the problem. Rather, the therapist joins the family as a guide looking for the buried treasure that is within the family.

Blocking tactics.   Blocking negative family interactional patterns is a useful technique in working with the codependent family. Blocking makes family patterns explicit. It also forces the family to find other ways to interact than the destructive methods they have developed.

Blocking means that the therapist intervenes directly in the family's normal way of doing things when those patterns are destructive and keep the family trapped. For example, in Ron and Ruth's interaction, Ruth played the part of the helpless and depressed wife. In the first session, Ron admitted that he was afraid of therapy because he might lose "control" of Ruth. Toward the end of the session, Ruth was talking about her desire to get a job. Ron interrupted her to say to me, "She thinks it is easy out there. It's a dog's world and she will be eaten alive by the sharks." His mixed metaphor was emphasized by a harsh tone that seemed to convey disdain for her feeble attempts in that world as much as his evaluation of that world. "How is it that you have a need to stop Ruth and keep her weak?" I asked. My intervention was designed to make explicit and block Ron's pattern of control and Ruth's unconscious acquiescence to that control.

Blocking involves direct tactics and gentle confrontation. Therefore, it must be used with care, especially in the first few sessions. The object is never to shame or to control, but to educate and prepare the family for the changes that are necessary.

Sculpting and making family portraits.   *Sculpting* is a technique used with benefit by many family therapists. It ranges from the very simple repositioning of seating arrangements to the enactment of rather complex family patterns. The former is accomplished by the therapist requesting that each person in the family go and sit beside the person they feel closest to in the family. When the family has finished moving about, they process what has occurred and how they feel about it.

In the more complex use of sculpting, the therapist dedicates the majority of the session to the exercise. One family member is selected to do the family portrait. This person is the director, and his or her task is to arrange all the family members in the room so as to symbolize their role in the family as the director sees it. First, the director places the family around the room in such a way as to represent the closeness or distance of the various family members. The director then asks each person to take a customary pose. That is, the director places each person in the family in a posture that symbolizes their characteristic place in the family. For example, power persons may be asked to stand on a chair, while the powerless may be asked to sit on the floor. The uninvolved person may be asked to turn his or her back to the group. Rageful persons may be asked to shake a fist or point a finger. Next, the director gives each person in the family a typical sentence to say. Finally, the director strikes a pose and selects a sentence for himself or herself to say. (Sometimes the therapist may have the director select someone else to play his or her part in the family. The director then plays that person's part.)

When everyone is in place, the director gives the signal and the family, one person at a time, recites their lines. They continue to do so until the director signals them to stop. The family may be asked to raise or lower volume at the director's request. Without leaving their positions, family members are asked to talk about how it feels to be saying the lines they have been given. It is not significant at this point whether they agree or disagree with the position and sentence they have been saying. The therapist should take care not to allow the discussion to degenerate into a debate on whether or not the director's perceptions are correct. What is important is how everyone feels in their appointed positions and saying their appointed lines. The exercise may end at this point and the family return to their seats and process what the experience meant to them. Or the therapist may ask the director to reposition the family and assign new sentences that reflect what the director would like to see in the family. In either case, the family needs to have time to talk about the exercise after it is concluded.

Sculpting is usually a very powerful technique to help reveal hidden patterns of family interactions. The discussion provides an opportunity for family members to become aware of many of the less obvious structural and dynamic aspects of the family. It also has the advantage of helping family members bring to the surface emotions they might otherwise have trouble getting in touch with.

Learning to play and have fun.   Codependent families are generally families that do not have much fun together. They have limited ways to get joy out of life. The therapist may want to help them discover ways to have fun together. An exercise that is fruitful in this regard is to encourage family members to talk about what they would like to do for fun. Frequently, children ask parents to share more about their work. This request is ordinarily predicated on the intuition of children that parents place great importance on their work and is an appeal by the children to be included in what is important to the parents. It can lead to a discussion of ways parents can involve their children in the more meaningful elements of their lives.

For example, Delbert, a compulsive codependent, loved his work as an advertising account executive. He did not enjoy playing games with his fourteen-year-old son. When his son said that he would like to know more about Delbert's work, he opened up a natural avenue for Delbert and his son to be together and have fun at the same time. They talked more about the work of the advertising world. Delbert took his son with him to his office and even took him on a trip or two that involved his work.

One therapist friend reported that she has families fill out a list called, "Ten Things I Enjoy Doing." As part of this exercise, she has them code each item on the list to indicate whether they prefer to do the item alone, with family members, or with people outside the family. After they have completed the list, the family discusses what they have written.

Involving younger children.   In an article in which he appeals to all family therapists to involve children in the therapy process, Keith (1986, p. 3) asserts that children are the guide to the family unconscious. They see through the facade that the parents and the therapist want to present, and they help us get in touch with what is really going on. Keith's point is that the mere presence of children in the session can be therapeutic for the family. The actions of the child can reveal much about the nature of the family and about what is going on in the session. Keith relates the following experience:

> A therapist worked with a 4-year-old autistic boy and his parents for nearly a year. The boy was making loud kissing noises as he played in the corner behind the sofa. The therapist was suddenly aware of his strong feelings of affection for the mother at that moment. The child was able to sneak in behind the therapist's professional face.

Normal preschoolers allow their emotions to operate in a natural fashion. They are less inhibited than their older counterparts, and their feelings are much closer to the surface. Older children from codependent families, along with their parents, have learned to evaluate the appropriateness of emotions. They therefore attempt to hide the emotions they perceive their system regards as invalid.

Simply observing the interaction of parents and the small child can be helpful. Wyckoff and Unell (1984, p. 1) write, "At their best, preschoolers are curious, inventive, eager, and independent. At their worst, they are obstinate, inhibited, and clinging." The therapist may simply note at which end of this continuum the child is more frequently found. How does each parent relate to the child and how does that seem to correlate with the self-perception of the parent? The counselor looks for patterns and how these fit into the family as a system.

It is important not to ignore the small child's emotions. If a child is demonstrating an emotion, the counselor may ask the parent to talk with the child about it. Physical closeness is always good, and the therapist may want to suggest that the parent sit close to the child or touch the child while the child talks. The counselor may also need to encourage the parents to open up and share their feelings with the child. Frequently, parents in codependent families are unaware of the important effect of modeling healthy emotional openness for the child.

Now let us turn our attention to how the therapist can help the adult child in individual therapy.

REFERENCES

Andolfi, M., Angelo, C., Menghi, P., Nicoló-Corigliano, A., (Translated by Chodorkoff, C.) (1983). *Behind the Family Mask: Therapeutic Change in Rigid Family Systems*, New York: Brunner/Mazel.

Bernard, C., and Corrales, R. (1979). *The Theory and Technique of Family Therapy*, Springfield, Ill.: Charles C Thomas.

Dorn, L., with P. Eldridge-Martin. (1983). *Peace in the Family: A Workbook of Ideas and Actions*, New York: Pantheon.

Gravitz, H., and Bowden, J. (1985). *Guide to Recovery: A Book For Adult Children of Alcoholics*, Holmes Beach, Fla.: Learning Publications.

Keith, D. (1986). "Are Children Necessary in Family Therapy?" in L. Combrinck-Graham, Ed., *Treating Young Children in Family Therapy*, Rockville, Md.: Aspen.

Minuchin, S. (1974). *Families and Family Therapy*, Cambridge, Mass.: Harvard University Press.

Whitfield, C, (1987). *Healing the Child Within: Discovery and Recovery for Adult Children of Dysfunctional Families*, Pompano Beach, Fla.: Health Communications,.

Wyckoff J., and Unell, B. (1984). *Discipline Without Shouting or Spanking: Practical Solutions to the Most Common Preschool Behavior Problems*, New York: Meadowbrook.

10

CORE ISSUES OF THE ADULT CHILD IN INDIVIDUAL THERAPY

David Keith (1986, p. 4) describes the case of Joan, a twenty-one-year old client whose parents brought her in for treatment. Joan was obese. The parents treated Joan as if she were ten years old, but they described their family as being perfectly normal. In the middle of the second interview, Joan handed the therapist a picture she had drawn of an oversized bug in a landscape. At the center of the bug was a small door, one by two inches. The door flipped open to reveal a little bug, a replica of the big bug. According to Keith, the message of the picture was that, in Joan's mind, a tender little girl lived hidden in the midst of the pseudo big girl.

Joan's problems are an apt description of the essence of codependence. She saw herself as an overstuffed "bug," a powerful metaphor that conveyed simultaneously her perception of how her parents saw her and of how she saw herself. It further conveyed her self-feelings about that perception. Joan despised that useless bug. Joan also saw that this painful description of herself was somehow not what she really was. The reality was hidden deep inside. But Joan did not know how to get free to let the reality out.

Working with codependents is the process of getting them to see that the outward perception is not the reality. Inside lives a child. Whitfield (1987, p. 9) states that this inner child is the person's true self. The problem is that the child has a family past that is still powerful and continues to affect the person's life in destructive ways. Getting that child free of the family's detrimental influence is what codependent therapy is all about.

Sandy's experience demonstrates how powerful the past can be and how deeply buried these destructive patterns are in our lives.   Sandy, a forty-one-year-old daughter of a very enmeshed and abusive family, was an overresponsible, compulsive, and histrionic codependent. Her father, a physician, had physically abused her and her three younger brothers. The mother was emotionally unavailable but present in the abuse as a controlling and judging agent. Both parents were alcoholics. There was some evidence that the father sexually abused Sandy, although she had not been able to bring any memories of actual sexual activity up to the conscious level.

The parents made all family members extensions of themselves. Sandy had no sense of boundaries between herself and other members of her family. On the other hand, the parents rigidly set the family apart from the environment. Father and mother both taught the children that they could trust no one outside the family.

Sandy's family could be described as chaotic and enmeshed, and Sandy was having great trouble separating emotionally. At the time I saw her, her mother had died of a heart attack and she had cut off all contact with her father for more than three years. The only communication she had with her brothers was a telephone conversation with them at Christmas.

Yet, she continued to have vivid and dramatic dreams that frequently involved her in some activity with her parents and brothers. These dream activities most frequently took place at her parents' home. Usually the dreams contained a motif that demonstrated the father's violent and destructive control over her and her mother's distant disapproval. A year of individual therapy and participation in twelve-step support programs produced enormous changes in Sandy. She improved in her self-feelings and in her behaviors. She achieved an inner harmony and serenity that was energized by deep spiritual experiences. But the dreams continued. Then Sandy reported the following dream:

> I dreamed that I bought this big house in Crystal Lake where I lived as a child. It was lovely, with big rooms and hardwood floors and the sun shining through the windows on the first floor. I bought the house not to live there but to rent. There were Madonnas and dolls, all different, in different places in the house. Some were pretty; some were plain. Then a nice, attractive lady, whom someone said was a peacemaker in Washington, came to get her things. She had several beautiful daughters. I gave them two weeks to move which was more than they needed.

> I think this dream shows that I am getting comfortable with the little girl in me (the dolls) and the woman in me (the Madonnas and the peacemaker woman who is moving out). I am going back to my parents' neighborhood where I was a child to learn about being a girl and a woman. *But I don't live there anymore.* The house is a rent house, an investment that will profit me.

> Lately as I travel, I look for dolls and Madonnas. Over a year ago, I got a little doll and named her Sandy Diane, the name of my favorite childhood doll. She has helped me get in touch with the child in me. I was able to celebrate Mother's

Day this year for the first time in my life. Recently I saw a plaque that said, "I love Mom." I almost bought it because it communicated my love and acceptance of myself. I am the Mom I love. All this shows the tremendous self-acceptance and healing that is taking place in my life. I think my dream means that I have moved out of my father's house. *That is not where I live anymore*!

The goal of all codependent therapy is aptly stated in Sandy's last sentence. Therapy helps the adult child to move out of the past and leave behind the self-limiting patterns of thought and feeling that are the result of the dysfunctional family. This chapter offers suggestions about doing psychotherapy with adult children in private, individual sessions to bring that goal about. The nature of codependence is such that, as described in previous chapters, it is amenable to both group and family therapy. Effective therapy can also be done with codependents in individual sessions. This chapter helps to familiarize the therapist with the core issues with which the adult child must deal to overcome the destructive influences of the past.

THE NATURE OF INDIVIDUAL THERAPY

Effective therapy with the codependent must center on several matters in the adult child's life. Previous chapters have covered many of these questions as they relate to group and family therapy. This section considers these issues from the perspective of individual sessions.

According to Sugarman (1986, p. 1), individual therapy can occur in the midst of group or family therapy. In his thinking, individual therapy does not refer to how many persons are in the room when the therapy occurs. Rather, individual therapy happens when the primary unit of analysis is a single person. Thus, Sugarman perceives as individual therapy any process of assessment, diagnosis, and outcome measurement that has the person as its focus.

While I concur that individual therapy can and does go on in group and family settings, that is not the emphasis of this chapter. Sugarman wants to highlight what he calls the "interface" of individual and family therapy. That is, how can we use the methods of one when we are engaged in the other? No such question will occupy our attention in this chapter.

Rather, we will conceive of individual therapy in this chapter in a more traditional manner. That is, the therapist meets with the individual alone for the purpose of helping the individual understand, cope, and change so as to lead a more healthy life.

CORE ISSUES IN INDIVIDUAL THERAPY

The following are some of the concerns that emerge when the therapist works with the codependent in individual sessions. These have been addressed in earlier chapters in connection with other topics. Our interest in these chapters is in considering these issues as they apply to individual therapy.

Childhood Roles

Children habituate behaviors that help them to function in their families and in life in general. These learned and habitual behaviors are like roles in a play. In the healthy family, the roles lead to a mature and adjusted adult. Just the opposite is true of the dysfunctional family. The roles the child learns in order to survive a sick family most frequently are self-destructive in the long run. In dysfunctional families, roles *disguise* the individual's most urgent needs. They become the mask under which the true self is hidden. Wegscheider (1981, pp. 104–149) summarizes four such roles. She calls them the *hero*, the *scapegoat*, the *lost child*, and the *mascot*. Let us look at each of these roles and see how each applies to individual therapy.

The family hero.   The person who plays the hero role engages in compulsively successful behaviors that are designed to make the family look good in the community. Children who play this role are overachieving people-pleasers who are super-responsible. This child gets attention by being what adults expect. Therefore, he or she is usually a miniadult who accomplishes much in school, in the community, and in church. This child tries to present the image of being perfect.

Hero children grow up to be what Chapter Four described as *the over-responsible codependent* and *the compulsive codependent*. These codependents seek positive attention for themselves. They become enablers for other people. They are perfectionistic, compulsive, and manipulative. They exhibit passive aggressiveness and have trouble with intimacy. They sacrifice themselves for others and yet cannot get enough attention for themselves.

In adulthood they continue the zealous caretaking and overresponsible behaviors they practiced as children. They get a sense of personal worth from being perfect and from giving others what they need. Thus, they feel responsible for everyone around them. They get their feelings of being loved by serving others. They do not feel loved unless they are working to take care of someone else's problems.

Gil is a hero child. A fifty-one-year-old college professor, Gil works long hours and expects no rewards for doing so. He is sensitive to other people's needs and is always making sure that everyone is comfortable. Gil is devastated when anyone criticizes him. On the surface, Gil is a loving and concerned person whose life and work are nearly perfect. Underneath, Gil is angry because he senses that everyone overlooks his needs. But, to admit his anger or ask that his needs be met is more than Gil can manage. To do so threatens the hero role he has always played. Gil does not know what to do.

The goal of therapy for the overresponsible and the compulsive codependent is to help them accept themselves as they are and to learn to take responsibility for themselves, not for others. Some of the signs of recovery for this type of adult child are to ask for help, admit mistakes, admit negative feelings, and learn to say no.

The scapegoat.   The family scapegoat is the child who acts out the family's problem. He or she is the opposite of the family hero. This is a defiant child who is hostile and has "behavior problems." He or she engages in openly deviant behaviors in an effort to get negative attention. As an adult, this person may be addicted to a chemical substance. He or she may be financially irresponsible and have poor coping skills in the face of life's pressures. This person continues to bear the family shame in the self-destructive life style he or she follows.

The scapegoat child typically grows up to be the *antisocial/narcissistic codependent* referred to in Chapter Four. The defiance and hostility may come out in harsh, insensitive behaviors that may produce financial success. The scapegoat grows up to thrive on competition and actually seek negative attention that comes in his or her perception that others feel inferior and jealous.

Margie was the family scapegoat. She grew up to be a "loser." Twice pregnant by different men before marriage, Margie worked as a secretary in a law firm. She was hospitalized for depression and drug use before she finished high school. Her father was an Episcopal priest, intellectual but aloof. Her mother was obese and very angry. Margie had a string of affairs with older, married men. She wanted to "settle down and get married."

Cliff was another scapegoat child. He demonstrated his defiance as a teenager by following his alcoholic and abusive father's example. He drank a lot, wrecked several cars, got in trouble a couple of times with the law, and got at least one girl pregnant. At twenty, he became interested in making money. He opened a sign painting business in a neighbor's garage. He had a talent for this work and his business prospered. Cliff invested his profits in real estate. By the time he was thirty, he was a wealthy man. Cliff was brash, harsh, sarcastic, and cruel. He hid his pain by being a success and flaunting it in the presence of others.

Antisocial/narcissistic codependents rarely come into therapy. When they do, the major goal is to help them develop a sense of trust. They need to know that they can be what they are and do not need to seek negative attention. But, it is difficult to break through their wall of bravado and help them lose their suspicions of other people. Recovery signs for antisocial/narcissistic adult children are to admit mistakes without blaming others, to accept the consequences of their behavior, to develop a sense of humor about themselves, and to begin to accept compliments.

The lost child.   The lost child learns to withdraw from the emotional chaos of family life. If this child cannot actually get away physically by leaving the scene, he or she shuts down all emotion. Wegscheider-Cruse (1984, p. 2) calls this withdrawal a "cope-through-avoidance" defense that leaves the individual isolated from the joy and richness of life. This child feels unloved and unworthy of love. He or she learns to run away from those situations that cause pain.

The lost child grows up to be either the *schizoid/avoidant* or the *paranoid codependent* discussed in Chapter Four. The loneliness and need to run away show up in the adult as superindependence and aloofness. This adult child exhibits a flat affect. Any attempt to have fun may be nothing but an effort to copy what others are doing. The individual has successfully avoided vulnerability, but at an enormous cost; he or she feels cut off and isolated.

Tina always hid when her mother and father fought. She went into her closet and closed the door. Later, when she could not get away, she learned to tune them out. Soon, no one ever even seemed to notice her. Now as an adult, she could adjust to any situation. At the office or at home with her husband and kids, she just held her emotions in and no one paid her any attention. Tina was a lost child.

Courage to become involved in the social environment is the major need of the schizoid/avoidant and paranoid adult child. Recovery signs are to start talking, to begin identifying feelings, to begin to demonstrate feelings, to disagree with significant others openly, and to ask for what they need.

The mascot. The function of this person in the family is to provide comic relief. As a child, the person is cute. He or she gets attention as the family clown at whom everyone laughs. The laughter disguises deeper emotions like anger and fear.

As an adult, the person attempts to remain the center of attention by entertaining. Thus, the mascot child grows up to be what Chapter Four called the *histrionic codependent*. This person tries to get attention by being cute. He or she may continue to dress and act like a child. The mascot may try to be funny but has no real sense of humor. Mascots do not entertain; they make fools of themselves. More frequently than not, they are seen as pests by others. They have "incongruent humor"—that is—they laugh at things that are not funny.

Denny was a mascot in his family. At thirty-one, he lived alone with his cat, Nobody. He tried to be funny any time he sensed anxiety in a situation. At parties, he dominated anyone who would listen by telling stories that only he would laugh at. Denny tried also to get people to like him by ingratiation. He complimented everybody for everything. He never disagreed with anyone. Denny wanted friends, but people avoided him. Denny tried to kill himself when he was in high school. He had always regretted that he had failed. In the session in which he revealed his suicide attempt, he said, "I'm so screwed up I can't even kill myself." Denny's laughter was unconvincing.

Histrionic adult children need to learn that they do not need to protect themselves by entertaining and making others happy. They do not need to continue to be the center of attention. Recovery signs for the histrionic codependent are insightful comments, owning feelings, taking oneself seriously, disagreeing with others, and asking others for help.

Black discusses (1981, pp. 16–27) the same four roles. She calls the hero the responsible one. She calls the scapegoat the acting-out child. Her term for the lost child is the adjuster. Finally, for her, the mascot is the placater.

I have found it helpful in individual therapy to get some idea of the role the codependent is playing in life. Most people are a combination of more than one and will go from one to another according to the situation. However, each has a dominant orientation that fits one of these roles. When we determine which of these outward masks the individual has chosen to wear, it makes the task of freeing the inner child easier. Positioning the individual in one of these roles also helps to draw a clearer picture of the nature of the dysfunctionality of the person's family.

Denial, Deception, and Dishonesty

In childhood codependents learn several methods of avoiding truth as much as possible. The therapist must be aware of these dishonest methods in order to help the adult child change the self-destructive life style he or she developed in childhood. But of equal importance is that the therapist be aware of these denial patterns in the therapy itself. The past is painful, and individuals are unsure of their ability to handle it. Changing present ways of thinking, acting, and feeling can be a frightening thing to do. Becoming responsible for oneself and giving up responsibility for others means restructuring all of one's close relationships. Denial and deception are effective ways of avoiding doing the therapeutic work that the adult child must do. Let us look at some of the adult child's reasons for deceit and denial in therapy.

Avoiding truth. Adult children use denial because they want to avoid the truth. To do so, they deliberately deceive. That is, they say things that are not so. "Who me? Angry? Of course I'm not angry," they say when asked if they are angry. "Whatever you want is okay with me. I want to do what you expect of me," they respond when asked for a preference. "I am really enjoying myself," they comment, when in reality they are not. "I am really getting a lot out of therapy. You sure are a skilled counselor," they comment when leaving a session.

Avoiding conflict. Codependents have learned to lie to avoid unpleasantness and conflict. "I was sick" is a useful excuse to avoid the truth that the adult child did not want to participate or was unprepared or was too afraid to face a situation. Once the lie is set in motion, an extensive coverup becomes necessary to keep the charade going. Woititz (1983, p. 31) tells about Joan, a twenty-six-year-old counselor who had trouble with lying. Joan wrote:

> I used to make up stories in order to be noticed, I think, and I think I feel bad that I didn't get caught, because if people had talked to me, and listened to me, and known me, they would have known that I was bullshitting, and I was really good at it. I'd start out faking being sick sometimes, and then get really sick. I was really an expert at it. It was so much easier to do that than to say that I just couldn't do what others could do. I felt like it would be terrible not to be able to cut it, I'd lose face. It was sad, though, and I didn't like doing it. There was always this panic about being caught....It seemed to me that I didn't believe I could keep it up. I just didn't know how to do it, and then I would start making things up. It gets very complicated.

Avoiding self-disclosure. All the lying is designed to help the adult child avoid self-disclosure. In his or her dysfunctional family, the child learned that letting others see what is going on leads to pain. R. D. Laing (1970, p. 1) illustrates in poetry the child's view of lying in a dysfunctional family:

> They are playing a game. They are playing at not playing a game. If I show them
> I see they are, I shall break the rules and they will punish me. I must play their
> game, of not seeing I see the game.

Avoiding responsibility.   Adult children hide the truth to avoid taking responsibility for themselves. Then they are surprised when they are told that what they are doing is dishonest. For example, Ann told me that she had been invited on a weekend trip to Mexico with a man to whom she was attracted. "I was afraid to go, but I told him I had to work." "So you lied to him," I responded. She looked confused, like I had hit her, and she did not know why. "Well," she finally said, "I guess that is what you call it when you tell something that is not the truth."

Avoiding pain.   In life, adult children have learned to avoid confrontation and protect themselves from the risk of rejection and abandonment by hiding the truth about themselves. They remain silent and bury their feelings. They deny the reality of a situation by making excuses for the other person's behavior. "He's just tired," "She's having a hard day," "The weather's too hot to be polite." They make similar excuses for their own behavior. "I don't want to say that to him because it would hurt him," they say. The truth is that they really want to avoid the risk of making the other person angry at them.

In therapy, the adult child practices the same denial. "Let's don't deal with this because it causes too much pain," they say. They have learned to use denial to avoid pain in their dysfunctional families. Just so, they will use denial to stay away from the pain of truth in therapy.

Robby, an overresponsible and compulsive codependent, is an example. He came in to see me to talk about whether he loved his wife of eleven years. He was thinking about leaving her and his three children. Robby was the problem solver in the family and felt responsible for everybody. A blue-collar worker who was very religious, Robby felt a lot of guilt about his unsure feelings toward his wife. He especially felt guilty about leaving his children. In the opening phase of the first session, as I was collecting information about his social history, Robby told me that his parents were divorced when he was six. Later in the interview, when I returned to that subject to explore its implications, Robby said, "Look here, that happened over twenty-five years ago. I don't need to talk about that and I am not paying you my money to go into the useless parts of my history." We worked for six unsatisfactory sessions during which Robby consistently refused to discuss his father's divorce from his mother. He finally left therapy saying that it was not helping him.

Learning to Trust

Trusting the self.   The adult child has grown up in a family in which emotions were discounted. That is, the family did not pay attention to the child's emotions.

Furthermore, people did not do what they promised. Moods swung wildly and unpredictably. What nurturing did occur came sporadically and with no consistency. Frequently, decisions were left hanging, with no final resolution. Important things happened, like death or a geographic move or some sudden conflict in the family, and no one ever sat down with the child to talk about what it all meant. Children who grow up in such an atmosphere do not develop trust in their own ability to know what is occurring and to make decisions for themselves. They have experienced their personal world as an elusive and changing and untrustworthy place. They have no sense of personal competency in that world. Fossum and Mason (1986, p. 100) say that such a child grows up "tossing their hat into every door before entering." That is, the adult child lives life very tentatively.

Patty is an example. A thirty-seven-year-old schoolteacher, Patty had been divorced for seven years. She had no children. She was an attractive woman who related well with men but could establish no long-term relationship. Both her father and mother had been alcoholics. Her father had died drunk in an automobile accident and her mother lived alone in Chicago. Patty rarely saw her.

Patty wanted to go to the seminary. To do so would mean giving up the security of her job. She felt uncertain and confused because she did not know what she would do with a seminary degree. She didn't even know why she wanted to go, but she had been "agonizing over it for three years." "I think God wants me to go," Patty declared, "but I can't separate God's voice from my own. I can't trust myself even to know what I want, to say nothing about doing it."

Trusting others. The conditions that cause the adult child to lack trust in his or her own self contribute to the inability to trust others. The whole family system of denial and duplicity leads the child to the inevitable conclusion that others are not to be believed. Excuses that cover up adult behavior may exonerate the adult, but they leave the lasting impression on the child that the world is a deceitful place. Physical abuse is redefined as punishment that is "for the child's good." Overeating is having a "sweet tooth." Hangovers are the "twenty-four-hour flu." Sexual abuse is being a "dirty old man." Sometimes enmeshed parents explicitly teach a child that the outside world is evil in order to keep the child dependent on them. All this deceit is further complicated by the "No talk" rule, which means that the child has no one who can help deal with the confusion that he or she feels. Family secrets must be protected. Having no one with whom to talk further reinforces the child's conclusion that there is no one to trust.

Shannon shows how hard it is to learn to trust. She is the young woman whose story appears at the beginning of Chapter One of this book. Her father committed suicide and she was later sexually abused by a stepfather. Her mother was lost in her own alcoholism and not available at that time to help her work her way through the problems. Shannon learned that people are distant, that they will hurt you, and that they will let you down. Four months into therapy, she wrote the following:

I went to a wedding yesterday. Maybe that's the reason that I'm so sad. Seeing someone so happy makes me realize how empty I am. I am incomplete, so alone. I try to be outgoing, more friendly. But I still come home alone. I still sleep by myself. I have no one to be close to me, to love and care for me. There is no one whom I can love and care for. I know that I am a special person. The problem is that no one else has found that out yet. I have tried to make them see but it's too hard. *They do not want to see.* And I don't know how to make them. I am ready to give up.

Shannon cannot believe that other people will ever be there for her. "They do not want to see" is her evaluation of how much she can trust other people.

Establishing Boundaries

Most of the adult children with whom I have worked have problems with boundaries. The only notable exceptions are the *antisocial/narcissistic codependents.* All other types have overt problems with boundaries. The problem is that they do not have the ability to determine where others end and they begin. They lack a clear sense of their own emotional and spiritual perimeters. Intimacy is confused with fusion. For the codependent, to be close to a person is to be like that person in values, attitudes, and behavior. When this fusion occurs, one of two undesirable things happens: (1) Codependents change to make themselves like other people. Cermak (1986, p. 18) refers to this condition as the codependent becoming a mirror; (2) codependents try to control other people into becoming a carbon copy of themselves. They say, in essence, "If you love me, you will become like me."

When there are no personal boundaries, any potential change in the partner is seen as a threat to the codependent's identity. The feeling of not being loved emerges as the codependent defines the relationship in terms of enmeshment. The codependent seems to be saying, "If you change, you are abandoning me."

April was a schizoid/avoidant codependent. She suffered great anxiety because she had no sense of clear boundaries. A twenty-five-year-old, very introverted young woman, she lived a few blocks from her forty-nine-year-old mother and stepfather. It was her mother's third marriage and according to April, it was not a happy relationship. Another divorce seemed imminent. April described her mother as a "dry drunk." That is, she was a person who had given up alcohol but had not dealt with the reasons that she had become an alcoholic.

April began a session by announcing that she was angry at her mother. It was a mock anger that had no real feeling behind it. She explained that she had been helping her mother move, and her mother had called her a bitch because she wasn't packing things as her mother had told her. As we talked, April continued to uncover anger at being used by her mother. It became evident that April had served as the parental child to her mother through the mother's years of distress and problems. April wept softly as she described her mother's pain in her struggle with alcoholism and during divorce. When I asked if April would consider giving up her responsibility for her mother, she responded, "She has no one to turn to except me. If I turn away from her, there will be no one to look after her. She needs me and I must help her." April saw herself as an extension of her mother. She had no existence, no feelings or needs outside her mother.

Overcoming Self-doubt and Establishing Autonomy

Self-doubt for adult children is the feeling that they have no control over their lives. People who suffer the loss of control experience the world as overwhelming and themselves as unable to effectively direct their own life. For them, the world has no order or organization. It is unpredictable and makes no sense. For such a person the world is unfair and they are unprotected in the face of life's vicissitudes. Their fortunes go up and down in a random fashion over which they seem to have no control. What they do does not produce the effects they desire.

Suppose one night a young woman senses that a strange man is following her on her way home from the bus stop. She has always felt safe on the well-lighted streets of her part of town. Tonight, because she is being followed, she feels alone and afraid. She hears the quick footsteps behind her and feels that her would-be attacker is getting closer. Panic-stricken, she can no longer restrain her fear. She screams and runs desperately to her apartment. She makes it home safely, but she is convinced that she was being pursued and no argument can persuade her differently. After this episode, she is never the same again. From that point onward, she does not feel safe out alone at night. She has lost the sense that she can control her life and her safety. Although she was unhurt in a physical way, she feels vulnerable and afraid, as though she has no power over what is happening to her.

Codependents frequently have this impression of being out of control. Their sense of powerlessness arises in the unpredictable nature of the family in which they grew up. Goodwin (1972) has shown that a positive correlation exists between powerlessness scores of mothers and their sons. Renshon (1974) found the same positive association on powerlessness in college students and their parents.

Thus, it is no surprise that codependents report the experience of self-doubt. Some say that they live with a sense of dread that some catastrophe is about to occur. These feelings come when they think that things are going well or when they realize they do not have something to worry about. When things are going well, they expect them to go badly. Others simply have a constant dull feeling that life is slowly swallowing them and there is nothing they can do to save themselves. For others, self-doubt comes out as the belief that they will never have what they need. Still others believe that they will have to do things they do not want to do to get the things they want.

Responses to self-doubt vary. Some codependents become hostile and bitter. Brehm and Brehm (1981) report that anger is a normal response to the feeling of powerlessness. The self-doubt that began as a child for the codependent in his or her family can result in a cynical bitterness. Consider Mary. She had been married three times and her present husband was nine years older than she. He was a carpenter and handyman who did not provide for her as she wished. She berated him for his ineptness.

Mary was afraid of getting old. Somewhat attractive, Mary had always tried to ensure a relationship with a man by her sexiness and physical beauty. Now she was growing old and losing the one thing which she felt protected her from being without a man and thus alone. She had grown up with an alcoholic mother and a father who was never home. One of her mother's constant sayings was, "You can't trust men." Consequently, Mary never did. That is, she refused to be vulnerable and real with a man because she believed that he would leave her, as her father left her and her mother. She was cynical and harsh with Don, her quiet and devoted husband. "Life has brought me nothing but pain," she said angrily. "I will never get what I want. Fuck it."

Another response to self-doubt is apathy and hopelessness. Seligman (1975) has demonstrated that the loss of a sense of personal control over one's life can lead to what he calls "learned helplessness." In the codependent person, hopelessness leads to a lack of motivation and a deterioration in performance. Poor performance, in turn, leads to a greater sense of helplessness. The adult child defines the situation as a function of his or her *character*. That is, what is going on is a result of the codependent's inherent inability to do anything right. The result is more helplessness and apathy, which keeps the whole negative cycle going.

Surmounting Self-blame

After an unpleasant event occurs in life, people try to determine an acceptable answer to the question, "Why did this happen to me?" When they do, they are making *attributions*. Few people appear uninterested in the question of Why. Determining what caused an event helps us to put it into perspective and to accept it. Thus, making attributions appears to be a universal human trait.

According to Sears and researchers (1988, p. 118), the central issue in answering the question about why something happened is the "locus of causality." That is, was the act caused by an *internal* state or by an *external* force? Internal states include all causes inside the person: moods, attitudes, personality traits, abilities, health, preferences, or wishes. External forces are causes outside the person, such as pressure from others, the nature of the situation, factors over which others have control, and the weather. Thus, an internal attribution for failing a test would be "I am stupid." An external attribution for the same event would be "The professor's lectures were ambiguous."

Codependents have a proclivity for internal attributions. They blame themselves when things go wrong. They think they are responsible for whatever happens in their own life and in the lives of others. One therapist friend of mine describes the codependent's penchant for self-blame by saying that they feel they are responsible for the rust on the Statue of Liberty. If anything is not perfect in their life or environment, they are sure it is because of something that is wrong with them.

Jackie is an example. The attractive twenty-nine-year-old wife of a lawyer, Jackie had never been to college. Very involved in social causes, she hid her childhood shame behind her highly energized life style. "I really want to go to college," she said one day. I asked what kept her from going. "I'm terrible at English," she sighed. I asked her to consider saying that in a different way. "Would you say, 'English is not an easy or good subject for me'? That sentence describes something about English. Your first sentence is a put-down of you." She laughed with resignation and commented, "I am *terrible* at English."

According to Michener and coauthors (1986, p. 251), individuals who consistently make internal attributions suffer long-lasting negative effects. They blame their own enduring character traits and see the results as stable and unchangeable. Peterson (1981, pp. 253–259) found that these persons are more easily depressed. They give up more easily and have a greater sense of despair about the future. If, however, the individual finds external causes for unpleasant events, he or she is more likely to interpret them as temporary, and therefore the individual is more likely to continue to strive for change.

Les helps us to see the connection between self-blame and the dysfunctional family. He was a seminary student who had always played the hero role in his family and in life in general. His father was an alcoholic, and his mother was a rigidly religious person who depended on Les to get her through her trials with his father. "She used to say, 'I would have left him a long time ago if it weren't for you kids.' That made me feel so responsible," Les confessed. For this young man, like so many other codependents, his mother's unthinking statement was translated into self-blame.

Accepting Personal Limitations and Conquering Omnipotence

As noted above, codependents feel that they have lost control of their lives and that they are to blame for all the bad things that happen to them. They have a sense of being worthless. At the other extreme of the continuum, they feel that they have unusual power to control events and make others happy. Walter is an example. He combined the qualities of the overresponsible codependent and the schizoid/avoidant codependent. Forty years old and recently divorced, Walter was afraid that he would never find a woman who would genuinely love and respect him. He had struggled with intimate relationships since childhood. In high school and in college, he had never dated much. In fact, he had never had any close friends. He married a woman when he was twenty-three. She was the first person who had paid any attention to him.

After his divorce, Walter found that he was not able to break off relationships. He could not bring himself to tell the women who expressed interest in him that he wanted to date other people. He strung them along with all kinds of explanations and promises that he never kept. Sometimes he would see a woman for the purpose of telling her that he was not going to see her again, and they would end up spending the evening together. Once he had two dates on one evening because he could not say no to either one.

"I just don't want to hurt them," was Walter's honest explanation of his motivation for this behavior. Walter suffered from an awesome case of omnipotence. He felt that he had the power to make these women very happy by falling in love with them. He could make life complete for them and they would be content to have him. Their pursuit of him indicated how much they wanted him. He could not do such a cruel thing as tell them that he was not interested in a total commitment to them. That would devastate them. In Walter's view, he held the key to their lives.

Developing a Sense of Humor

Adult children are typically superserious. They were frequently assigned adult responsibilities while still quite young. As a result, they often have no memory of themselves acting like children. Many report that they always felt like an adult. Therefore, it is important that they develop a healthy sense of humor and to learn to have fun. Somehow they must recapture the spirit of that lost childhood. Usually, this goal comes in the later stages of therapy, because they have to learn to get in touch with a lot of pain and to take their loss seriously. In the normal process of recovery, grief comes before relaxation and fun. But at an appropriate point, the therapist must start the process of helping adult children to loosen up and take themselves less seriously.

Some pressure is removed when the codependent individual realizes that others are not that dependent on him or her. When he or she establishes boundaries and then sees that others do not cease to exist by this action, the adult child can say, "Hey, I'm not that powerful." That feels good and can help the codependent to relax a little.

It also helps to begin to give the codependent permission to do spontaneous and impulsive things. "Letting out the kid in you," is a neat term by which the codependent can begin the difficult task of understanding what fun and relaxation are all about. This statement also strengthens the resolve of the adult child to have fun. After all, through many years, life has stifled and repressed the natural playfulness of this child. This restraint has nearly squelched the child's spirit. Who can deny the child the right to fun and uninhibited joy?

These are some of the concerns with which we must deal in working with the adult child in individual therapy. They become the guiding forces of the sessions with the adult child. Now, let us look at some of the methods of intervention that are at the disposal of the counselor to work with these and similar matters.

REFERENCES

Black, C. (1981). *It Will Never Happen to Me*, Denver, Colo.: M.A.C.
Brehm, S., and Brehm, J. (1981). *Psychological Reactance: A Theory of Freedom and Control*, New York: Academic Press.

Cermak, T. (1986). *Diagnosing and Treating Co-dependence*, Minneapolis: Johnson Institute Books.

Fossum, M., and Mason, M. (1986). *Facing Shame: Families in Recovery*, New York: W. W. Norton.

Goodwin, L. (1972). *Do the Poor Want to Work?* Washington: Brookings Institute.

Keith, D. (1986). "Are Children Necessary in Family Therapy?" in L. Combrinck-Graham, *Treating Young Children in Family Therapy*, Rockville, Md.: Aspen.

Laing, R. (1970). *Knots*, New York: Pantheon.

Laing, R. (1972). *The Politics of the Family and Other Essays*, New York: Vintage Books.

Michener, A., Delamater, J., and Schwartz, S. (1986). *Social Psychology*, New York: Harcourt, Brace, Jovanovich.

Peterson, C. (1981). "Self-blame and Depressive Symptoms," *Journal of Personality and Social Psychology*, 41, 253–259

Renshon, S. (1974). *Psychological Needs and Political Behavior: A Theory of Personality and Political Efficacy*, New York: Free Press.

Sears, D., Peplau, L., Freedman, J., and Taylor, S. (1988). *Social Psychology* (6th ed.), Englewood Cliffs, N.J.: Prentice-Hall.

Seligman, C. (1975). *Helplessness: On Depression, Development, and Death*, San Francisco: Freeman.

Sugarman, S. (1986). "Individual and Family Therapy: An Overview of the Interface," in S. Sugarman (Ed.), *The Interface of Individual and Family Therapy*, Rockville, Md.: Aspen.

Wegscheider, S. (1981). *Another Chance: Hope and Health for the Alcoholic Family*, Palo Alto, Calif.: Science and Behavior Books.

Wegscheider-Cruse, S. (1984). "Co-dependence: The Therapeutic Void," in *Co-dependency: An Emerging Issue*, Pompano Beach, Fla.: Health Communications.

Whitfield, C. (1987). *Healing the Child Within*, Pompano Beach, Fla.: Health Communications.

Woititz, J. (1983). *Adult Children of Alcoholics*, Pompano Beach, Fla.: Health Communications.

11

WORKING WITH THE ADULT CHILD IN INDIVIDUAL THERAPY

Sandy, whose story was introduced in the previous chapter, related the following dream as a breakthrough in her therapy. She was a physician's daughter who had been physically and psychologically abused in her very chaotic family. Both parents had been alcoholics and her father had a cruel streak that came out in totally unpredictable ways. Here is her account of the dream that had made such an impact on her:

> I was waiting for my turn to speak to a priest in a beautiful monastery with wide corridors, high ceilings, and walls covered with dark and rich wood. Just as I started into the room to see the priest, he changed the sign over the door to MOLESTED. I understood that he was now ready to see those who had been molested. I went in.
>
> As I talked to him, I related all the men who had molested me: my father was first on the list. The priest asked me to tell him about it. I described the waste, the injustice, the pain, and the enormous shame. I told him that I was damaged by the molestation. I told him that I felt sick, sad, and angry because of the loss of love, joy, peace, and sense of being alive.
>
> As I left the church, a very large lady was standing outside. She had been abused as a child and she was wailing in long, angry sobs. I went over to comfort her and she said that I should not try to stop her from crying.

This dream says that I must face the fact that I have been molested. I do not need to deny the pain but rather must grieve the loss which my dysfunctional family has cost me. I must cry, *wail* for the deep pain which I have suffered. But I am not just the lady outside the church, I am also the strong priest. I am able to help me to my own healing. The monastery was a holy place, beautiful and comforting. These are all parts of me that are there to help me feel the pain and grief until it goes away.

After I wrote down the dream, I found myself holding my doll close to my heart. I stayed there for awhile just holding that doll and comforting her. Then I realized that what I was telling that doll, I must be willing to tell the little child in me that was so beat up in my family. I have been unwilling to listen to the child and hear her pain. I have been trying to get her to stop crying. Now I will listen and believe her. We will get through this pain together.

Counseling with Sandy was one of the most pleasant experiences I have had in working with adult children. Not all cases are as easy to work with, nor are all concluded with such great change in the client. Although she was one of the most deeply hurt individuals I have ever personally worked with, Sandy was able to pull herself out of the abyss into which her dysfunctional family had thrown her. Her dream and her interpretation of it represents the desired goal toward which all codependent therapy moves.

This chapter offers suggestions of interventions the therapist may use in counseling with the adult child. Of course, these recommendations are in addition to all the normal tactics and strategies that therapists have at their disposal. They have been developed specifically with the adult child in mind.

THERAPEUTIC GOALS IN WORKING WITH INDIVIDUAL CLIENTS

The therapist must keep several specific objectives in mind in working in individual therapy with adult children. These goals are helpful in developing treatment strategies and are useful in evaluating how therapy is progressing. Among the goals of effective therapy are uncovering the past, clear thinking and understanding, hope, skill development, change, and detachment.

Uncovering the Past

Adults who grew up in dysfunctional families need to deal with the past. They must bring to the surface the pain of childhood that they too often pushed into their unconscious. These memories, like Sandy's, are typically very painful. To look at them, the adult child must break powerful family rules. Two such rules are "Don't feel" and "Don't tell others negative things about this family." Thus, the adult child tries to repress the past. They often say, "I just can't remember anything from my childhood." Sometimes they say, "I just don't see what good it does to dig these things up. They are in the past and I have them under control. Why disturb them?"

Clear Thinking and Understanding

Codependents need an understanding of where they are and how they got there. They need to see how the past still exists and influences the present.

Identification of Shaming Events

Adult children need help in clearly identifying events of the past that have shamed them. They need to name the abusive events. Sandy had to be willing to enter that room that was for molested persons before she could get healing. Typically, adult children seek to protect the persons who have hurt them by saying things like, "I had a really good family and my parents loved me the best they could. Who am I to criticize them?"

Hope

Adult children frequently need help in developing hope that they can change and that they can get their needs met. Sandy's dream was very positive because it reminded her not only of the pain but offered the optimism that she could deal with it and it would go away. To develop that hope, the adult child needs to understand reality and learn healthy methods of dealing with it.

Skill Development

Adult children need help in developing the skills necessary to have better relationships. They need to learn new rules of communication and they need to look at their own expectations. They need to learn how to differentiate between their needs and their wants.

Change

Codependents need help changing their own thinking, feeling, and acting patterns. They need practice and encouragement to try new things outside therapy. In individual therapy, they have no one other than the therapist with whom to experiment with innovative exercises. The therapist must be patient and gentle when they experience painful failures outside therapy.

Detachment

Adult children need to learn to detach and stop taking responsibility for other's feelings and behaviors. They need to quit being the hero and trying to fix others.

With these goals in mind, let us now look at specific intervention tactics that can help the adult child.

INTERVENTION TACTICS IN INDIVIDUAL THERAPY

Dealing with the Past

Facing the past honestly is hard work. It is also scary. It is especially difficult for the codependent because the past is the burial ground of the fears, threats, pain, and doubt that the codependent seeks to avoid. Indeed, the codependence itself is a defense designed to *protect the codependent from facing these unpleasant facts of his or her life.*

For some people, especially the more feeling types, remembering the past and grieving the hurt comes easier. The therapist gives permission and encouragement and they spill out the pain in the midst of a torrent of tears. When this occurs, the therapist must be aware that such emotional outpouring is necessary and good and not try in any way to stop it. Sometimes in our own fear of powerful emotions, we will try to "comfort" the client to stop the emotional release. When we do this, we are stopping the therapeutic effect of grieving.

Other clients may have a more difficult time getting to the repressed material of the past. The therapist must work with gentleness and patience at this point. Some people are more logical and rational in their approach to life. The therapist must not try to force these persons into a feeling role. They will get in touch with the emotions of the past much more slowly than feeling-oriented individuals. They try to be more analytical and controlled as they recall the past. The task of the therapist is to give permission, encouragement, and guidance.

I sometimes give the following to clients to help them get memories up to the conscious mind:

Tips for Remembering

1. Let the memories come on their own. Don't try to force them. That is, give yourself permission to remember. Sometimes it helps to stimulate the memory to look back through scrapbooks or picture albums. Or, sometimes it helps to talk with relatives or friends who knew you as a child. Or, if possible, you may want to visit the places in which you grew up.

2. Pay attention to glimpses. Memories do not always come back full blown. Sometimes they come in bits and pieces like a puzzle. Don't miss a memory simply because it doesn't tell the whole story.

3. Listen to your dreams. Dreams are a way the unconscious gets in touch with the conscious mind. Your dreams reveal the way you feel about yourself in your world and they can help you get in touch with the past. Write dreams down in a notebook and keep up with them over time. See if you can find patterns and trends in your dreams. Keep in mind that all persons and things in your dreams are really symbols of parts of yourself.

Getting in touch with the past is sometimes a little like fishing. One must believe that there are things under the surface, that they can be caught, and that the catch is worth the wait.

Telling One's Story

There is great therapeutic power when individuals simply describe what is happening to them today and what happened to them growing up. The adult child rarely has been in a situation in which he or she has felt free to describe life's experiences. There has always been too much shame or the fear of rejection or the belief that the other person will not be interested. It comes as a great relief to be listened to and accepted as the individual says, in effect, "This is me."

Telling one's story should not be thought of as restricted to a single incident. That is, the client may tell part in one session and another part in another. One may tell the story at deeper and deeper levels. New insight comes as the key elements of the story are repeated.

The therapist gives permission and encouragement basically by door-opening questions. All it takes for some clients is the simple question, "How was it when you were a child?" Other clients are more resistant to talking about their past. When they are, the counselor simply continues to probe gently and patiently. Moving the client back and forth from the present to the past is a useful method of helping unwilling clients to relate their pasts.

Clients should be encouraged to tell their stories to safe persons outside therapy. Members of the adult child's family of origin are not generally considered safe. They will frequently seek to justify their behavior and exonerate the family when the client begins to share his or her experience. For that reason, we must warn clients early in therapy against trying to tell their story to their immediate family. At the same time, we must encourage clients to begin the process of developing relationships in which they practice self-disclosure. The storytelling that happens in the therapy sessions is modeling and practice for the same behaviors in real life.

Grieving

To recover from the effects of the dysfunctional family, the codependent must learn to grieve. To grieve is to feel the pain by acknowledging and facing the loss. The act of grieving may be the hardest for the codependent. Our culture makes it difficult to grieve openly. We require that people cover up their grief with a charade of strength. "He didn't break down once in the entire service," we say with admiration of the person who did not cry at a funeral. In our culture, not grieving is erroneously considered appropriate grief.

Codependents must grieve at least four things: (1.) the loss of their own childhood; (2.) the pain of the shaming events the codependent has endured; (3.) the loss of the unconditional maternal and paternal love which codependents were denied in their childhood and for which they have continued to look through their codependent ways; (4.) the loss of the compulsive behaviors and thinking that the codependent has used to avoid the pain since childhood. Recovery means giving up the old, comfortable, though destructive, way of life and developing new ways. New roles must be developed and the loss of the old role must be grieved.

To help the codependent deal with grief, I take him or her through the *Cycle of Healing*.

1. Acknowledge the *hurt* that hides the loss and loneliness.
2. Acknowledge the *loss and loneliness* that hides the lack of self-worth.
3. Acknowledge the *lack of self-worth* that hides the anger.
4. Acknowledge the *anger* that hides the denial.
5. Acknowledge the *denial* that hides the hurt.
6. Begin at number one again.

Grief, then, is a prerequisite of healing. In fact, in its first stages, the process of recovery is the process of grieving. So long as the client holds on to the old ways and old thoughts, he or she is unwilling to grieve. Conversely, so long as he or she refuses to grieve, to that extent the client holds on to the old ways. And the result of it all is that the client blocks the process of healing.

Reggie was a man who denied the pain and grief that is necessary in recovery. He was a compulsive codependent and was, at forty-one, a successful businessman. His attractive wife had attended a couple of his therapy sessions and was very supportive of him. They had a son, Steve, who had been hospitalized for drug addiction and with whom Reggie had a hard time relating. The son was coming home from college for the summer and Reggie was there to "learn better relationship skills." In the process of working on these issues, Reggie brought up his mother. He was enmeshed with her and could not even think of displeasing her in the smallest way. "Nothing could be worse than having your mother mad at you," he said, fully believing that nobody in his right mind would disagree with that statement.

Reggie described a scene when he was in his early twenties. He had offended his mother by something he said and she had not spoken to him for four months. "That was the worst period of my life," Reggie confided. His face was contorted as he spoke, indicating that even the memory of it was very painful to him. "My mother really loves me," he quickly added. "She loves me unconditionally. I will never believe anything but that," Reggie lied to himself. "But," he smiled pleasantly, "enough of this sadness. Let's get back to my problem with Steve."

Imagery

I have found that the use of guided imagery is a useful tool in working with individual clients. Some of the tactics described in the chapter on group therapy are useful for work in individual therapy. In addition to those methods, I use imagery in two ways in working with individuals: by changing powerful images and by refinishing the past.

Changing powerful images.   Becky was an example of a client who had trouble with powerful images. She was a schizoid/avoidant and paranoid codependent and was easily defeated by life and often gave up in a deep depression. An artist by profession, Becky lived alone and thought frequently of suicide. She wrote the following as a part of a four-page description of her sadness with life and her desire to die.

> God, I'm so lonely and all I do when I'm alone is cry. I've tried to let people know me like you've told me to. I've tried and tried. I just can't do it anymore. I feel like I'm on the edge of a big deep black hole. I know that any minute I will fall in and keep falling and never return. Maybe this is a premonition that I'll go crazy. All I know is that it has been there for the longest time and I don't know what it is and it scares me.

When Becky brought me this to read, she was very depressed and tired. The deep black hole that she feared became my focal point. I encouraged her to talk about what she had written. She free-associated about how miserable her life was and how she would rather be dead than go on as she was. I asked, "Would you tell me about the black hole?" She described it in her creative way, exquisite in detail and vividness. She was very afraid of that black hole. I asked her to do a guided imagery with me. We had done guided imageries before and she quickly agreed. I took her through the breathing exercises to relax her. Then I continued:

> Now I want you to see the deep, black hole. Walk carefully and slowly up to the edge of it. Look at its blackness. It is as black as polished marble. It *is* polished marble. It is solid. Bend over and touch the solid black marble. Put one foot on it and feel how solid it is. Now, you are a child and the marble is a frozen lake. (Becky grew up in Ohio and was familiar with frozen lakes.) Picture yourself as a child and step out on the smooth, strong, solid ice. You have on ice skates. See yourself skating skillfully across the black, frozen surface. (As a child, Becky had won several local prizes for her ice skating abilities.)

> Feel the air as it rushes through your hair. See the blue sky and the trees on the banks of the lake. Notice the other skaters on the lake with you. Hear the happiness of their laughter. See yourself laughing with them. Feel yourself skating with skill and zeal.

After I brought the imagery to a close, Becky talked about her experience. The skating had been exhilarating. She had recaptured some of the joy of life in that experience. "The black hole is your image," I explained. "You own it because you created it like one of your pieces of art. And you can change it any time you wish. If it scares you as a deep hole, make it a beautiful valley into which you descend to enjoy its delights." Such tactics help the individual to restructure frightful images.

Refinishing the past.   Many adult children have images of the past that they carry with them and which cause them pain. These are images of things that they remember having happened to them or to others in their family. Or the images may be of things they feared happening to them. Guided imagery can be useful to them in finding relief. They can change the picture or complete the story by refinishing it so that it no longer causes pain.

Ross is an example. A short man who managed a restaurant, Ross was thirty-seven and exhibited many of the characteristics of the histrionic codependent. He was divorced and he went around taking care of others to get their approval. Ross had little self-confidence. In our first session, Ross related this picture of himself. "My mom and dad didn't care a damn about me. They were both slobs. My dad was a drunk and my mom a nagger. I would come home from school and clean up the house. They didn't even notice." Ross wept softly as he described his efforts to get his parents' love by being a "good boy" and cleaning up after them. He continued his story and described himself as the kind of person who had great compassion for other people. His great goal in life, he said, was to take care of others.

"Are you open to changing the way you see yourself?" I asked. He gave a hesitant but affirmative answer. I asked him to do a guided imagery with me in which he changed the way he saw himself in childhood. In the imagery, I asked him to see himself as a messy kid and his mother and father trying to get him to clean up. He saw himself coming home dirty and throwing his clothes about in the house. He ate food and left everything out of the cabinet. His mother and father came to his room and asked him to clean it up. I then asked him to decide whether or not he wanted to clean things up as they had asked and then to visualize himself doing what he decided. I gave him a couple of minutes to complete the image and then asked him to open his eyes. We talked about how he felt now as he was changing the picture of himself as a youth. We finished as Ross described ways he could change his adult behavior of cleaning up other people's messes.

When clients refinish the past, they do not fool themselves into thinking that the past is now different. Rather, they are changing how they are *seeing* themselves in the past. This exercise is not unlike refinishing a piece of furniture. The desk remains the same in shape and structure. What changes is the outer cover and thus the way we see the desk. Clients can change the way they feel about the past and by so doing change the meaning and the emotional impact of the past.

Les, the seminary student mentioned in the last chapter, is an example of how the past can be refinished. Les was an outstanding high school athlete who played on a winning football team. His dream was to play in a game for the state championship. His dream came true in his senior year. But his father turned it into a nightmare. He showed up at the game drunk and made a fool of himself. Les did not tell me what his father had done, but it embarrassed him greatly in front of his coach and some of the spectators. Les's team lost and Les wept along with the other players. Only his tears were not because they had lost the game. He wept for the shame he felt because of his father's drunken behavior.

When Les related his memory of this event to me, I asked if he was open to changing it. "I guess so," he responded with some uncertainty. I asked that he do a guided imagery with me. After relaxing him with breathing exercises, I asked that he go back in his memory to the night of the high school championship game. I asked that he see his father's behavior with all the vividness of which he was capable. I gave him a brief time to reexperience the feelings and sights of that evening. "Now," I directed, "I want you to see yourself from the eyes of your high school coach. He sees your father's behavior and he sees your courage and strength in going on and playing the game. See him coming up to you and saying something to you about it. Listen very carefully to what he says to you." I allowed Les a few moments to visualize the exchange between the coach and himself. Then I ended the imagery.

"What happened?" I asked gently. Les wept. "He said he *admired* me," Les replied through his tears. He talked on about seeing the whole thing in a different way. That night had been a shaming event for Les. He had taken on his father's shame and defined himself by his father's negative behavior. The refinishing imagery had helped him to see the event as reflecting his strength and courage. Others saw him in a positive way, not negatively. Les was able to change the meaning of the event for himself. He felt differently about it and therefore about himself.

Family Mapping

Laing (1972, p. 7) writes about the "internalized family." By this term he means the family "picture" or "map" that individuals carry around in their heads about their family. Internalization is the process of transferring family relationships from reality to perception, memory, imagination, and dreams. The internalized family is the set of images that the individual has about his or her family. According to Laing (p. 4), members may "feel more or less in or out of any part or whole of the family." He cites one description (p. 6):

> My family was like a flower. Mother was the centre and we were the petals.
> When I broke away, mother felt she had lost an arm. They [sibs] still meet round
> her like that. Father never really comes into the family in that sense.

The internalized map is a powerful factor in how individuals relate not only to their family but to others also. This family map is influential in how people feel about themselves. The place of the family in this regard is central and is shared by no other institution in society. The individual who grew up in a dysfunctional family needs to bring the family map into clear focus. Family mapping is a useful method of making that internal image conscious.

Bob was depressed when his mother brought him to our clinic for counseling. After several sessions, his counselor reported on his work with Bob in a supervisory meeting with our staff. They had met weekly for one hour each session. Bob was from an upper-middle-class family and was the oldest of two children. He was eighteen and his sister was five. The counselor reported that the mother was an "obsessive, compulsive, and controlling" person and the father was gone a lot traveling in his work. Bob felt closest to his sister, for whom he baby-sat frequently. His therapist described Bob as robust, healthy, and handsome.

In the course of the therapy, Bob's counselor asked him to draw a picture of his family and his place in it. The next week, Bob returned with the picture as shown in Figure 6.

Bob and the therapist spent that session talking about Bob's map and what it showed about his feelings about his family and himself. Four important things came from the discussion:

1. Bob felt separated from his family. He drew himself in one circle with two friends. He put his mother, father, and sister in another circle that does not touch his circle. He said that he was closest to his sister, but he drew his mother and father coming between himself and her.

2. All people who represent his friends and his schoolmates were looking to the side rather than straight ahead. When the therapist asked about this, Bob responded that no one really sees him. The school, which is drawn in great detail, looks like a prison. Bob described it as such. "In fact," he stated "I feel trapped everywhere."

3. Close inspection of his mother, his girlfriend, and the figure in the church circle reveals something covering parts of their faces. Bob described these face covers as *blinders*, which they wear to "keep them from seeing the truth about me and life."

4. In the picture of himself, Bob had drawn knives in his hands. When his counselor asked about the knives, Bob said "I feel that I must be on guard all the time." He felt that he was being shut out and that he was trapped. No one was really aware of him and his needs. He was angry about the condition of his life.

Overall, the family map that Bob drew shows the separation he feels from his family and the estrangement he is experiencing in life in general. The therapist used the map to continue Bob's cognitive understanding of what is happening to him. It helped him to understand the source of his stress and where his depression came from.

Writing

Some clients respond positively to the suggestion that they write down what is going on in their lives through the process of therapy. Others do not. I have found that for those who do, three areas of writing are profitable.

Autobiography. If I think it might be appropriate, I suggest that the client write an autobiography. This is an ambitious task and is not for everybody. It should be done only if the client enjoys it and should not be a laborious or distasteful task.

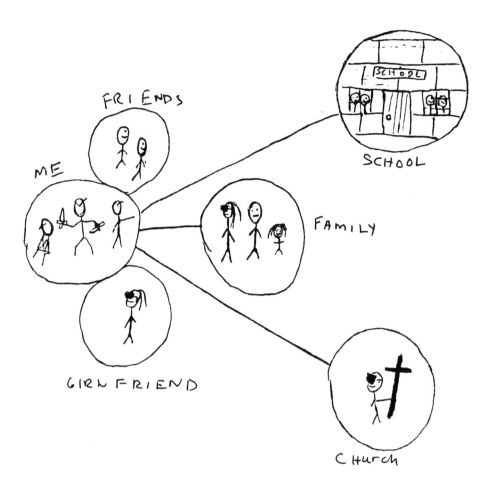

Figure 6   Bob's family as drawn by himself.

The client decides if he or she wants to participate in this exercise and how extensive he or she would like to make the writing.

The following is a suggested outline that the client may wish to use in writing his or her autobiography:

Writing Your Autobiography

1. Description of your family.
    (a) Family map (including grandparents, uncles, and aunts)
    (b) Physical description of each person in the family. Include significant social, educational, religious, psychological, and medical facts.
    (c) Relationship description. Indicate the type and quality of relationships between the major persons in the family.

2. Write a brief answer to the following questions:
   (a) Did any of your family use drugs, including alcohol?
   (b) Who talked to whom? Who did not?
   (c) What were the major secrets that individuals in the family sought to keep?
   (d) Who made the money in the family? Who controlled the family money?
       Who spent the family money?
   (e) How was religion handled in the family?
   (f) Describe the major unwritten rules in the family.
   (g) Describe important family rituals.
   (h) Describe any other factors that you feel are important to your family.
3. Write a brief narrative describing what you know about your mother's and father's families of origin. Were they happy as children? How were they treated? What impact did these things have on their personalities and on the way they parented you?
4. Write a narrative of your memories and what people have told you about your life before you were three years of age. Include any experiences of your mother when she was pregnant with you. After recording the facts as you remember them, write a description of what you feel is important about this part of your history. How does it make you feel about yourself?
5. Write a narrative of your life from age three to age six using the instructions in #4.
6. Divide your school years into at least three segments and write a narrative description of each segment. Comment on the kind of person you see yourself becoming in each segment. What are the important things you see happening to you during these periods, and what are your feelings about yourself during these periods?
7. Select the three or four most important events in your adult life and use these events as major dividers of your life. Write a description of each of these segments of your life. Follow the same instructions as given in #6.
8. Write an essay dealing with the conclusions and feelings you have about the biography you have written. Conclude with your hopes and plans for the future. That is, where do you hope to go with your life from this point forward?

Letters to persons of the past.   Clients frequently respond positively to the suggestion that they write letters to significant others in their childhood. This procedure is very useful for people who have a difficult time getting in touch with anger for the hurts of childhood. Individuals who have a hard time forgiving others also can use this technique profitably.

The letters are spontaneous and unpremeditated exercises. That is, the client sits down with several sheets of paper and writes, "Dear _____, There are some things that I want to say to you...." Whatever comes out on the page is okay. The client should not try consciously to direct the flow. At this point, grammar, spelling, even chronology are not important. What is important is what the individual remembers and how he or she felt about it then and feels about it now. That information needs to come out of the person and onto the page.

When the writing is done, clients can do one of three things:

1. They can tear up the letter and throw it away. The destruction of the materials can be more than a perfunctory act. It can be very symbolic. The client can see it as symbolizing getting rid of the offenses described in the letter. Thus, destroying the letter can be an important ritual that connotes the laying down of a burden.
2. Clients may want to share the letter with someone they trust. After doing so, they are to destroy the letter as a ritual of putting the past away.
3. They may want to bring the letter in and share it with the counselor. Then the client destroys the letter.

Maggie, an overresponsible codependent who had been brought up in a rigidly controlling family, brought the following letter in for me to go over with her.

January 28

Dear Dad,

I understand that you have had a painful life. I understand that you feel unloved and persecuted. I understand that it is too painful for you to admit and that you need to express anger and power and control so that you don't have to deal with your fear and impotence. You lie to hide what's real.

However, when you expect me to suppport your lie, I lie and then I hate myself. When you blame me for your troubles, I feel responsible for your troubles and for figuring out how to fix them. I am not responsible for your pain and I do not have the power to fix things for you.

You have hurt me. You have used me. You continue to say and do things that are designed to hurt me.

You will not change. You don't even want to change. You have made that clear to me.

But I can change.

I don't have to lie. I don't have to be around anyone who hurts me.

For that reason, I will not see or talk to you ever again. I will no longer consider in any way the accusations and demands you have made of me since I was born. I reject your way of defining me and my life. As soon as I recognize a thought came from you, I will dismiss it because I will realize it was something you said to me to control, dominate, and hurt me. I will not feel sorry for you anymore, nor will I consider you an innocent victim.

I, this moment, turn my back on you and your influence on me. I, this moment, turn toward my life as it is today and will be from now on. I am loved, understood, comforted, and cherished by my husband and friends. I have a God who is a loving Father who gives me good things and wants me to live. I turn toward Him.

Clients also may write a letter to themselves as a child. This exercise, described earlier in Chapter Four as a part of group therapy, helps clients "reparent" themselves. They return, as it were, to the hurt child of the past. The letter gives them the opportunity to express to the child the unconditional love that was absent in child-hood. I usually ask the client to give the letter to me. I keep it, unread, and a few weeks later, I mail it to the client. Many individuals have reported that receiving the letter in the mail and reading it has been a very moving and healing experience.

Journaling. I encourage some clients to begin keeping a journal. Journaling is the simple process of writing a brief description of each day and what meaning one finds in it. Simons (1978, p. 13) says, "Thus a journal is a day book, a diurnal, a book of days, a book of the single day which is my life. It is the ongoing book which will be a continuing response to the nagging question, 'Who am I?'... The journal records the journey, the events and the distance traversed each day and in the sum of days."
There are books that describe extensive methods of journaling. Progoff (1975) and Simons (1978) are examples. Baldwin (1977) has a book that is especially helpful to women. If the client wants this more complex experience, I recommend their books. However, a simple method is sufficient. My instructions are that clients buy a spiral notebook. They begin each entry with the date and they write down briefly what is going on in their lives and what they see as significant about those things. They may wish to record their dreams. A journal, I note, is different from a diary. The diary records events. A journal, on the other hand, records the meaning of occurrences and how we feel about them. Baldwin (1977, p. 3) points out that the journal is more informal. It is "looser in definition, may allow for more creative expansion of the entries, and doesn't imply an obligation to write every day." The journal is an effort to describe day by day how we feel. Clients may wish to include pictures which they draw of "where they are" on that day. Mary, as an example, drew herself as a small ship on a stormy sea. A week or so later, she drew that same ship in a calm harbor. These pictures were vivid images that helped Mary understand and record what was happening and how she felt about it.
The journal helps clients make their experiences concrete. Writing down the experience and their interpretation of that incident forces individuals to look at what is going on in their emotions. Life becomes more than a blur. The journal also helps the individual to keep up with the *process* of life. Looking back over last

week's (or last year's) entries gives the client a sense of the progress that he or she is making.

Active Loving

Carnes (1983, p. 82) has shown that the core belief of individuals who grow up in dysfunctional families is, "I am basically a bad, unworthy person." Therapists can help individuals who live with that conviction to love and appreciate themselves. "Active loving" is one effective method that the therapist can use.

Consider Lennie, a woman who despised herself. Lennie combined the characteristics of the overresponsible and compulsive codependent. She was a participant in one of my groups for adult children and one afternoon called to request a private session. She was very articulate and had shared willingly in the group about her abused past. It was evident that Lennie had lived all her thirty-four years as the object of conditional love. She wept openly that night in the group when she told how she had tried to get her father's love and approval by being a great athlete. Now she was overweight by twenty-five or thirty pounds. She was married to a man who was emotionally distant, as her father had been. Lennie described him as a "good man, but never showing his love." She wanted out of the marriage but "did not believe in divorce."

The afternoon she came for the individual session, she arrived weeping and defeated. She felt helpless and spoke derisively of her failures in life. She described herself as a fat, useless person. I listened quietly to her bitter words. Finally I said, "You do not love yourself enough." "I know that," she shot back. "I know I should love myself more. But how?"

"I do not mean that you should *feel* loving toward yourself," I replied. "I mean that you should *act* loving toward yourself. The fact is, you are *abusive* to you. You treat yourself today as you were treated as a child. Stop doing that." "How?" she repeated softly. I made four suggestions:

1. Be aware that you are being abusive to you and that you are saying things to yourself that you would not tolerate another person saying to someone else. *Every* time you find yourself doing that, get a picture of yourself as a girl, ten or twelve years of age. See that child clearly and reach out to her. Hug her. Tell her that you love her and you will take care of her. Tell her that you will not tolerate anyone hurting or abusing her any more. Your abused past has deprived you of these acts of unconditional love and now you can give them to yourself. When you do, you are actively loving you.

2. Give yourself positive affirmations instead of negative disaffirmation. For example, you seem to feel pretty helpless today. What affirmation can you say to yourself that might help you get rid of that feeling? Immediately she responded, "I can have what I want." I suggested that she repeat the phrase several times a day: "I, Lennie, can have what I want."

When you give yourself affirmations, you are changing your self-talk. In this way, your mind is like a computer; what you put in is what you get out. Start putting better stuff in.

3. Give yourself hugs and physical strokes. Patting your own face and saying, "I love you," is a good thing to do. Stand in front of a mirror and look into your face and say, "I want to thank you for being you. Here are some things I like about you." These are all things you would do for another person who was down on herself. Why not do it for yourself?

4. Make a list of things you like people to do for you and special things that you enjoy doing for yourself. Make a space in your life to give these things to yourself. Do not be sporadic in this effort. Rather, make a planned and conscious attempt to put these self-affirming things in your life. Also, give yourself permission to avoid the things you do not like. Tell yourself that you are doing all this because you deserve it.

Finding Strengths

Strength-oriented counseling is very appropriate for adult children. Typically, they feel enormous shame and doubt and have negative self-perceptions. They have carried these feelings since childhood. Many of them will allow the therapist or anyone else, for that matter, to do problem solving for them. They will sometimes feel so much relief in grieving that they will "stay in the problem." For these reasons, helping the adult child find strengths is an effective method at an appropriate point in therapy.

Emphasizing strengths stresses the client's vitality and the options that he or she has in life. When using this perspective, the therapist spends less time attempting to help the client understand and explain the problem and more time on the client's strengths in solving it.

I have found two things to be of special use in this area. First, many clients suffer great pain when they lower their defenses and deal with the past. They feel like *victims*. Grieving the losses of the past is, as noted earlier, a necessary step for adult children.

Therefore, I encourage them to experience and express these feelings. But at an appropriate time in the sessions, I point out that they are not victims, but *survivors*. That is, while they have been through great trauma, they have lived to tell it. The deeper the pain and the more abusive this past experience, the greater is the strength they have shown in surviving. I refer to the courage and grit that was required for them to live through their past. In such a manner, strength-oriented counseling reframes the negative experiences of their life in a way that contributes to the client's self-perception. It also helps the client internalize a much-needed method of self-affirmation.

The second use of strength-oriented counseling is to point out the client's inherent capacity to deal with whatever problems he or she is facing in the present.

Clients are their own best problem solvers. They need to be told that they are moving in the right direction to find the solution to their problems. They do not, of course, need to be abandoned to their own resources, a condition which they perceive having happened to them in their families of origin. Rather, they need the gentle reminder that they are strong and resourceful and that they have everything they need to find the solutions to their problems. Therapy provides them the environment and time to work it out.

When emphasizing strengths, we must exercise care not to be (or to give the appearance of being) condescending or manipulative. Clients need honesty, not flattery. Jonathan is an example. His wife, Carol, left him after three years of a stormy marriage, taking their two-year-old daughter. It was our initial visit and Jonathan, a handsome young Cadillac salesman, told me about all the things he had done wrong in his marriage to make his wife leave him. He fought back the tears as he blamed himself and related how he had told her repeatedly the ways he would change if she would only come back.

Jonathan saw himself as "lost" without her and feared that he could not go on with life. It was near the end of the session and I wanted to conclude with some reference to his strengths. I asked him what he had been doing to improve his life since his wife had left him. In his rambling, imprecise answer, he made a reference that gave me the opportunity I was looking for. He said, in essence, "I have been trying to understand me." I went back to that statement when he finished by saying, "You said something a moment ago that caught my attention because it shows how much strength you have. You commented that you are trying to understand *you*. I like that about you and would like to suggest that you continue that practice."

I went on to give him a couple of simple exercises that would help him see his own value. I suggested that he think less about what he had lost when Carol left and more about the positive things he had contributed to their relationship. I asked him to look at what *Carol* had lost and what she was giving up in losing him. I also suggested that he think some about what positive qualities he could bring to future relationships with other people, including his daughter. We took the last ten minutes of the session to discuss how this strength could help him solve the problems which he faced.

Incrementalizing Relationships

One of the most beneficial tactics I have discovered in helping the adult child is to teach them to incrementalize their relationships. Codependents characteristically look for approval and acceptance in *every* relationship. They generally interpret this approval as love, and they measure their worth in each relationship by how much of this acceptance they get. What they are looking for is an experience of intimate acceptance by all the people with whom they interact. If they do not get it, they feel rejected. This thinking sets the adult child up for defeat and a feeling of being unaccepted in most relationships.

In using this exercise, I point out this fallacious thinking to the individual and help him or her clearly understand it. I encourage the client to think of examples of how they have expected people in nonintimate relationships to give them these feelings of intimate acceptance. Then I suggest that they place all their relationships on an incremental intimacy scale. One's relationship with a spouse or a child, as an instance, would be a 9 or 10 on the intimacy scale. On the other hand, one's relationship with a boss would be a 3 or 4 on the intimacy scale. Codependents who are dating can use this exercise. They frequently expect a relationship that is just starting to be a 9 or 10. This expectation typically sets them up for disappointment and they interpret it as personal failure and unacceptability. I suggest that they begin with a lower expectation. They can, for example, enjoy a relationship as a 5 and see if it grows to some higher level.

For clients who respond positively to this suggestion, I may recommend that they actually write out a list of their troublesome relationships and assign them each a number on the intimacy scale. For others, I may ask them only to do this exercise with one or two relationships. Beth is an example. She had grown up in a family that was undistinguished in any way as far as abuse was concerned. In fact, it appeared normal and even functional except that it was emotionally distant. Beth did not feel loved. She was a sensitive child, and the lack of emotional support in her family left Beth hungry for acceptance. Despite a loving and accepting marriage, Beth spent her professional career and much of her social life feeling rejected. Bosses, co-workers, and friends could not satisfy the longing she had. She was looking for the mothering she never got and measured herself as unworthy when she did not get that kind of love from each person with whom she interacted. Beth was a compulsive codependent.

Beth was a member of a women's group in her church. She suffered feelings of rejection when she attended its monthly meetings. The leader as well as group members were warm and friendly to Beth, but Beth did not feel that she really belonged. I talked with Beth about her expectations of intimacy from that group and asked her to place the group and the leader on the incrementalized intimacy scale. She agreed that she had them at a very high level in her expectations but that they realistically needed to be about a 4. Over the next few months, Beth reported a lowering of her feelings of rejection from the group. She also found that she was less anxious as the time for the meetings approached. When she did feel unaccepted by the group or the leader, she simply reminded herself that the group was only a 4. Beth was able also to use this method with success in her work and in other areas of her life.

Support Groups and Group or Family Therapy

Many clients in individual counseling can profit from participation in some kind of support group or in group or family therapy. I often suggest that they combine individual counseling with some group experience. They may find local support groups by calling the Alcoholics Anonymous number in the Yellow Pages of the telephone book. Many cities now have twelve-step programs for codependents, adult children of alcoholics, sex addicts, overeaters, and the emotionally overwrought.

These groups vary in their quality according to the individuals who constitute the group. If specific clients do not enjoy a particular group, I encourage them to try another. Success in these programs differs from one person to another. Therefore, if they find the whole concept of the twelve-step program uncomfortable or if they cannot find a group with which they are satisfied, I do not insist that they continue.

TERMINATING INDIVIDUAL THERAPY

We must give special consideration to terminating therapy with the codependent client. Cermak (1986, p. 92) points out that termination skills are among the last ones most therapists develop. Nonetheless, termination represents an integral part of therapy. Indeed, it is the goal toward which all the other parts of therapy are moving. It is, Cermak says, "a process, not an event." Thus, the termination procedure may occur over the last several sessions. The therapist has the opportunity during this time to deal with specific issues that cannot be dealt with until that point.

Emotional Pitfalls of Termination

The codependent faces a number of emotional problems in terminating therapy. The therapist must be aware of these potential pitfalls and prepare the client for them. They should be brought up and dealt with openly during the process of termination. The client's capacity to look at these issues and face them squarely is a measurement of his or her readiness to terminate therapy.

Anger. Many codependents must get angry in order to leave therapy. Anger, in this case, is not a healthy emotion. Anger is frequently present in terminations that are client originated and occur before the client is ready to leave counseling. For the codependent, anger is the only way to get out of relationships. He or she has never had a relationship end that did not involve anger at some point in the process. For that reason, some adult children terminate counseling with anger. The anger gives them permission to quit.

Stewart had to get angry to leave counseling. He struggled with a codependent background that included sexual abuse by his mother. Stewart worked courageously for nearly seven months, during which his pain and fear were enormous. For the last several sessions before he quit, he mentioned that he was thinking about leaving therapy. He complained that he came to me for relief and all he felt when he left each session was depression. He was agitated and irritable. He arrived one day to say that he was too tired and did not want to talk that day. We sat in silence for about ten minutes. Stewart finally broke the silence to say that he did not want relationships with people. He always had thought he did, but he now realized that he did not. He was happy as he was. He left that day saying that I could not help him and he would have to look for someone else. His wife called the next week to say that he would not be coming back.

Stewart needed to be angry at me so he would not have to take responsibility for the despair and helpless exhaustion that he felt. He was unwilling to look at these emotions and as a result missed the growth and change that had occurred through the pain he was experiencing.

Fear of success.   Paradoxically, the adult child fears success. The experience of even a single occasion of success is threatening, because the codependent fears that others will expect him or her to keep it up. Success reminds the codependent of the pain of not succeeding. Codependents have much more experience with failure. They expect to be wrong or judged inadequate. When they do not fail, they feel set up and prepared for even greater failure. One individual told me that some of the worst evenings she spent as a schoolchild in her home were those evenings when she had some good thing to report to her family. Her father's praise was worse than his criticism. She thought, "Oh no, now he will expect me to keep this up and I'm afraid I can't."

Termination often raises similar fears in the adult child. The responsibility of succeeding and the fear of failure come to the surface. "If I am being released," the codependent reasons, "it must be because my therapist thinks I am well. I know that I will not be able to keep everyone thinking that I am doing okay. I know that I will fail and this is my greatest failure because I have been in all this therapy and I should be okay."

Fear of abandonment.   Two levels of fear of abandonment come to the surface as codependents think about leaving therapy. The first is the fear that the therapist is abandoning the codependent. Wayne said to me the first time I mentioned the possibility of termination, "Well, you are getting tired of me, I see." He laughed nervously as he said it and there was pain in his eyes.

The second is the codependent's fear that the counselor might feel abandoned by the client. Codependents experience a sense of guilt that they are leaving someone who has given them love and hope. For the codependent, to think of leaving someone who has given them so much is an act of ingratitude.

Anxiety.   Adult children may feel doubt about their ability to make it on their own without the therapist. The knowledge that there will be the next regularly scheduled meeting gives the client the assurance that he or she can handle whatever will come up in their life. Now they are facing life without that knowledge. They will not have someone to help them deal with the problems which they know are going to come. This realization can bring anxiety that ranges from mild to severe.

For some codependent clients, even the counselor's summer vacation can be traumatic.

Abandonment, anger, and the fear of separation are familiar issues for the adult child. He or she has dealt with them from before early childhood. Termination raises them again, and the client may actually regress significantly when we bring up the discontinuation of therapy. Cermak (1986, p. 92) concludes:

> This is a time of mixed sadness and joy. When a client is capable of experiencing and tolerating this complex blend of emotions, he or she is probably ready to begin thinking seriously about terminating therapy.

The Process of Termination

Signs of recovery.   It is hard to establish a line beyond which the individual is ready to leave therapy. No hard and fast rules exist for the therapist to follow to determine when a client is finished. There are signs that the therapist can look for. But even these are ephemeral and not always clear. The therapist will find the most responsible clients moving back and forth between being prepared for termination and still needing more work.

The following are some of the signs that a client is ready to leave therapy.

1. The client has become comfortable communicating at a feeling level. He or she is able to identify feelings in himself or herself and in others. There does not seem to be the need to deny or hide feelings. The client practices this behavior spontaneously as part of his or her natural framework of behavior and seems not to need other people's permission to engage in it.

2. The client will ask for help instead of thinking he or she has to do it all. In other words, the client has surrendered the need to be responsible for everybody and everything.

3. The client will admit "negative feelings" without a sense of guilt or shame.

4. The client has no "secrets" that he or she must keep hidden from everybody. Conversely, the client does not "share" promiscuously with every person he or she meets. In other words, the client is able to differentiate between safe and unsafe persons.

5. The client can appreciate his or her effort as much as a completed project. There is a willingness to accept something less than perfection. The client is no longer devastated by failure. In other words, the client has begun to accept his or her limitations and humanness.

6. The client is able to loosen up and play.

7. The client is able to turn down honors that would overextend him or her. That is, the client can say no to opportunities to rescue, save, fix, or in some other way make himself or herself indispensable. In other words, the client has given up omnipotence.

8. The client is able to accept responsibility for his or her own behavior. Not blaming others, accepting the consequences of behavior, and having a sense of humor about oneself are all signs of taking personal responsibility.

9. The client is able to accept others as they are and no longer needs to control their behavior. There is less need for others to behave in a certain way for the client to feel good about himself or herself. The individual can be happy even if other members of the family are not happy. The client can accept failure and imperfection in others.

10. The client has shown evidence that he or she can be aware of and withstand the efforts of other people to make him or her return to the way they were before therapy. In other words, the client has met the pressure of the family and others to give up the changes that recovery has produced.

11. The client believes that he or she has inherent worth. There is evidence that clients believe that they *can* have what they want from life, that there are other people who care about them, and that there are ways of taking care of the pain. They show a sense of hope. They are burdened neither by self-doubt nor by the depressing thought that there are no choices they can make.

Stages of Termination

Exactly how the process of termination occurs and how long it will take will vary from one client to another. We must consider the nature of the specific issues with which they have dealt, the severity of their codependence, the nature of the social and psychological milieu in which they live, as well as other ingredients. In general, there are three stages through which any termination should pass.

Initial stage. This stage begins the process of termination. Sometimes the client initiates this stage by the question, "How much more therapy do I need?" Other times, the therapist will begin the procedure with a comment like, "I feel that you have made significant progress and that it is time for us to begin thinking about termination. How do you feel about that?" The therapist makes the statement and observes the client's reaction. The client may want to talk about whether he or she feels ready to go on their own and why the therapist thinks they are. The purpose of Stage 1 is to open the subject for consideration.

Intermediate stage. The second stage allows the therapist and client time to deal with any emotional issues that leaving therapy may cause for the client. For some, this stage may be so brief as to last only one session. Other clients may need two or three sessions. Others may reveal during this stage that they are not finished and will need to remain in therapy.

Final stage. When the client has completed the work of the intermediate stage, he or she is ready for a session dedicated to closing. I spend this session going over with the client what he or she has accomplished in therapy. We look at what specific issues brought the client there, the various things we have done to deal with codependent problems, and how the client has changed. I ask the client to finish a sentence stem or two like, "The most important thing that I see changing about me is ...." or "The thing I like most about me is ...."

The purpose of this session is primarily to recapitulate. My major goal is to fix in the client's mind what he or she has accomplished. If the client wants to praise and thank me, I accept the compliments without resistance. Then I say something like, "The good work that I did was based on the decisions which you made. I provided the environment and you provided the courage and strength. Your growth and change came because of the choices that you made. You brought that capacity with you when you came and you take it with you as you leave."

R E F E R E N C E S

Baldwin, C. (1977). *One to One: Self Understanding Through Journal Writing*, New York: M. Evans.

Carnes, P. (1983). *Out of the Shadows: Understanding Sexual Addiction*, Minneapolis: CompCare.

Cermak, T. (1986). *Diagnosing and Treating Co-dependence*, Minneapolis: Johnson Institute Books.

Laing, R. (1972). *The Politics of the Family and Other Essays*, New York: Vintage Books.

Progoff, I. (1975). *At a Journal Workshop: The Basic Text and Guide for Using the Intensive Journal Process*, New York: Dialogue House Library.

Simons, G. (1978). *Keeping Your Personal Journal*, New York: Paulist Press.

INDEX